Captain James Fairweather
Whaler and Shipmaster
His Life and Career 1853 - 1933

By his Granddaughter
Nancy Rycroft

Published by Fairweather Books

Printed in Great Britain by
Pennine Printing Services
Ripponden, West Yorkshire, England

ISBN 0 9551739 0 6 paperback
ISBN 0 9551739 1 4 hardback

Front Cover: The "Aurora" in the Nips off Cape York. From a photo taken at the time
Inset: Captain James Fairweather

Captain James Fairweather

His life and career,
by his granddaughter Nancy Rycroft,
in association with Keith Mackay

LIEUT.-COMMANDER JAMES FAIRWEATHER R.N.R.
Shipmaster
July 22, 1853 - March 23, 1933

I dedicate this book to Christopher
without whose total commitment and
single minded perseverance it would
never have reached publication.

Scarr House
September 2005

This work has been produced by a troika of myself,
my husband Christopher and my kinsman Keith Mackay.
It has taken over eighteen months of painstaking work
with each of us making our contribution; myself as the primary writer,
Keith researching and Christopher our mainstay on the computer.
I need hardly say how grateful I am to Keith and Christopher for their
wholehearted support in my effort to record my grandfather's
life and career, and to perpetuate his memory.

Contents

*"In all his fifty-two years of dangerous sea-life
he lost, with the exception of one man who went
a-missing, neither a single life nor one of his ships."*
The Scots Magazine

Introduction

I never knew my grandfather, he died when I was just over three years old. We did encounter each other at least once, however, when my parents took me in my organdie-trimmed carrycot from Halifax to Newport on Tay for my grandparents' inspection. My mother was Captain James's second daughter and I was told later that he was charmed at the sight of Tan and Dick's little girl, an afterthought, for my parents were both over forty when I was born.

The journey was arduous in those days. They would set off in the Lagonda Coupe at 6am and reach Newport about 6pm with stops for picnic lunch and tea, not to mention morning coffee. Going over remote, wild Shap Fell filled my mother with horror. They had been making this journey with my brother Alastair, ten years my senior, since coming to Halifax from the Shetland Islands in 1923.

My brother Alastair is now the only person alive to remember Grandpa, for unfortunately Dorothy Newell, the youngest of the 'Carlisle cousins', died on May 8th, 2004, aged eighty four Alastair remembers him as 'down to earth and quick tempered.' He was good with children but understandably stood no nonsense from little boys, which is not surprising as Alastair and his cousin Duncan were a very lively pair.

I need say nothing here about Grandpa's character and personality, both will be revealed in abundance in the narrative, which follows. I will only state that his memory has influenced succeeding generations. He was a hero figure not only to the immediate family but to the Duncan and Craik branches. His career was both long and varied and also it was constructive and adventurous.

To clarify matters at the outset, I must mention that there were two Captains Fairweather: Captain Alexander, and his younger brother Captain James. Both were whaling masters sailing from Dundee. Alexander was approximately seven years older than James and his career was well established before his young brother went to sea. Alexander died aged forty-nine or fifty in May 1896 at the height of his career, whilst James after fifty-two years at sea died in retirement in March 1933. Although Alexander is mentioned from time to time in this narrative it is primarily an account of the life and career of my grandfather Captain James Fairweather.

As Norman Watson rightly says in his recent book The Dundee Whalers, 'They (the Whaling Captains) were famous names among anyone venturing beyond the 60th parallel North. They were said to know the Polar Regions as well as the gateway of the Earl Grey Dock. They were Arctic Navigators and explorers in their own right with an impressive practical knowledge of the frozen regions . . . The maps of the Polar Regions bear witness to their pioneering activity,'[1] which included going well into the then only partly explored North West Passage.

The information about Captain James' career has been to hand within the family for years; the impetus to write it up now came from several sources, in fact this narrative is long overdue.

In the summer of 2003 at least two sources published incorrect information about the Fairweather brothers, of which one actually reached the internet. This confusion had occurred before, with authors stating they were father and son, sometimes the wrong way round, or ignoring James existence altogether. Episodes in James' career were credited to Alexander. There was complete ignorance of Captain James' memoirs,[2] though the articles in the 'Scots Magazine' were in the public domain[3] as was David Moore Lindsay's book *A Voyage to Arctic in the Whaler Aurora*.[4] Also excellent obituaries were published of both men in the Dundee newspapers.

It was a chance remark by my kinsman and colleague Keith Mackay to the effect that recognition of the achievements of lesser participants in polar voyages was long overdue; coupled with my conviction that the record must be put straight which led me to write this narrative. Captain James' life and career deserves to be recorded for posterity. It has been a pleasure as well as a duty to ensure that this has been achieved.

Family Tree of FLEEMING

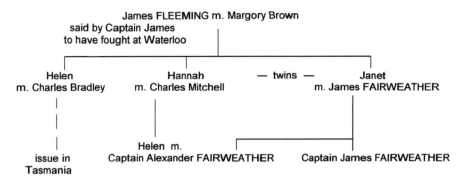

James FLEEMING m. Margory Brown
said by Captain James
to have fought at Waterloo

Helen m. Charles Bradley	Hannah m. Charles Mitchell	— twins —	Janet m. James FAIRWEATHER

issue in
Tasmania

Helen m.
Captain Alexander FAIRWEATHER

Captain James FAIRWEATHER

Family Tree of DUNCAN

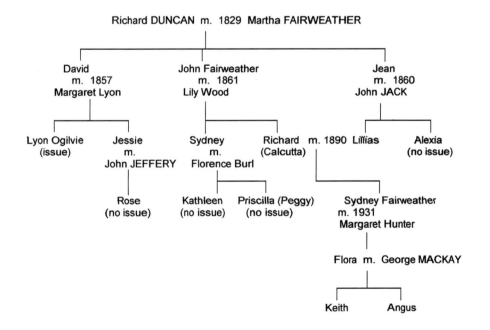

Richard DUNCAN m. 1829 Martha FAIRWEATHER

David
m. 1857
Margaret Lyon

John Fairweather
m. 1861
Lily Wood

Jean
m. 1860
John JACK

Lyon Ogilvie
(issue)

Jessie
m.
John JEFFERY

Sydney
m.
Florence Burl

Richard m. 1890 Lillias
(Calcutta)

Alexia
(no issue)

Rose
(no issue)

Kathleen
(no issue)

Priscilla (Peggy)
(no issue)

Sydney Fairweather
m. 1931
Margaret Hunter

Flora m. George MACKAY

Keith   Angus

Family Tree

David FAIRWEATHER m. Agnes Palmer

- John Malloch
- JAMES m. Janet Fleming
- Alexander m. Mary Ann Sharp

JAMES m. Janet Fleming:
- Alexander
- Hannah

Alexander m. Mary Ann Sharp:
- **JAMES 1853-1933** m. Mary Ann CRAIK

June WALKER descendant of John Malloch

JAMES m. Mary Ann CRAIK children:
- Elizabeth m. James CORR
- Alexander
- Charles m. Eva Hughes
- William
- Mary Ann m. Stuart BOLTON
- David
- Helen (Ella)

- James m. Nellie Denby
- James (Jimmy)
- Ethel m. Rupert BURTON
- Duncan

- Evelyn
- Helen m. John HOPE
- Dorothy

- Alastair
- **Nancy** m. **Christopher RYCROFT**

- Martha m. Richard DUNCAN
- John
- Richard
- Sidney
- Flora m. George MACKAY

- James (Jim)
- James (Jimmy)

issue in Australia

issue

issue

issue

issue

Keith MACKAY

Captain James Fairweather

Family Background

Other people's family history is often tedious to read, so I have to start with a small apology for boring the general reader. This apology is immediately qualified in at least two ways.

Firstly, to understand a person fully, it is essential to know their background and forbears; the forces which moulded them.

More generally, the second half of the nineteenth century, the flowering of the industrial revolution, offered in my opinion, optimum conditions for individuals with talent and drive to succeed in life, often from very humble beginnings, and found prosperous families.

Thus the Jute magnates of Dundee and Calcutta including the Duncan family, and in a smaller way the Fairweather and Craik families, thrived. Examples such as ours abound throughout the British Isles and many families of today have cause to give thanks for the initiative of their industrious and enterprising ancestors.

It has been possible to trace the Fairweather family through the Old Parish Records (OPRs) back to Alexander Fairweather of Little Crief, Kirriemuir. Kirriemuir is a country town, about nineteen miles north of Dundee, in the nineteenth century the home of a thriving handloom weaving industry.

Alexander had five known children, the eldest being Alexander, and the second our ancestor **James**, christened on August 11th 1748 at Kirreimuir. At this date mothers were infrequently mentioned in baptism entries so we do not know her name. James is known to have had eight children christened at Kirriemuir, likewise to an unnamed mother. Their seventh child was **David** - Captain James Fairweather's grandfather.

Much more is known of David than of his predecessors. He was christened on September 22nd 1787. On October 15th 1807 he married at the unusually young age of twenty, Agnes Palmer aged twenty-two of Lintrathen, a village about six miles west of Kirriemuir. Agnes was the daughter of James Palmer of Drumend and Elizabeth Ogilvy. The marriage took place at Lintrathen.

David and Agnes had nine known children, and their place of christening gives an idea of the family's movement over the next twenty-one years. Their first four children were christened at Kirriemuir. The eldest christened in 1808 was Martha Adamson Fairweather, great great great grandmother of Keith Mackay - my kinsman and helper, Elizabeth followed in 1810, next was John Malloch in 1812. He was the great grandfather of our kinswoman June Walker of Australia. David was baptised in 1814 and then **James** was born, the only child of David and Agnes for whom no christening has been found. James, Captain James's father, must have been born between March and October 1817.

The family evidently left Kirriemuir about this time, for the sixth child Alexander was christened at Auchterhouse about twelve miles out of Kirriemuir in 1819. The last three children, Isabella christened in 1825, Charles in 1827 and Andrew in 1829 were all baptised at Lundie & Fowlis, about fourteen miles south west of Kirriemuir.

It would seem that David and Agnes left Kirriemuir as a consequence of the decline in the handloom weaving trade there and moved, as many others did, inexorably towards Dundee. The next sighting of David is as "miller of Lundie" when on the 19th of November 1829 his eldest child Martha Adamson was married at Lundie & Fowlis to Richard Duncan, a shoemaker of Newtyle.

In a letter of the 8th of September 1937 written from 46 Great King Street, Edinburgh by Alexia Jack to Kathleen Duncan, the writer gives an amusing account of a visit to Newtyle with her cousin Lily Duncan to meet their cousin Jessie Jeffery; all three ladies being grand daughters of Richard and Martha, she quotes:

"Martha Fairweather's father was the miller of Lundie, a village over the hill from Newtyle . . . Richard as a boy and a young man often went over the hill to visit his uncle and so met Martha Fairweather whom he married when she was 18 or 19. They were married at Lundie . . . Fifty couples were present at the wedding and after the ceremony and the feast the whole company set out with the bride and groom to walk over the hill to Newtyle and see the young couple installed in their house. The company had a marathon race to the house of the newly-wed and whoever reached it first was to have a stroke of good luck. One of the company - a friend of Richard's, spied a horse in a field, took possession, mounted and on bareback, and at daredevil speed reached the house first and welcomed the newly-wed and the guests . . . This Martha Fairweather was aunt to Captain Alexander and Captain James as their father was her brother. These two boys were brought up in Dundee and from early childhood made the docks their playground; played truant from school and were always found at the docks. Nothing could prevent them from taking a sea-faring life. Yet so far as we know, no ancestor had anything whatever to do with the sea."[1]

I have heard it suggested however that the boys might have been inspired by the career of Admiral Duncan of Camperdown, a local hero. And we now know that their father may have spent some time at sea.

At this stage I must mention the years of endeavour spent trying to link our great grandfather James into the family of David and Agnes. There is no baptism for him and the census returns of 1841 for Forfarshire and Dundee were thoroughly trawled. Both the Duncan family and my mother's kinsman Sir Charles Craik Cunningham knew by word of mouth of a relationship. Keith's mother, Flora nee Duncan, remembers a snowy owl mounted in a glass case, at her grandparents' home in Edinburgh, which had been presented to her grandfather Richard Duncan by Captain James. Proof came like 'eureka' one morning when I belatedly set eyes on an obituary of John F Duncan in grandfather's scrapbook annotated in his own hand 'my cousin John Duncan'. I could not get to the phone quick enough to tell Keith.

The last sighting of David and Agnes is in the Dundee census of 1841 which reads as follows:

Book 17

Sea Gate		born in Parish
David Fairweather	53 Hand Loom Weaver	No
Agnes	56	No
Isabella	15	Yes

David Fairweather died on 13 January 1843 and Agnes on 15 March 1845. Both are buried in St Peter's Churchyard, Dundee; a pleasing location, which we have visited.

By 1850, Dundee, which had been a very depressed port and market town in the late seventeenth and early eighteen centuries, had experienced a century of fluctuating industrial and commercial growth. By 1851 the population had reached 78,931 and its trade exceeded that of any Scots town but Glasgow. Conditions for the inhabitants were however poor; there was no adequate piped domestic water supply, and disease, particularly cholera, typhus and tuberculosis was rife. Poor wages meant a miserably inadequate diet of meal and potatoes. By 1860 housing for the poor consisted of crowded apartments in tenement buildings intersected by wynds or narrow alleys. The Craik family was living in one such building, number 3 Crescent Street, at the time of the 1861 census.

The industry of the 1850s and 60s was dominated by linen and then jute production and there was a constant stream of immigrants from the hinterland to take up employment in the factories. The Fairweathers and Craiks were two of many families who migrated to Dundee as a consequence of the decline in domestic production.

The sea was never far from Dundee life, for the Tay Estuary was a busy waterway for national and international shipping. On the dockside, in roads called Whale Lane and Seagate, were oil yards and refineries for processing raw blubber. The stench which issued caused annoyance to many of the populace. It was not surprising that wealthier members of the community began to leave for more salubrious neighbourhoods nearby.[2]

James Fairweather 1817-1857

James senior is a shadowy figure, finding facts about his life has been a struggle. The initial problem was a lack of a baptism, though for a long time we strongly suspected that he was a child of David Fairweather and Agnes Palmer, and brother to John Malloch Fairweather who, like James, was a cabinet-maker in the 1841 census of Dundee. As every census entry for Forfarshire and Dundee was searched without success, one possibility is that he was at sea. The first documented reference to James is his marriage entry in the OPR (Old Parish Records) in which he is referred to as being a 'wright'. This raises the possibility that he may have been a ship's carpenter, as he was on his final journey to Australia in1854.

James married on the 20th of April 1846 in the parish of Dundee, Janet Fleming, both of this parish and it seems appropriate here to write a few words about the Fleming family (sometimes spelt with one e, sometimes two).

Janet was the twin daughter of James Fleming and Margory Brown living at Princes Street in the 1841 census. Her twin was Hannah and they were both handloom weavers aged 17. James is termed a labourer aged 55 the same age as his wife. William their son is aged 14. Next door lived their daughter Helen aged 20, married to Charles Bradley also aged 20.

The history of these girls is very relevant to the family. Whereas Janet married James Fairweather senior and was grandfather's mother, her twin Hannah married Thomas Mitchell of Dundee, and their daughter Helen Mitchell married Captain Alexander Fairweather, grandfather's brother and her first cousin. This was a particularly close cousinship as the mothers of the bride and groom Janet and Hannah were twins (see family tree of Fleming). Thus 'Aunt Ella', Captain James's youngest daughter, was named Helen Mitchell Fairweather. The Bradleys are also interesting for Helen and Charles emigrated to Tasmania and I remember a lady called Enid Bradley visiting my girlhood home Invermark in Halifax sometime in my early life. Charles and Helen's sons John and George Bradley both had distinguished careers in Tasmania. Enid was doubtless a descendant of one of them.[3]

To turn to James Fleming, Captain James' maternal grandfather, he is referred to by his grandson in two letters. The first dated 14 January 1930 is to his own grandson Jim Fairweather (now in Australia) on the occasion of his fourth birthday. In it he tells Jim that his grandfather on his mother's side was in the battle of Waterloo, and how proud he had been of this as a boy. In a letter to Jim's mother Nellie dated 18 January 1930 Captain James also mentions that it was his mother's father who served under Wellington at Waterloo. Incidentally I get a small mention in this letter as a footnote after Granny's bilious attack, as he writes "I cannot remember if I told you that Tan (my mother's nickname) *had a daughter on the night of the 13th inst and that both are doing well.*"

8

Despite employing a military researcher I have been unable so far to trace any record of James Fleming's military service or of the Waterloo Medal to which he should have been entitled. I have even made contacts in Tasmania in case Helen took the medal with her.

The next reference to James Fairweather is in the Dundee Street Directory of 1850 where he is listed as a cabinet-maker at 28 Meadow Entry.

The 1851 census gives us our last picture of James with his family, though grandfather was not yet born, and reads as follows:

Book 69
143 Meadow Entry

James Fairweather mar.	33	Master Cabinet Maker employing 5 men b. Kirriemuir
Janet	26	b. Dundee
Alex	4	Scholar b. Dundee
Hannah	2	b. Dundee

It was not until I saw this census entry that I knew James and Alexander had a sister. I never heard her mentioned. The only knowledge I have of Hannah comes from her death certificate, which reads as follows:

Death   Newington City of Edinburgh 6855/60
1904 January 21
Hannah Fleming, Weaver (single) at Longmore Hospital
Edinburgh (usual residence 26 Forfar Road, Dundee)
Age 54 daughter of James Fairweather Cabinet Maker
(deceased) and Jessie Forbes previously Fairweather. M.S.
Fleming (deceased); chronic bronchitis and asthma 4 Years,
cert by George Blaikie M.D. Informant, George Ritchie,
nephew by marriage, of 5 Roxburgh Place.

I believe there is an Edinburgh connection which was likely to be on the Fleming side, but this is still to be researched. To return to the census there is an entry for James snr's brother John Malloch Fairweather, a cabinet-maker at 18 Bell Street, with his wife Agnes and two small children.

Thus it would appear that at this stage in his life James Fairweather was in a good position with a business, employing five men, and living with his wife and two children, yet in just over three years all this was to change dramatically.

On the 22 of July 1853 Captain James Fairweather was born. What impelled James Fairweather to leave his wife and children, with James under one year old, and embark on the ship *Kurrajong* for Sydney, Australia, on the 20th of June 1854 has been a matter of debate and enquiry for years. 1851 seemed on paper to show him in a good position, but was the census entry misleading? There seem to be three possibilities, firstly the possibility of a matrimonial dispute springs to mind, desertion of one's wife and family happened then as it does today. However, there is no evidence this was the case, on the contrary his sons continued to respect his memory. Secondly, there is the possibility that his business collapsed, for trade in Dundee was badly affected by the Crimean War. Perhaps he made the voyage in order to establish a base for his family to join him at a later date, this was a frequent procedure for emigrants then as now. For the whole family to travel together would be a major and uncertain enterprise. A foothold in this remote colony would be an advantage whereby they could in due course join him. A third theory is that of ill health, which might have forced him to abandon his business as a cabinet maker. It seems certain that James suffered from tuberculosis. His death certificate of the 7th of May 1857 gives the cause of death as 'rupture of blood vessel after a four day illness'. This is the identical description given in an account of the death of my Bolton great aunt's brother who emigrated to New Zealand in the 1880s and took up farming there for the sake of his health. His death is reported in the newspaper for 'Hamilton' in detail and the expression 'ruptured a blood vessel on the lungs' is used. He was known to suffer from tuberculosis. An additional factor is that William Craik Fairweather, Captain James's talented son who wrote short stories some of which were published as an addendum to my grandfather's book, *With the Scottish Whalers*,[4] tragically died of TB in April 1906 at the age of twenty one; of which more later. Tuberculosis was said to run in families, though it is now recognised as an infection.

To return to the Kurrajong. In the second half of the 19th Century there was considerable emigration from Scotland as a result of economic conditions at home and a desire for a better life in the new colonies. Many vessels left Dundee for Australia and Canada in particular, and the arrivals and departures of vessels were announced in the *Dundee, Perth, and Cupar Advertisers*. The ship was usually in dock for some days or weeks loading a cargo of mixed goods, and embarking passengers and crew, and it was possible 'to get up and go'. However James signed on as a crew member, as ship's carpenter, unassisted, aged 37, under Captain Robertson.

The ship left Dundee on the 20th of June 1854, and arrived in Sydney, New South Wales, on the 14th of October. Nothing is known of James's time in Australia, though an internet site shows that there was an unclaimed letter in Melbourne which may be of interest. James died on the 7th of May 1857. His death, registered in New South Wales, was at Clarence Street, Sydney, aged (this time) 33, styled Carpenter, cause of death, - Rupture of Blood Vessel 4 days, father and mother not known, informant A Walbum, carpenter, Clarence Street, buried on 8 May in the Scotch burial ground

Sydney. The only witnesses of the burial appear to be the undertaker and the minister. Born in Scotland he was three years in New South Wales, married (particulars unknown) children unknown. Altogether this death certificate appears to reflect a sad and lonely life.

My late kinsman Keith Barrie of Australia told me that the Scotch burial ground was part of the Devonshire Street Cemetery which closed in 1863. The graves were moved to La Perouse Cemetery and two others; the undertaker's premises were in Crown Street. Interestingly my cousin Ethel records that Captain James "went ashore at Sydney on a voyage to look for his father's grave and found that Sydney Town Hall had been built on the site of the graveyard."

To return to Dundee; in 1854 Janet is left with three children aged seven, five and one, and almost certainly with no means of support unless any were forthcoming from her brothers-in-law John Malloch Fairweather and Alexander Whyte Fairweather.

John was an established cabinet-maker, and Alexander, who was well known in the public life of Dundee, carried on an extensive business as a house painter and decorator. Apprenticed to him was his nephew John Duncan, Keith Mackay's great-great-grandfather. Alexander's widow Mary Ann Sharp died in 1881, and the estate was put into an ongoing trust to offer scholarships for the children of poor families in Dundee to enable students to go to college or university in Scotland. The fund was to be known as *The Fairweather Bursaries*.[5]

By the time of the 1861 census Janet had moved to Princes Street and was living at number 99 Neans Land, the entry reads as follows:

Janet Fairweather	Head Widow	34	Weaver
			b. Forfarshire Dundee
Hannah	dau	12	Mill Worker
			b. Forfarshire Dundee
James	son	6	Scholar
			b. Forfarshire Dundee

Alexander was not at home; we know from his obituary that 'his first voyage was on a small coasting vessel when he was only ten years of age'.[6] He was born circa 1847, so he would be approximately fourteen and away at sea at the time of the census.

On March the 21st 1864 Janet, now reverted to her maiden name Fleming, married Benjamin Forbes. She is termed Housekeeper, widow aged 36 of Princes Street. He is mill overseer, widower aged 37 of 19 Queens Street (parents given). The marriage took place at 18 Queens Street, Dundee, Free Church of Scotland. They were therefore married at his home. There is no mention of her children who would be aged approximately seventeen, fifteen and ten years old.

The Career of Captain Fairweather

We should remember at the outset that that Captain James never knew a father, James senior having disappeared from his son's life before he was one year old. In consequence it seems that his older brother Alexander fulfilled this role in his early years. We have no date of Alexander's birth but from other information he appears to have been between six and seven years older than James, and signed his apprenticeship certificate in loco parentis. Alexander must have been a major influence on James's early life and no doubt encouraged him towards the seafaring career that he pioneered. We now know that contrary to Alexia Jacks's comment, the boys did have associations with life at sea, for it is possible that their father was a ship's carpenter before his marriage and he certainly sailed to Australia in 1854 in that capacity.

Alexander's long and fulsome obituaries (see appendix) state that his first voyage was in a small coastal vessel when he was only ten years of age. This would be approximately 1856 or 7. By the time he was sixteen he had completed his apprenticeship.

We know nothing of the boys' schooling, but they both write well and grandfather's prose is vivid, spontaneous and humorous. They must have been of excellent intelligence, learning on the job and attained their Master's Certificates, James at the early age of twenty-four. In addition the responsibilities they assumed so young were awesome by modern standards.

In 1928 Captain James published privately his memoirs entitled *With the Scottish Whalers, The Story of a Shipmaster's Fifty-two Years at Sea.* He commences his racy account by telling us that at a very early age he worked for a period at a factory in Dundee. This would be necessary in view of the poor circumstances in which his mother had been left. A cutting in Grandpa's scrapbook entitled 'an honoured son of Dundee' announces the appointment of one Dr Ramsay as chief magistrate of Blackburn. Captain James annotates this with the comment "An old friend of my youth". The cutting states that Dr Ramsay began life in a humble capacity in the service of Baxter Brothers & Co, in Dens Works. Baxter's were large jute manufacturers and it seems likely therefore that grandfather also spent his early years there, probably from the age of seven to fourteen.

From this period also derives a story told by my cousin Ethel Burton, daughter of Elizabeth Corr, eldest daughter of Captain James Fairweather and Mary Ann Craik. It is here that my grandmother enters the picture, for Ethel states that Mary Ann Craik worked in a jute mill from the age of seven. She says that the Fairweathers and the Craiks lived up the same stair in Dundee and the children became friends. The housing consisted of tenements containing a number of flats, for instance 3 Crescent Street where the Craiks were living in 1861[1] and still there at James and Mary Ann's marriage in 1874, consisted of eleven dwellings of two to three rooms, each accommodating between two and eight persons. The Craiks lived in flat number 8, seven persons occupying two rooms; a stairwell linked the flats. Granny Fairweather told my cousin Ethel that James was "a puir wee laddie". He and Mary Ann would sit on the stairs, and she would give him 'a jeelly piece' because he looked cold and hungry. She was two years and two months older than he.

Captain James's memoirs begin with the following account of his early life. It is clear from this and other references that the lure of the sea was powerful to Dundee lads in contrast to the dreary life of the factory. The desire was there, but also the opportunity, with the proximity of the Tay, the harbour and the ships that thronged it in those days. There was also the example of his older brother Alexander to follow.

> To every boy there comes at some time or other the desire to go to sea in search of fame and adventure. In my case, the impulse came after I had worked for a period as a boy in a Dundee factory, where I had started to earn my living at a very early age — a common experience amongst Dundee boys of the sixties of last century. I tried in various ways to get a ship, but my age and size were against me. One ship-owner, I remember, told me to go home, sup more porridge, and then come back.
>
> Nothing daunted, I made it up with another boy to run away to Shields to look for a ship — a procedure that was common amongst adventurous lads in those days. We arranged to start on Saturday with our week's wages in our possession. This amounted to only a few shillings, but it seemed a lot to us.
>
> The first stage was to cross the Tay on the "Fifie." We got to Fife all right, but no further. My chum's mother was on our trail and ran us to earth at Newport pier. Our wages were taken from us, and we found our plans thwarted and our resources gone.[2]

However early in 1867 James was engaged as a boy on the Dundee barque *Stork*. He would be fourteen years of age upon joining the ship at Dysart with all his belongings in a pillowcase, for a voyage to Archangel during which the ship was damaged.

On the 11th November 1867 James was contracted as apprentice to William Crighton ship owner of Dundee for a period of four years; he was then fifteen years of age. His father is named as James Fairweather deceased, so his brother Alexander consents in his stead. His wage was £27, though he states it as £24 in his memoirs, four pounds to be paid in the first year, five pounds in the second, six in the third and twelve pounds for the fourth and last year, with a gratuity of three pounds if time is served with satisfaction. In return Crighton binds himself to teach the business of a seaman and provide him with meat, drink, lodging, washing, medical and surgical assistance (excluding apparel and sea bedding!). On the back dated Dundee 13 November 1871 is the note "I hereby certify that James Fairweather the within named apprentice has completed the terms of his apprenticeship to my satisfaction, Wm Crighton.'

James' apprenticeship was served on Crighton's brig *Wycliffe*. In his memoirs he mentions a voyage from Genoa to London, and also states that he had been across the equator and as far south as Bahia on the Brazilian coast and up the Mediterranean as far as Alexandria. In his book Captain James states that when his time was out he made a voyage to the Baltic and to the White Seas on the Dundee barque Stork. Later, in 1871 he joined the whaler *Tay* and subsequently became the mate of the *Victor*.

Regarding the *Tay* the following extract from grandpa's book is of interest:

> Nevertheless, for all the risks and adventures that are to be found on a voyage to the Arctic, it had its advantages over the ordinary merchant sailing vessels of these days. I well remember how I felt when I went on my first voyage in the whaler 'Tay' as a seaman. The galley fire was allowed to bum night and day. We got all the oil we wanted to burn in the lamps of our quarters. Plenty of food, and above all, three watches, so that we had only eight hours' duty out of the twenty-four, except when fishing. I could not believe it, and thought it too good to be true, it was all so different from what I had been accustomed to. Then we were going from and to Dundee direct, where our homes were, and last but not least, we had the winter at home. So all these advantages were well worth a few risks.[3]

Whaling and Sealing, a short history

The history of whaling is a vast and well-researched subject and it is possible here to give only the briefest facts, and refer readers who wish to know more to other sources. Suffice to say that the whale was hunted from earliest times.[1] Although by 1570 the Basques were sailing in large numbers to the Newfoundland whaling grounds, and explorers seeking the Northwest Passage reported large numbers of whales in the Davis Straits, the origin of the Arctic fishery was the North Atlantic, around Spitzbergen. The first British voyage to the Arctic was in 1610 when the Muscovy Company sent one ship to examine the industry's capabilities.

In the Seventeenth Century, the Dutch dominated the industry and their influence is perpetuated in the names of whaling personnel. Harpooner, spectioneer (he who had charge of the equipment), and schieman (captain of the hold) "are relics of our forerunners the Dutch, who had 300 sail in the fishing of 1665", according to Captain Hector Adams.[2]

By 1720, whaling in Spitzbergen waters was a thing of the past. The whales had been hunted out of existence and there was a headlong rush to exploit the new grounds of West Greenland and the Davis Strait. Hunting the small bottlenose whale however continued in the North Atlantic. The success of the British whaling industry fluctuated over this period, affected by trading conditions and war.

1808 was the start of a period of successful seasons but the Greenland whales caught were juveniles, for the second time an entire area had been fished out and attention again moved to the Davis Straits. The quest for whales moved northwards and large numbers were taken on the west coast of Baffin Bay. This was the peak of the industry. In 1813 Dundee had eight vessels.

By the late 1840s two voyages were often made in the season, the first to kill seals in the Greenland Sea, and then to the Davis Straits to hunt the whale. The most successful British ports were Hull, Peterhead, Aberdeen and Dundee. By 1857 Hull was the only English port persevering, and sealing (at which the Norwegians excelled) was becoming a lucrative business. The major technical advance, the advent of the steam engine, brought a new prosperity to the trade for a number of years. About 1857 several sailing vessels were converted to steam, including Captain James's first ship the *Tay;* many more were soon under construction. The old sails and rigging were still in place and the ships looked much the same as before, only the added funnel being conspicuous.

In 1859 Hull and Peterhead experimented with sending iron ships to the Arctic for the first time. In consequence Alex Stephen & Sons of Dundee built the *Narwhal*, the first custom built auxiliary steam whaler but constructed of timber. On the whole the wooden Dundee vessels fared better than their iron relatives, and wooden ships were considered the best ice ships for many years to come.

These steamers had the ability to pass through the ice, which would have stopped a sailing ship and thus had the edge over their competitors, Dundee leapt into prominence as a whaling port.[3]

There are two distinct groups of whales, those with teeth that are known as *Odontoceti* while those without are named *Mysticeti*. Among the former group is the Bottle-nosed whale (*hyperoodon ampullatus*) of about 13 to 16 feet in length and found mainly in the North Atlantic. Though primarily hunted by Norwegians, many were brought back to Dundee by Scottish Whalers, and noted in the records. The 'white' whale (*delphinapterus leucas),* also a toothed whale, was killed in great numbers by Dundee ships, usually when the Right whale had eluded them; most adults are only approximately 6 feet in length and highly gregarious. Captain James gives a good description of a 'white' whale kill.[4] (see pages 58 and 59).

The Narwhal (*monodon monoceros*) was also caught, but in much smaller numbers. A cousin of the 'white whale, it is distinguished from it by the presence of a long tusk growing out of the head of the male which may average 6 feet in length.[5]

However, as Norman Watson tells us "The chief quarry of the Dundee Whalers was Balaena Mysticetus, the Greenland Right whale, so called to distinguish it from the wrong one to catch. It was 'right' in that it was slow-moving, easy to hunt and floated when it was dead."[6] This whale, also known as the bowhead, was a docile giant, up to 65 feet long and weighing up to 100 tons or more. Its tail alone could be 30 feet across and its tongue weigh over a ton. In the cold Arctic waters it swam ponderously on the surface with its awesome mouth open, and its food was caught in the long slabs of its 'whalebone'. This was not actually bone, but a soft, springy tooth substitute called baleen that hung from its upper jaw in overlapping plates and acted as a filter for its intake of krill from the large mouthfuls of water taken in and expelled. No other whale had such a mass of baleen, making the Right whale a prime commercial target. Its cavernous mouth could yield a ton of this valuable bone and, as the years passed, fashions changed and whales grew scarce, 'whalebone' rose in price to £3000 per ton on Dundee's wharves. While the Right whale's flesh was not used, its heavy layer of fat, or blubber, the thickest of all whales at between 12 and 8 inches, was another valuable commodity and could produce as much as 7000 gallons of marketable oil after it was boiled on return to port."

This was done in factories near the docks, a messy and smelly procedure.

Initially the oil was used for lighting, but this use was superseded by gas. The trade in Dundee was then stimulated by the development of the Jute Industry. Jute was a cheap natural fibre imported from Bengal. Its use was stimulated by the invention of linoleum in about 1847, in which it was used as a backing material. Jute had many other uses and was made into canvas fabric for sails and sacks, and in time of war for tents and wagon covers. Oil was necessary as an agent for 'batching' or softening the raw

The ARCTIC, with boats fast to a "FISH".

jute. By 1913 mineral oil was underselling whale oil for this use, a factor in the decline of the whaling industry.[7] In passing one must mention that in whaling ports whaling was referred to as 'fishing', and the whale as a 'fish' In the nineteenth century it was not generally known that the whale was in fact a mammal.

The Dundee fleet continued to expand, and in 1861 consisted of eight steamers, rising to twelve in 1867. The returns for 1874 show how profitable the business could be. Seal skins were 4/6 each, the estimated value of a catch — around £30,600. Whaling was equally profitable, oil fetching £40 per ton and whale bone £540 per ton. The catch was valued at £87,500 minus the expense and fitting out eleven ships. By the end of the century the value of whalebone had risen to £2,500 a ton, perhaps the most important element in the catch economy.[8]

It has already been mentioned that for some time the Dundee Fleet had undertaken two voyages in the season. The first consisted of a sealing voyage to the Greenland Sea in the vicinity of Jan Mayen Island due north from the Orkneys. Ships would leave Dundee in late February or early March and sail via Lerwick in the Shetland Islands or Stromness on Orkney, returning to Dundee in April or early May. I remember reading that fortunate ships returned laden with seal skins and blubber to such an extent that there was barely room for the crew to bunk down. However if this was the case the voyage had been successful and the crew were delighted.

After unloading, the ship embarked within a few days on a second trip, to the Davis Straits for the whaling, usually returning to Dundee in the late autumn.

When the whalers left for the Davis Straits in April, the departure often coinciding with a local holiday, "the harbour was thronged with sightseers watching the boats put out to sea. It was a festive occasion enjoyed by all. The ships were bedecked with flags and bunting, and good luck tokens were thrown onto the vessels as they passed the lock gates".[9] Captain James confirms that the crew was usually drunk, and they often had to anchor in the river until the men were sober enough to put to sea.[10]

Captain James's career mirrors the above pattern. Nine out of ten voyages of the *Victor* and *Active* between 1872 and 1881 consist of two trips, the first to the Greenland Sealing, return to Dundee, followed almost immediately by a second voyage to the Davis Straits for the whaling.

By the middle of the 1870s whales taken were undersized, indicating impending scarcity. Whaling had its ups and downs but the general trend was a decline, whilst sealing continued to be profitable. Captain James indicates in his memoirs that it was the advent of steam whalers that enabled the Dundee owners to take advantage of the immensely seal-rich fishing grounds of the Newfoundland Seas. Although seals had been taken there in increasingly large numbers since at least 1805, it was much later in the century before a new pattern was established for Dundee ships. "The Western Ocean passage could be made earlier in the year, and the sealing taken *en route* to the whaling. It became necessary to arrange with agents at St John's, or to build yards where the cargo of seals could be taken care of, leaving the vessel free to proceed north."[11]

Chafes's Scotch Records state that "The first attempt to capture seals by steamer instead of the old fashioned sailing vessel was the SS *CAMPERDOWN* and SS *POLYNIA* originating from Scotland in 1862 in which year the SS *POLYNIA* had to put into St John's for repairs."[12]
Basil Lubbock lists the early Dundee voyages:
"In 1876 *Arctic* (Adams) first voyage to Newfoundland.
In 1877 *Arctic* and *Aurora* to Newfoundland.
In 1878 Close time commenced. *Arctic, Aurora, Esquimaux* and *Natwhal* to Newfoundland."[13]

There was however an initial snag as Captain James explains in his memoirs:

When in command of the Aurora, the season of 1884 was one of great anxiety to me in so far as I was, for various reasons, the only Master in the fleet of steamers leaving Dundee that spring who was to continue in command during the sealing trip. The others were superseded by Newfoundland Masters on arrival at St. John's. They went the trips, gaining experience, until the sealing was all over. They then again took over for the whaling.

The feeling among Newfoundlanders when Dundee steamers first went there was — that they welcomed the steamers very much, but they did not want Dundee Masters to command them during the sealing. The Newfoundland Masters were all more or less chieftains in their way, and drew their crews from the districts they came from themselves. The men were also to a great extent dependent on their Masters for their summer's work at the cod fishing, so that they viewed the advent of Dundee Masters as a breaking-up of old customs. As a "freelance" I was able through our agents to pick up a good crew, numbering something over three hundred all told, including the Dundee portion which was about sixty[14]

By 1881 the total number of seals taken in Newfoundland was 447,903 of these, six Dundee ships took 139,885.[15] In earlier years the catch had been even greater. Captain James went to St John's once with the *Thetis* in 1882, and his six voyages with *Aurora* all included Newfoundland. The pattern was straight to Newfoundland via the Shetlands Islands, then a major sealing voyage, followed by a shorter one possibly to Labrador, back to St John's with the cargo, then a long whaling voyage to the the Davis

Strait as far north as Cape York and Lancaster Sound. Late summer fishing in Cumberland Gulf was followed by return to Dundee in the autumn. Some Dundee ships, however, continued sealing in the Greenland Seas, sometimes sailing from St John's to Cape Farewell on the southern tip of Greenland, in pursuit of the old Hood Seals during their migration north.

The seals hunted by Dundee crews were not the fur-bearing variety from which seal skin jackets were made. These animals were found in the Behring Sea and the Aleutian islands in the North Pacific. The three species hunted by the Dundee men were known as hair seals, and comprised the Hooded Sear, the Bearded Seal (Ogjucks in Eskimo parlance) and the Harp or Saddleback Seal. All three species were to be found in the North Atlantic. The Hooded Seal produced pelts of high value, particularly from the young, which were known as blue backs, as well as oil. The Bearded Seal was hunted primarily for its pelt which was processed into industrial leather, also for food and oil. 'The skins and blubber had native subsistence use',[16] The Harp Seals are to be found breeding in huge numbers on the pack ice, and it was these animals which were slaughtered in their thousands off Newfoundland during the first annual sealing voyage from St John's. The young when born, are covered in stiff white wool which falls off in two to three weeks when hair takes its place. This white coat is in great demand, also the oil obtained from the young seal is of the finest quality. "Young seals are born on the Newfoundland ice, February 15th to 25th and are in perfect condition for the market by March the 20th."[17] The ships would lie in wait until the animals were in perfect condition and the slaughter by clubbing would commence before the pups took to the water. The second voyage was a much smaller affair when older seals and young who had taken to the water were shot, as there was now no necessity for silence.

I have written at some length about the sealing because it looms large in Captain James' memoirs, and he was master at a time when whaling was in decline, and sealing was the more economically important activity. "After the mid 1880's Dundee was the only remaining whaling port. By the 1890's lost ships were not replaced, the last whaler to be built being the Terra Nova in 1884."[18] We should not forget, however, that whaling was an extremely hazardous activity, requiring exceptional qualities in the men who undertook it. I do not intend to go into the gruesome details of sighting — from the crow's nest, taking to the boats, the harpooning, killing and flensing (removing the blubber) from the whale. The hunt is fully described in the articles by Captain Hector Adams printed in the appendix. The horrors of these activities can only be matched by the extreme courage and skill of the boat's crews, in the most dangerous conditions imaginable, sometimes in competition with boats of neighbouring whalers. In open rowing boats, armed with muzzle loading guns, and using hand lances on occasion to kill the whale, they sought their prey.

The attitude to wild life in those days was totally different from that of today. We can afford to take a high moral tone, but to Captains Alexander and James this was a business, and one in which they had to succeed in order to provide for their families. The same could be said of all the crew.

Nevertheless, the account by David Moore Lindsay of his voyage of 1884 with Captain James as master, makes gruesome reading, as they shot and killed every bird and animal possible with pride.[19] Whilst mate of the Victor, Captain James thought nothing of shooting a mother bear and her two cubs (later to adorn the drawing room floor), except as an achievement. These stories are too numerous to repeat.

By 1913 the Dundee whaling was almost at an end. The Arctic whales had been over fished, and mineral oil was underselling whale oil. Norwegian competition, in terms of oil production, from mother ships with steam powered whale catching vessels in attendance was more than the old fashioned Dundee wooden hulled whalers could compete with.[20] The demand for whaling products had diminished.

One aspect of the earlier voyages which impresses me is the lack of any technical communication; such as we take for granted today. From the point of view of the wives and mothers of the men, the ships disappeared down the "Silvery Tay" in the spring, and nothing further was heard of their loved ones until they reappeared in the late summer, probably to find a new arrival in their family. Casualties were common in such a dangerous enterprise, and women would not know if they were to be widows and destitute, with large families to feed and clothe. My grandmother always looked very serene, perhaps religion prompted acceptance of fate; such stress would be considered beyond belief in our comfortable era. Perhaps the families benefited from mutual support. Certainly the families of Captain Alexander and Captain James were close. According to cousin Ethel, James' family lived in East Newport, whilst Alex and family lived in West Newport. They were distinguished from each other in their generation by being known as the Faireys East and the Faireys West. With eight children and seven children respectively, Mary Ann and Helen were close in both family ties and experience of life.

To conclude this chapter, I quote from *Arctic Whalers* by Basil Lubbock:

The Qualities of a Greenland Whaling Master

In no other sea service was the personality of the captain so all important as in that of the Arctic whale and seal fishery.

First of all he had to be a natural leader of men, whose presence, whether on deck or in the crow's nest, gave his people perfect confidence and whose quietly voiced order was obeyed on the Jump.

He had to possess not only an intimate knowledge of a

whale's habits, but an equally deep knowledge of Arctic weather lore, of ice conditions, of Polar meteorology. He had to pilot his ship into unchartered bays and bights, where rocks offered shipwreck as well as ice, where currents brought towering bergs up against the wind and where a narrow channel between the land ice and sea ice was often the only navigable water.

Upon his skill the whole voyage depended. He had to decide whether to turn north or south; whether to take his ship into danger for a possible reward in blubber; to risk being nipped or even iced in for the winter, in order to complete his filled casks, or to turn homeward with the knowledge that his owners would have no dividend and his crew a hard winter before them and their families owing to a poor pay day.

Indeed the position of a ship master in the Greenland seas needed certain rare attributes of character which were as contradictory as those considered necessary in a General of Horse.

He had to be cautious and at the same time daring; he had to be as dogged and stubborn as a Chinese mule, yet as ready to change his tactics on the instant as a mongoose in fight with a cobra. He had to have that cold, cool courage, which even the most terrifying or desperate situation could not stampede; and by sheer force of character he had to put confidence into his crew when all seemed lost.

The correctness of his judgment meant the difference, often enough, between shipwreck and safety, between life and death. He had to size up a situation in one glance and unfalteringly take the right action where half a dozen alternatives offered.

In handling his ship he had to use a seamanship which no other form of sea trade required, for his heavy broad-beamed barque had to be handled like a passaging haute école charger. He had to stop her as quickly as if she had had four wheel brakes; back her down tortuous ice passages; turn her, whether to the wind or off the wind, short round on her heel, keep her dodging in a "hole of water" or under the lee of a protecting ice floe or berg, without making lee way; shoot her through narrow leads when heavy floe or field ice was closing in upon him, and when caught in a gale of wind in the pack keep her clear of the heavy chunks.

Ice seamanship, indeed, was a very specialised form of seamanship — of which we shall see a good deal as this book progresses. No present day seaman, unless he belongs to the Newfoundland sealing fleet, has probably ever heard of "overing" or "mill dolling" or "centipeding."

But on occasions the old-time whaling master had to resort to all those queer means of progress.

Our Greenland captain had to be possessed of a strong physique and tremendous stamina in order to stand the long hours of unceasing vigilance in his crow's nest when "on fish", or of nerve strain and endurance when he was navigating difficult ice or dangerous waters.

Most captains had grown up in the trade; indeed, I only know of one exception, the famous Captain Charles Yule who only recently (August 1935) celebrated his hundredth birthday; few ever left it except through compulsory circumstances.

Such men who had served their time in a whaler's half-deck and later perhaps filled every position on board before taking command were able to show each man on their articles how to do his work.

They were, of course, skilled harpooners, had a thorough knowledge of the shipwright's trade, could wield an adze or a caulking mallet, patch or repair a whale-boat, forge a whaling iron out of old horse-shoe "stubs," cut out and seam a sail, set up a cask, and use every weapon in the whaleman's armoury, whether it was the harpoon, hand-gun, lance, seal-club, ice-drill, blubber knife, king's fork, or closh.

But besides being a consummate master of his trade, the Arctic captain was usually a great sportsman and a keen naturalist; a good shot with a rifle, as keen an observer of fur and feather as of fin, and even a geologist, who was as quick to note a precious metal as a Rocky Mountain prospector.

Finally, he was a geographer and scientific explorer, who never neglected to survey a coast line or sound a new harbour or channel. To the two Scoresbys we owe our first knowledge of the East Greenland coast line. Many of the sounds on the west shore of Baffin Bay were discovered by whalers, notably that famous whale resort, Eclipse Sound, out of Pond's Inlet, which the daring Captain J. Gray of the Eclipse, Peterhead whaler, discovered in 1854.

Indeed, many an old whaling barque, many an ice-master, and even harpooner have been immortalised in the nomenclature of the Capes, Sounds, Bays and Inlets of the Arctic Seas.[21]

In the pages which follow, I believe it will become apparent that Captain James possessed most if not all these daunting qualities.

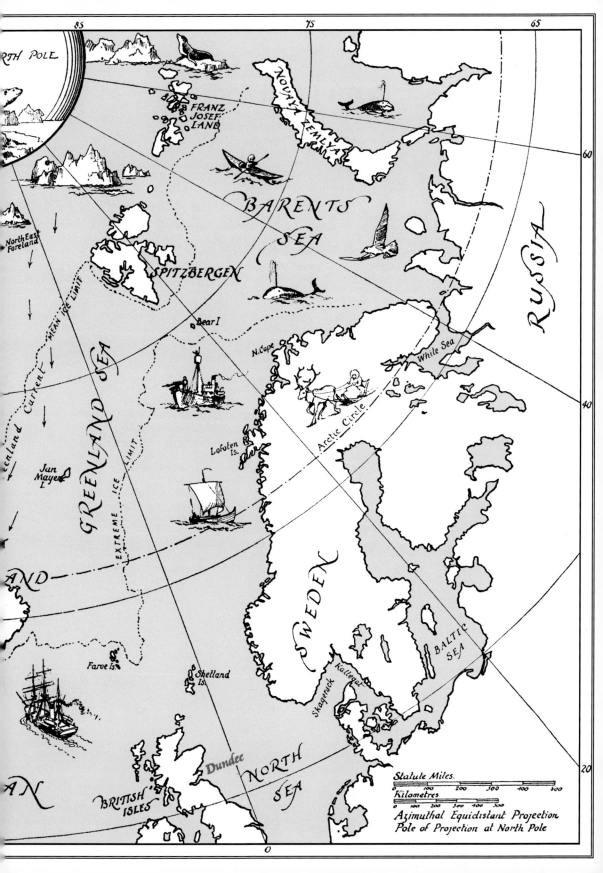

NORTH POLE

FRANZ
JOSEF
LAND

NOVAYA ZEMLYA

60

BARENTS
SEA

North East
Foreland

SPITZBERGEN

RUSSIA

MEAN ICE LIMIT

Greenland Current

Bear I

40

GREENLAND SEA

N. Cape

White Sea

Arctic Circle

EXTREME ICE LIMIT

Jan
Mayen
I.

Lofoten Is.

SWEDEN

LAND

BALTIC
SEA

20

Faroe Is.

Skagerack

Kattegat

Shetland
Is.

Dundee

NORTH
SEA

BRITISH
ISLES

AN

Statute Miles.
0   100   200   300   400   500
Kilometres
0   100   200   300   400   500

Azimuthal Equidistant Projection
Pole of Projection at North Pole

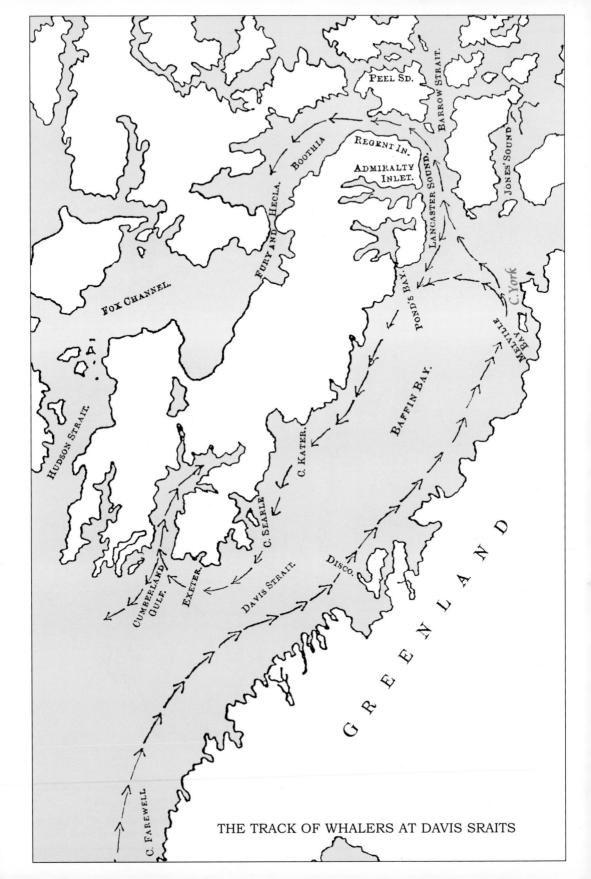

THE TRACK OF WHALERS AT DAVIS SRAITS

1872 to 1881 The Victor and the Active

It is clear from coverage in the press that the sealing and whaling industry was of great interest to readers, and must have contributed substantially to the economy of Dundee. Year by year accounts and statistics fill the columns of the 'Dundee Advertiser', the 'Dundee Courier' and other local and national newspapers,[1] particularly in the spring and autumn. The autumn figures were of most importance, and each year the yields and values are analysed and compared either favourably or unfavourably with those of the previous year. Early reports of the catches from Captains, with estimates as to the eventual tally were received, sometimes by telegraph from the first landfall, and printed. There is also a 'Dundee Year Book'[2] giving an annual summary of many aspects of Dundee life and industry, which printed sealing and whaling statistics.

The records of the Tay Whale Fishing Company,[3] who owned the *Victor* and the *Active*, have however provided what we deduce to be the most reliable information.

The information for the whaling years of Captain James' career comes largely from these sources. For certain years such as 1877 and 1884 an independent account of a voyage provides splendid supplementary material, and of course Captain James gives his own inimitable and sometimes very detailed recollections in his book.

One slight difficulty has been to get an absolute agreement between tallies of the catches in the various accounts. One can imagine that it was an impossibility to know exactly how many seals for instance were killed on a particular voyage. Sometimes too, the catches for the two voyages were not noted separately, so it is impossible to say how many seals were slaughtered on each. We have to be satisfied with the combined figure.

In 1872 the Dundee sealing and whaling fleet consisted of eleven ships. All were captained by well-known Dundee masters, the senior being Captain Adams of the *Arctic*. Alexander Fairweather is not named as a master in 1872 but captained the *Diana* in 1873, and the Active in 1874 and subsequently. However it is very likely that he sailed in the fleet in 1872, possibly as chief officer and first mate. James as a seaman on the *Victor* would know many men in the fleet, mostly his fellow Dundonians.

The fleet was both co-operative and competitive. It operated as a loose unit, parting and meeting throughout the voyages. Sometimes the competition in the fishing was intense, with rival crews from two vessels pursuing the same whale in small boats in conditions of infinite danger. Conversely in times of crisis help was at hand and in case of shipwreck, which was not infrequent, the masters gave every possible assistance to their rivals.

1872 This year Captain James entered the employment of the Tay Whale Fishing Company; his first ship was the *Victor* of 278 tons. According to a reference from G.W. Welch written on 17 November 1881, He 'served in the seal and whale fishing ships under my management for the space of nine years from 1872 inclusive in the several capacities through all the grades of office up to master of the (ss) *Active*, which you have commanded for the past three years."

We can assume that Captain James commenced in a fairly lowly capacity, but by at least 1877, he was chief officer (first mate).

In **1872** under Captain Edwards, the *Victor* made two voyages. She departed from Dundee on the 24th February for Greenland and returned on the 27th April. Her second destination was the Davis Straits, departing on 4th May and not returning until the 27th November.

The following is an account of the results of the fishing in 1872, from the 'Dundee Advertiser' of November 29th:

REVIEW OF THE DUNDEE WHALE
AND SEAL FISHING

The Victor, the last of the Dundee whaling fleet, having now arrived, we give our annual review of the results of the fishing. The seal fishing this year was a comparative failure, The vessels engaged in its prosecution were the following: — Arctic (Adams), Erik (John B. Walker), Esquimaux (Yule), Narwhal (M'Lennan), Camperdown (Gravill), Ravenscraig (Allan), Tay (Greig), Intrepid (Souter), Victor (Edwards), Diana (Kilgour), Polynia (Wm. Walker).

The respective catches of these were:

	Seals	Oil, tons
Arctic,	8000	80
Erik,	7000	70
Esquimaux,	5300	55
Narwhal,	4400	40
Ravenscraig,	3700	40
Camperdown,	3200	39
Tay	3442	35
Intrepid,	2764	32
Diana,	1400	23
Victor,	1402	15
Polynia,	13	-
	40,621	429

The price of seal oil has been £39 per ton, and the catch of the season is therefore represented by £16,731. To this, however, has to be added to the value of the skins. The price of each is 4s 6d and this gives for the whole £9139 14s 6d, so that altogether the seals taken by the Dundee vessels were worth £25,870 14s 6d.

Then, as regards the whale fishing, ten vessels were engaged as against eight last year; but the catch is 145 tons less than in 1871. It is, however, considerably in excess of that for the six previous years, and may be regarded as very successful. he result of this season's fishing is as follows:

	Fish (whales)	Oil tons	Whalebone cwt.
Arctic,	16	21013	13
Camperdown,	25	160	7
Intrepid,	16	130	9½
Esquimaux,	12	55	5½
Ravenscraig,	10	90	4
Narwhal,	6	80	4½
Victor,	8	70	3½
Tay,	7	70	3
Erik,	5	70	3
Polynia,	1	15	1
	105	1010	54

The same issue announced:

ARRIVAL OF THE *VICTOR* - On Wednesday, the whale ship Victor arrived in Dundee. She brings eight fish, which will yield 70 tons of oil and 4 tons of bone. The cause of her being so long behind the other whalers is explained by the fact that she was detained ten days by stress of weather. There have been no accidents on board during the whole of the voyage.

1873 Captain Edwards was again Master and the same two voyages were undertaken. The *Victor* departed for Greenland on the 26th of February returning to Dundee on the 25th of April. She then steamed to the Davis Straits, departing on the 3rd May and returning on the 4th November. Her combined catch:

Seals	8568
Whales	13
Seal Oil	75 tons
Whale Oil	75 tons

The fleet consisted of ten ships and the sealing was more successful than 1872, but still regarded as a 'comparative failure'. The whaling however is given good coverage, with an account in the 'Dundee Advertiser' of 19 September headed Great success of Dundee whaling fleet'. Captain Adams alone killed 28 whales in *Arctic*, this was calculated to yield 260 tons of oil, one of the biggest, if not the biggest cargo ever brought to Dundee. The excitement of the year was the fleet's involvement with the *Polaris*

Expedition, sent by the United States government to extreme northern latitudes in Smith Sound for polar discoveries and investigations for scientific purposes. The ship was wrecked and the survivors suffered extreme hardship before being picked up by the whaler *Ravenscraig*. They were transferred to the *Arctic* and arrived in Dundee to scenes of tremendous interest and excitement, 'A large crowd were waiting at the dock gates this morning expecting the *Arctic's* arrival. On the 22nd it was reported that crowds including the leading citizens thronged the West station to watch the departure of the American explorers for Liverpool and embarkment for New York.

One interesting feature of the year was the success of Captain Adams in penetrating the Gulf of Boothia (inland from Lancaster Sound and south of Prince Regent Inlet), which was fished for the first time.

1874 There is an abundance of information about the voyages of 1874 from the records of the Tay Whale Fishing Company, but also from accounts in the 'Dundee Advertiser':

> The *Victor* was fitted with new engines and boilers for this season and had a successful trial trip on February 14th cruising about the river until about six o'clock. A party of gentlemen — directors of the company, and a representative of Gourlay Brothers who constructed the engines, were on board and were highly pleased with the working of the engines and the sailing of the vessel.

As usual the first voyage was to Greenland and the ship under Captain Edwards left Dundee on the 28th February, and returned on the 26th April. News must have already reached Dundee because on April 16th the 'Advertiser' announced '*The Victor* has been damaged. She was struck by heavy ice'. The following day further comments were printed 'the season was not favourable to the successful prosecution of the fishing. Strong easterly winds with protracted fogs prevailed, and there was so much bay ice that the men encountered great difficulty in following up and killing the seals. Every day several members fell through and got severely chilled. Fatal results have occurred in two cases' (of the fleet). Interestingly the next paragraph reads:

> "It has been remarked that the seal packs seen this season were not nearly so extensive as those encountered in years gone by. By some, this has been attributed to the tremendous slaughter which has been carried on uninterruptedly and the old ideas of instituting a close season has again been suggested."

It appears that the Victor only brought back 850 seals yielding 7 tons of oil. The total catch for the fleet of eleven ships was 46,252 seals worth £30,601; it is not clear whether this was the total for one or both voyages.

The *Victor* departed for the Davis Strait on the 3rd of May, but with a new master. The 'Advertiser' announced that Captain Deuchars had been appointed for the whaling voyage, which proved very eventful for the fleet. Two ships were lost; the *Tay* and the *Arctic*, and the *Victor* had a narrow escape.

The *Tay* was the first to go. She was lost on June the 16th in the notorious Melville Bay, where, after getting into difficulties earlier in the day, she was later crushed amongst heavy ice and cut through by the ice floes; she sank in three quarters of an hour. Nothing of the vessel floated to the surface except the figure head — which was a full sized representation of Queen Elizabeth. All the crew succeeded in reaching the *Nova Zembla* which was only three miles distant.

In August a further drama occurred in the Gulf of Boothia, when the *Arctic* was lost and the *Victor* nearly also.

After great success in the whaling the 'Dundee Telegraph' states that on the 7th August a fearful gale was encountered. The wind blew fiercely from the southward, and rain fell in torrents. The *Victor* was severely squeezed and as already reported, the Arctic was lost. She first got into trouble at 8.30am on August 7th when she was squeezed heavily having been beset. At 9am the vessel was completely on her beam-ends and the port bow was stove in. The crew of 54 were walking about without shelter and drenched to the skin, though they had all their effects and provisions on the ice. At 6pm the Arctic caught fire, the ice then opened and the wreck went down stern first. For several days the crew had to live on the ice in two tents. On the 9th the crew were taken on board the *Intrepid*, but were eventually put on board the *Victor*.

The *Victor* nearly suffered a similar fate. "So alarming was the state of matters that the crew of the Victor had their clothes removed to the ice, and provisions stowed away to meet any emergency." Captain James Fairweather would be one of those who suffered this frightening experience. On the 12th the *Victor* got clear. The *Victor* left the fishing ground on 25th August and got to Thurso on Tuesday. Captain Deuchars brought home Captain Adams and Mr Edward, the mate on the *Arctic*; Captain Loffley, master of the *Tay*; twenty-five of the *Arctic* crew and six hands belonging to the *Tay*.

It was Captain Deuchars who, on his arrival at Thurso, telegraphed news of the loss of the *Arctic* to Mr George Welch of the Tay Whaling Company. This was a major loss to the company of its finest and most successful ship.

Captain Alex Fairweather brought home thirteen of the crew of the *Tay* on his ship the *Active*. He states that the season was very favourable for the successful prosecution of the fishing and that many whales had been seen.

The 'Telegraph' stated that this was Captain Deuchar's first voyage in the Victor, and the success which he achieved (is) very gratifying.

Other items of interest in the press this year included a report by Captain Alexander of the sad death of eskimo Ocacock who had been rescued at

Greenland the previous year and was being returned to his native land in the Ravenscraig.

An extract from 'Land and Water'[4] is printed objecting to the premature slaughter of pregnant seals and in particular those who have just given birth. The cruelty of this proceeding is highlighted and also the futility, as it would be more profitable to postpone the killing for five days until the young are grown to size worthy of value.

The *Victor* arrived back in Dundee on the 11th September, her Davis Strait catch was:
24 Whales yielding 140 tons of Oil and l20 cwt of Bone.

Tying the knot
Six weeks later to the day James Fairweather married Mary Ann Craik. James' elder brother Alexander had married his first cousin Helen Mitchell on the 24th of November 1868. Now it was James' turn to take a bride, his childhood sweetheart Mary Ann. They were to be married for over 58 years and to have eight children. Grandpa's memoirs bear the inscription dated the 23rd of October 1928, their 54th Wedding Anniversary:

TO MY DEAR WIFE
Who has shared with me the joys and sorrows
of the past fifty-four years this work is respectfully dedicated.
Bonavista
Newport Fife
23 October 1928

These touching words, reinforced by his letters, surely tell the story of their relationship. Their long marriage was fraught with periods of danger and separation, particularly in the later stages of James' career, when he was in the East for nearly three years; as well as extreme tragedy when three of their sons predeceased them. Through it all, my grandmother remained a calming influence on his more mercurial temperament.

The marriage took place at the bride's home 3 Crescent Street, Dundee after banns according to the forms of the U.P.Church.

James Fairweather, seaman M. S. (Merchant Service) aged 21, and Mary Ann Craik, powerloom weaver aged 23.
James's address is given as 86 Albert Street.
His father - James Fairweather, cabinet maker, master, deceased; his mother - Janet Forbes, prev. Fairweather, maiden surname Fleming.
Her father - Charles Craik, factory night watchman; mother - Eliza Craik maiden surname Smith.
Witnesses were Alexander Ramsay and Elizabeth Craik (the bride's sister).

It seems appropriate here to say a few words about the Craik family. The Crake or Craik family also had their origins in Kirriemuir. The earliest records go back to James Crake in the early 18th Century, whose son James was baptised in 1740. His grandson Charles, Mary Ann's father, was baptised on October 31st 1805. Charles married Eliza Smith daughter of Alexander Smith and Ann Jones, born in Ireland circa 1813. The search for Eliza's background is what genealogists call a 'needle in a haystack job'. Mary Ann baptised on the 14th May 1851 at Kirriemuir was the youngest of six children and the family followed the same migratory course to Dundee as had the Fairweathers. It is indeed possible that they were known to one another which would account for James and Mary Ann's early friendship.

The Craiks were handloom weavers in Kirriemuir in the linen trade. When this declined they moved to Dundee, where in the 1861 census Charles is listed as a jute weaver of 3 Crescent Street. By 1874 he was a factory night watchman, the occupation also given on his death certificate of June 20, 1891. He lived to be eighty three and his wife seventy nine; another long lived couple.

I have a photograph which I strongly believe to be of Charles and Eliza though one can never be certain when they are not identified in writing. In my opinion the Craiks were tall, dark and handsome, in contrast to the Fairweathers who were stocky and tending to be pear shaped in later years. Of James and Mary Ann's children, Charles, Elizabeth, and my mother Mary Ann Craik were of Fairweather build, whilst Willie, Helen (Ella) and David were very tall and striking in appearance.

The Fairweather and Craik families maintained close contact and in a letter dated 22nd of January 1988 my late kinsman Sir Charles Craik Cunningham states "She (Mary Ann) must have been a relative because the link with Captain Fairweather was often spoken of when I was very young. Indeed I had an 'eskimo' doll (which I admired but was rather afraid of) representing a gloomy little man dressed in seal skin which was said to have been given to me by Captain Fairweather."[5] Eskimo dolls were a common toy in Dundee. Little girls were the envy of the street if father or grandfather brought one home. They were called "Yacky Das"; yacky, yackie or yakkie being a whaler's name for an Inuit.[6]

On Saturday September 16, 1876, Mary Ann gave birth to their first child James at 6am, at 3 Crescent Street. Young James was to become father to my cousin Jim Fairweather of Australia, and also to pursue a distinguished career in the Merchant Navy. James and Mary Ann were probably still living with her parents and James was at sea at the time of the birth.

1875 The Master of the *Victor* for this and the following two seasons was Captain Nicholl, and in all three years the destinations were Greenland waters, followed by the Davis Straits. The *Victor* left Dundee for Greenland on 27th of February, but returned 'clean' ie. with no catch on 24th April. She departed again on 29th of April for a long voyage, returning on the 20th of November. This time she brought home:

54 Seals which produced ¾ tons of Seal Oil,
6 Whales yielding 35 tons of Whale Oil.

Captain James mentions this voyage in his memoirs and tells an amusing story of a football match on ice and its unexpected consequence:

In Davis Straits in the season 1875 the crews of all the steamers engaged in the trade had gone what our Captain called "fitba' mad.' On each of the steamers there was a football team, and when any two steamers met, either on ice or in a harbour, they had a friendly game. We had just come out of Dexterity Harbour, where we had met various steamers, and the crews had had a lot of football. We were working down the Straits, when it came on thick fog, and the vessel was made fast to the Land-Ice.

My watch on deck was from eight to twelve p.m. It was daylight, but, as I have said, very thick fog. The members of the watch asked if they could go on the ice and have a game of football. I gave the permission asked for, telling them to go far enough not to disturb the watch below, but near enough to keep within hearing of the bell. So off they went with their ball (which was made out of sealskin), leaving only the Harpooner of the watch and myself on deck. All went well for a while, but all of a sudden we heard a terrible noise, and on looking over we saw them all running to the ship, crying: "A bear! A bear!" There was only one ladder for them to get on board by, and that a swinging one. They were all trying to get up at once, which caused delay and confusion. When order was restored, I learned that after they had been playing for some time, one of them got a vigorous kick at the ball. Another ran for it, only to find a full-grown Polar bear running for it too, from the other direction. They had not seen the bear sooner because of the fog. Then it was a case of the bear catch the hindmost, even the referee joining in the race; and Bruin was left in full charge. But not for long. The Harpooner and I got our rifles, went on the ice, and shot the bear when it was still tearing at the sealskin ball.[7]

A letter to 'The Times' of March 8th 1875 was printed in the 'Dundee Advertiser'. Once again the subject of a closed season for the Greenland sealing is being debated and parliamentary papers have been distributed. The extreme cruelty of sealing early in the season is strongly emphasized and it is suggested that international law should prevent killing before April 6th.

1876 The *Victor* under Captain Nicholl departed for Greenland on February 28th, and returned on May 29th. She left for the Davis Straits on May 6th and returned on November 4 th; the combined catch was:

Seals   3272 producing 30 tons of Seal Oil
Whales   5 producing 52 tons of Whale Oil

Captain James' memoir contains an extract from this period covering a variety of topics, from his assessment of the eskimo character, to a whaling anecdote which is characterised by his humorous touch in recounting how the second mate lost his beloved pipe:

The Eskimo has always been considered a docile race. Referring to the individuals we met on the west coast of Davis Straits, they were docile, in my opinion, only because they could not help themselves. Given an opportunity, I think they could and would show their teeth. The master of the whaler "Alexander" of Dundee had the name of being very good to them. But when she was crushed and lost in Ponds Bay, just before my time, I have been told that the master and crew had a bad time with the natives.

A case that fell under my own observation occurred when I was mate of the "Victor." The steamer was hooked on to the ice in Admiralty Inlet. Two sledges with two men and a lad in each, all typical natives, came on board. They had nothing with them, but they told the master that they had skins and horns ashore, and if he sent a boat for them they would barter. So I was sent with a boat and boat's crew — taking the four adult natives with me in the boat, the lads driving the sledges to the land.

We pulled for a long distance, then landed at a place where there were a lot more natives. The four Eskimos got out of the boat, so also did two of my men, who were at once surrounded. One of them, the blacksmith, had on a large thick red worsted muffler. All at once I saw two of the natives trying to take it off, one pulling one way and the other pulling the other way, till the man was nearly choked. Then a general melee took place. I whipped off the gun cover of the harpoon gun, and fired the wad amongst them. That made them scatter. My two men rushed for the boat, got in, and we got away. Ever after that I refused to trust the natives when they were in the majority, but I always saw that they were well-treated when they gave us a visit.

When in Admiralty Inlet on that occasion, I got fast to a whale, and when the lines were running out, the bollard got heated, causing a lot of smoke. I had my back to the crew, so called for water to be thrown on the lines. It is the line manager's duty to wet the lines, but he had lost his head, so the man next me, an Irishman, got hold of a piggan, and the first thing that I knew was getting a douse bath. I yelled to him not to throw the water there. "Well, sir, that is where the fire is, anyhow," he answered. During the killing of this whale an incident occurred which was so unusual that I think it worth recording here. The whale, after being fastened, took under the fast ice off Admiralty Inlet. In time it became evident that it was not likely to come out to us, as the ice was so honeycombed that it was able to break it anywhere when it wanted to breathe, so it was a case of Mahomet and the Mountain. We went to it, carrying with us a rocket-gun and some hand lances. When near to where we expected it to show itself we spread out to wait. While waiting, the second mate, Thomas Burnett, thought he would take a smoke, so got his pipe filled and ready. Now, the whole tragedy hinges on that pipe. It was a meerschaum pipe, and according to Tom there never was such another. It had all the virtues that a smoker could desire. He made an idol of it, and spent much time cleaning it, or covering it with fancy-work. On this occasion, just as he got it agoing, the whale broke the ice right under his feet and lifted Tom up on its crown-bone. When it subsided again Tom was left in the water amongst the broken ice. Fortunately, we had about five fathoms of small rope attached to the rocket-gun, and, with the help of that, Tom was soon fished out of the water. But when it dawned on him that his beloved pipe was lost, then the atmosphere took on a most lurid hue. He certainly had a wonderful vocabulary.[8]

1877 In the back of a bound volume of Captain James' articles for the 'Scots Magazine' are pasted some excellent articles written by Captain Hector Adams for the magazine of the P.S.N.C. (Pacific Steam Navigation Company) which was called 'Sea Breezes'.[9] In order to bring this material into the public domain, they are printed in an appendix. There are thirty-two pages divided into nine chapters. Apart from the first chapter of five pages, the other eight are devoted to a very detailed account of the sealing and whaling voyages of the *Victor* in 1877, when Captain Fairweather was First Officer. As an account of a whaling voyage it could not be bettered, particularly on the technical side; which is lacking in David Moore Lindsay's account in *A Voyage to the Arctic in the Whaler Aurora* of 1884.

In 1887, the author of the account, Hector Adams, aged seventeen, was just beginning his career. Captain James was then aged twenty three-twenty four, and first mate under Captain John Nicholl.

The *Victor* left Camperdown Dock Dundee on the 20th of February 1877 and headed for Lerwick to complete the crew. They steamed northeast and entered the ice; by April the 22nd they had been as far north as 78.40 degrees North, 3 degrees of Longitude East, and it became evident that the Greenland sealing voyage was a failure. They had caught 500 seals, 3 bears and 15 sharks; the ship returned to Dundee.

On May the 3rd they sailed again, this time for the whaling, travelling up the west coast of Greenland to Disco Island where they had the usual dance with the eskimo maidens. They continued through Melville Bay to Smith Sound then west to the Carey Islands then south to Lancaster Sound, where, near North Devon Land they caught some white whales. These are small mammals of 10 to 14 feet in length.

By the middle of June they had three medium sized whales, 52 white whales, one male and four female Narwhal, and three or four Walrus, also six bears.

They then caught an enormous female whale; there is a gruesome account of the seven hour fight to kill her. She was 81 feet long and her estimated gross weight about 74 tons, yielding 18ft.of baleen. Basil Lubbock mentions this catch on page 407 of *Arctic Whalers*.

The summer fishing finished in early August and they sought harbour in Cumberland Gulf for 'cleaning down' and checking and repairing equipment. During the summer fishing the *Victor* took only six fish, yielding 68 tons of oil. The weather changed with the last day of August and the fall fishing yielded no results. They set off for home on October 3rd in a blizzard, and had a narrow escape with an iceberg before arriving back in Dundee on 9th November.

The first mention of Captain James in Hector Adam's account is in the crew list where his name is listed second, after the Master, John Nichol.

He then figures in the sad account of shooting a starving polar bear who approached the ship during the sealing voyage. "A terrible figure, gaunt and starving, that lopeing (sic) trot brought him within 200 feet of the ship, and he arose, erect on his hind legs, with his great paws extended — as if defying the ship and its puny occupants. He dropped, with a projectile from the mate's 'Martini Henry' which went under his chin and out through his brain. The contents of his stomach consisted of two pebbles. His hams were strung on the martingale stay for food and the skin was salted and packed away."

There is an account of a fracas between the crews of two whalers at Lerwick on the outward whaling voyage. The incident culminated in the miscreants raiding a hat shop, and they were escorted aboard wearing assorted headgear, by special constables. On sailing, the ship required some pumping after a strong south westerly wind and high sea. The mate ordained that the pumps be manned and relieved by the 'bad lads' who got adrift at Lerwick. A typical example, this, of Captain James making 'the punishment fit the crime'.

In mid-June , Hector Adams recounts the tally of wildlife taken so far, and records that "the deer and most of the bears had fallen to our chief mate

Mr J Fairweather, a keen gunner and a 'merciful' shot." This again seems totally in character and it is noted elsewhere that Captain James was a humane man, in a cruel profession.

On the same page is an account of a bear hunt on the ice by Adams and Captain James. Hector was on this occasion hailed by the mate to go with him 'after a bear'. The second mate had replied from the nest "There seems to be three of them." I ventured to ask Mr F. as we plodded along "What am I to do with a shot gun?" and "what's to happen if we meet them?" He gave a grim chuckle and replied "ye'r just to round them up to me, till I'll get a mark on them."

After a circular walk of three or four miles to get leeward of the bears they came to a high hummock. Poor Hector was angry and sore having been told to "keep out of line of fire". The outcome was that Captain Fairweather shot an old female bear. Her two half grown cubs were however rounded up by the crew and got aboard. The cooper made barrels into which they were hauled and they returned to Dundee well fed and kept clean and healthy with a daily good wash with the deck hose.

Captain Hector Adam's last mention of Captain James is of a meeting between the two at Antwerp in 1893: "He was then the master of a big steamer and I was chief officer of the ss. *Alberta*", he adds, "I am informed that in consequence of some legal action, as between managers and shareholders, he had been authorised by the judge to control the necessary expenses for the benefit of the company, and all concerned, and to report in regard to the same, to the Admiralty Court; than which (I may say) no greater compliment could be paid to his character and probity as a shipmaster."

He concludes with a reference to Captain Fairweather's war service, which is quoted later in this account.

The 'Dundee Evening Telegraph' contains an extract from that morning's 'Glasgow Herald'. The writer analyses the seal and whale catch for 1877 and points out the discrepancies between the catches of the ships, some of which return laden whilst others are less successful. The article also contains the observation, after emphasizing that the industry is in decline: "It is very questionable we think, if it were not that some of the manufactures carried on in Dundee require the aid of animal oil, if whaling would be continued to the extent it is. In some years very few whales are caught and although eighty-two right whales have been taken this year, there is no guarantee that fifty will be obtained at next year's fishing, or even half that number in 1879."

The *Victor* returned to Dundee on November the 9th, and on December the 22nd 1877, James was granted his Certificate of Competency as Master, by the Lords of the Committee of Privy Council for Trade:

Whereas it has been reported to us that you have been found duly qualified to fulfil the duties of master in the Merchant Service we do hereby in pursuance of the Merchant Shipping Act 1854 grant you this Certificate of Competency.

He was twenty-four years of age.

1878 was a very quiet and unsuccessful year for the Victor under Captain Adam. Only one voyage was undertaken, to the Davis Strait, sailing on the 7th of March and returning on the 3rd of November 'clean'; it seems hard to believe that the ship was out for such a long period with no result.

A list of provisions and stores for the *Victor* in 1874 gives us some idea of the crew's diet during a voyage of some months:

2	Butts beef
5	Butts pork
4	Casks bread
2	Casks flour
2	Casks meal
1	Cask pease
1	Cask barley
1	Casks rice
1	Cask treacle
2	Casks sugar
2	Cases limejuice
1	Box tea plus 1 chest tea (112lb)
1	Cask coffee
1	Bag tobacco (82 lbs)

The annual review of the seal and whale fishing in the 'Dundee Advertiser' tells us that *Camperdown* had been wrecked in the Davis Straits in October. Survivors were brought home by the *Erik* of London. Conditions must have been severe for the *Intrepid* (Captain Nicholl) had been unable to penetrate Melville Bay from east to west. The *Victor* had arrived on Sunday night 'clean'. The fleet had consisted of twelve vessels, four of which went straight to Newfoundland instead of Greenland. The *Victor* and the *Mazinthien* went straight to the early whale fishing without any success. There had been an increase in the sealing and a large decrease on the whaling compared with 1877. The Seals killed amounted to 77,411 yielding 1,106 tons of oil. Only 6 Whales were killed yielding 114 tons of oil and 6 tons of bone.

However, the end of 1878 was momentous for Captain James, who was appointed to his first command. One year after obtaining his master's certificate he was appointed Master of the ss *Active* at the age of twenty-five.

1879 *Active* was Captain James' first command and this is what he had to say about her: "Speaking about the *Active* reminds me that she was my first command, and I was very proud of her indeed, and viewed from any point, I thought her a thing of beauty, and in my opinion a joy for ever'.[10] He also said the following which may be regarded as surprising in view of subsequent events: The voyages on the *Active* were uneventful enough as voyages go . . . "[11]

For a start, the *Active* left Dundee for Greenland, and it was reported in the 'Advertiser': 'Captain Fairweather states that he left Dundee on the 3rd of March and reached Shetland after a splendid time of 25 hours." A heavy gale of wind was experienced and the Active shipped a sea which carried away one of her boats. In consequence of the severe weather she had to put back to Lerwick. She continued north and made ice on the 21st of March. A dense fog prevailed for three days before the sealing began and when it cleared away the ice had broken up in consequence of the southerly winds. The seals were so spread that only a few could be got at a time. On the 3rd of April 1,000 seals were caught and 300 on each of the two following days, and 100 were caught during the rest of the time. The weather on the whole was good and the health of the crew excellent. The *Active* left the ice on the 13th and had a fine passage home, arriving at Dundee on April 20th.

They left for the Davis Straits on Saturday the 26th of April and once again Captain James has stories to tell about the voyage. Having no doctor on board he had problems with a seaman who wanted a tooth pulled out, a problem which Captain James solved in his inimitable manner by a combination of horseplay and psychology, until medical help became available. Towards the end of the voyage the following incident took place which shows what resourcefulness had to be exercised alone and far from help:

> The Arctic is a hard school to pass through, and resource is forced on those in charge. As the whaling voyage alone generally lasted six months, we ourselves had to do any necessary repairs as best we could.
>
> The fall of 1879, when I was on the "Active," came very near to being a disastrous one, as at one time it looked as if we were to be caught in the pack-ice for the winter. I still think that, had it not been for a long spell of south-west winds, such would have happened, at least to the smaller vessels, of which the "Active" was one one. In September all the vessels were at or about Cape Kater. The weather was good, and there was little ice in sight, but some of the older masters were getting suspicious. The sea was keeping too smooth and inclined to freeze over on the least provocation, and other symptoms were there for those who could see them.

The *Active* berthing in the Dundee Docks.
Captain Alexander Fairweather was master in 1874, 1875, 1876, 1887 and 1888.
Captain James Fairweather was master in 1879, 1880 and 1881.

It was agreed that we would all go off to eastward and make sure that our retreat was not cut off by the ice coming down the middle.

We only too soon found out that the latter was the case, as we came against a very heavy pack of ice, stretching away to the north and south, how far none of us knew. At first we followed the edge of it to the south, but found it trended to the west, and finally we were satisfied that it was against the land to the south of us. So we were in a trap.

The fleet by this time had separated in pairs. I had the "Narwhal" for a companion. We came back North as long as we could make some easting. Then there was nothing else for it but to take the pack and work due East. The southwest wind had come away by that time, and holes of water were showing here and there, and we were getting on fairly well until the engineer came to me and said that the main sea-cock had choked up with ice, and that we would have to stop, as he could get no water for the boiler. We tried every known expedient to clear the valve, but without success (we had not reached the stage when a steam jet was fitted into the valve), so we were driven to a most drastic cure, which was no less than a decision to take off the cover and chance being able to put it on again.

It was really a dry-dock job, but we had no dock near us, and had the possibility of a winter in the pack if we did not get out of it soon. We had lost sight of the "Narwhal" some nights before that. All the pumps were put in order. The sea-cock was on the starboard side. So the vessel was stopped in a hole of water, with the wind on the port side, then ropes were passed under and around the vessel. The best topsail we had was spread out and pulled down head first under the ship's bottom, on the off-chance of its covering the outside of the sea-cock.

When all was ready, the cover was taken off and the valve cleared itself at once. With the precautions taken, the rush of water was not so great as we expected. Still it was only with a lot of trouble and many attempts that the cover was got on again. I was assisting the engineer throughout the job. and when right in the thick of it, with water flying all over us, a cry arose that the ship was on fire. I could just see by looking over my shoulder that she was burning under the boiler, so told them to turn the hose on it. That was done with good effect, and it was soon put out. It was the boiler-seat that had caught on when the fires were drawn

The getting of the topsail on board again was no mean job. However, it was accomplished, and in time we got safely out of the pack, quite close to the east side of Davis Straits. For some days before that, we were burning one third each of wood, rope and coal. When we got free, there was just sufficient coal left to do the cooking. So the passage home had to be made by sail alone. But that was no hardship with the "Active".[12]

The *Active* returned to Dundee on the 3rd of November and the total returns were as follows:

Seals	1721
Whales	3
Seal Oil	22 tons
Whale Oil	23 tons
Whale Bone	30 cwt

Captain James appears to have had modest success in this his first season of Greenland sealing and Davis Strait whaling on the *Active*.

The main news story for 1879 was the loss of *Our Queen* which was captained by Alexander Fairweather. 'The 'Dundee Advertiser' of September 2nd gives the following account. The ship had previously undergone a trial trip on March 5th. A subsequent account gives further details:

THE LOSS OF THE OUR QUEEN

Captain Fairweather, who has come home on board the Arctic, reports that his ship, Our Queen, was lost in Admiralty Inlet on the 18th July. The Our Queen was bought by a company of Dundee gentlemen last year, and converted into a steamer. She was a very strong ship, and was fortified in the most substantial manner. At the Greenland fishing she was the most successful of the Dundee fleet bringing home a cargo of 36 tons. After refitting, she left Dundee for Davis Straits on the 28th April, and having completed her crew at Shetland, she sailed from Lerwick on the 1st May. An unusually stormy passage was experienced, and the ship did not reach Holsteinborg till 31st May. Melville Bay was crossed on the 22nd of June and Lancaster Sound was entered on the 25th. The first whale was caught the following day, and by the 10th of July 14 whales had been got on board, the yield of oil being calculated at 120 tons and six tons of bone. From the 11th till the 17th June numbers of whales were seen, but they could not be got at, on account of the ice being so closely packed together. On the latter date, when the ship was in Admiralty Inlet, she got beset and was fastened in a large dock off Cape Charles York, beside a floe nine inches thick. At half-past eight o'clock on the morning of the 18th July, while the vessel lay in this position, the ice borne along by the currents, broke the dock, and came down upon the ship, carrying away her rudder and sternpost. An hour later it was found that there were ten feet of water in the mainhold, and the crew got their chests and clothes ashore on the ice. At half-past ten the ice again came crashing in, breaking the vessel right across the middle, and five minutes thereafter she sank under the floe. At this time the Nova Zembla and Ravenscraig a mile or two distant, were also in danger of being crushed, but fortunately they escaped, and the crew of Our Queen were thereafter taken on board those vessels. The ship and cargo were insured. The vessel with fittings was estimated as worth £14,000.

Early on Monday morning the Dundee whaler Arctic, Captain ADAMS, anchored in the Tay from Davis Straits, being the first arrival from the whale fishing this season. She brings 115 tons of oil and 6 tons of bone, the produce of 8 whales, captured between 22nd June and 16th July. Although the cargo of the Arctic will prove remunerative, the reports as to the other vessels show that the season on the whole will not be productive. The Arctic had on board Captain Fairweather and 28 of the crew of the whaler Our Queen, which was crushed to pieces in the ice off Admiralty Inlet on 18th July. So suddenly did the ice come down on the vessel that the crew had barely time to escape with their lives. She had on board a valuable cargo of oil, which was totally lost, as she broke right across the middle and sank under a huge ice floe. Both vessel and cargo were insured. The crew were distributed amongst the rest of the fleet.

This loss was compounded by the wreck of the *Ravenscraig* on October 8th. She struck a reef in a gale with heavy snowfall off Cape Austin; no further details are given. Her master for the whaling voyage was Captain Adams, an earlier disaster having occurred when Captain West committed suicide by jumping overboard, her crew having refused to proceed to the Davis Straits owing to the ship's leaky state.

Once again James had missed the birth of a child to Mary Ann. Elizabeth Craik Fairweather had been born at 9.50am on Tuesday August 5th at 5 Baffin Street. She was to marry James Corr and be the mother of James (Jimmy), Ethel and Duncan. The move to Baffin Street was to better, though still cramped accommodation. Number 5 is a handsome stone-faced building with a pedimented entrance door and central staircase. There are eight flats.

Baffin Street is singularly appropriate for grandpa's residence as it is named after Baffin Bay the northern section of the Davis Straits with which he was all too familiar.

1880 was a much more successful year for Captain James and the *Active*. He had one of the best catches at the Greenland sealing and the 15 whales caught in the Davis Straits was the best haul of his career.

The 'Dundee Year Book' for 1880 states that of the Dundee Fleet, eight steamers proceeded to Greenland, and five to Newfoundland for the fishing. The *Active* under Captain James left Dundee for Greenland on the 4th March and arrived back on the 25th of April; her catch was: Seals 3286, yielding 47 tons of Oil. She left Dundee for the Davis Straits on the 4th of May, and left Lerwick on the 8th.

Captain James had a doctor with him on this trip, but unfortunately he was very untidy, and also slow to rise for breakfast. Grandpa took drastic measures to make him change his ways, with the equivalent of an Edwardian 'apple pie bed', in this case putting a one pound blasting keg under his bed and lighting the fuse. The keg was of course empty but the spluttering fuse had the desired effect of ensuring that the doctor was never late for breakfast again. Later in the voyage in Eglinton harbour (on the west coast of the Davis Strait) the doctor got his revenge. Boarding the ship after a hunting trip in which his shot got damp, he put on a fresh cap and snapped it between the Captain's legs. Captain James recalled, "The explosion made me jump, my head came in contact with the mizzen boom and I fell back on the doctor. We both fell down the cabin stair, and the doctor underneath got the worst of it. He was full of apologies. Then as soon as I could speak I said 'Doctor, I threatened to blow you up, and now you have blown me up. We are quits now'."[13]

The *Active* returned to Dundee on the 22nd September. At the whale fishing in Davis Straits, her catch was: Whales 15, yielding Whale Oil 140 tons.

On *Active's* return the following account of her voyages in 1880 appeared in the 'Dundee Advertiser':

THE WHALE FISHING
ARRIVAL OF THE ACTIVE

The whaler Active, Captain J. Fairweather, passed Wick about one one o'clock on Monday afternoon, on her return from the Davis Straits whale fishing. Captain Fairweather sent ashore a telegram reporting his arrival on the coast, and stating that his cargo consists of fifteen whales which are expected to yield 145 tons of oil and 8 tons of bones. No particulars are given of the catch of the other vessels, but as the Active has added one whale to her cargo since the departure of the Arctic and Aurora on the 2nd August, there is every reason to suppose that the other vessels have likewise been successful. The Active obtained 3300 seals, equal to 46 tons oil, at the Greenland seal fishing in the spring, so that her voyage this year will prove very profitable to the owners. Late last night the Active brought up abreast of the Lights. She was expected to leave her anchorage about midnight, steam up the river, and dock about four o'clock this (Wednesday) morning.

DAVIS STRAITS WHALE FISHING
SUCCESS OF THE ACTIVE

The steamer Active, Capt J. Fairweather, which arrived in the river on Tuesday night from the Davis Straits whale fishing, was berthed in Earl Grey Dock yesterday morning. Her voyage has proved very successful, as she is "full ship", her cargo consisting of fifteen whales, which will yield 150 tons of oil and eight tons of whalebone. The Active prosecuted the seal fishing at Greenland in the spring, and got a cargo of 3300 seals, which produced 47 tons of oil. After refitting, she left Dundee on the 4th May for the Davis Straits whaling. Calling in at Lerwick to complete her crew, she left Shetland on the 8th May, and a fine passage was experienced to Davis Straits, Disco being reached on the 3rd of June. In company with the Jan Mayen and the Polynia the Active proceeded northward, and an easy passage was made through Melville Bay, which was remarkably free of ice. This seems indeed to have been a most exceptional season, as more open water was visible in high latitudes than had been seen by our Arctic explorers for a long series of years. The west side of Davis Straits was reached on the 7th June, and Captain Fairweather then proceeded to what is known as the "middle ice fishing". Here the first whale was caught on the 28th June, and the fishing was subsequently prosecuted with success in Pond's Bay and southwards along the west coast to Cape Eglinton, fourteen whales having been captured between the middle of June and the beginning of August. On the 31St July a large whale was harpooned: but after being 'fast" for two hours the harpoon snapped at the blade, and the fish was lost. The whale had died from the effects of the wounds, for the carcase was descried floating in the water several weeks afterwards. A furious gale was raging, however, and the boats could not be launched to secure it. The Active was in company with the Dundee fleet at Cape Kater, and left them there on the 27th August, when she steamed southward to Cape Hooper, where a number of whales were seen. On the 1st September the crew were successful in capturing a large fish, yielding 18 tons of oil and 22 cwt of bone. This completed the vessel's cargo, the fifteen whales yielding: 150 tons of oil and 8 tons of bone, and entirely filling the ship's tanks. The Active left for home on the

6th September, and reached the Tay after a pleasant passage across the Atlantic.

Captain Fairweather reported that on the 27th August, when he left the Dundee fleet at Cape Kater, their catches were the same as reported by the *Arctic* and *Aurora*, with the exception of the *Nova Zembla,* which had secured an additional large fish, bringing up her cargo to 80 tons of oil, the produce of six whales.

A live bear has been brought home on board the *Active.* It was seen disporting itself on the ice along with its mother and another cub, and the old bear and one of her young having been shot, the other was captured alive.

At the present time whale oil is selling about £28 a ton, and whalebone brings in about £1100 a ton. Whalebone fetched as much as £1200 lately, it dropped, however, to £1000 after the news of the successful fishing, but it has again begun to rise in value, and is now quoted at £1100. The total value of the *Active's* catch at Davis Straits is therefore over £1200, and the expenses must be comparatively small, as the voyage has occupied only four and a-half months:

FATAL ACCIDENT ON BOARD THE NOVA ZEMBLA

Information has been brought to Dundee by the crew of the Active of a sad accident, which happened on board the whaler Nova Zembia. One of the crew, a lad named Tosh, belonging to Dundee, was engaged aloft on the 12th August, when he accidentally lost his hold and fell on the deck. He received such severe injuries to his spine that he died two days after the accident. His body was taken ashore and buried at Cape Kater, his grave being beside those of two Dundee seamen, who had been interred there in previous years.

This year the *Xanthus* of Peterhead was lost in Melville Bay.

In December 1880, Captain James was awarded an accolade by the Tay Whale Company, receiving the following letter:

Whale Lane
Dundee
23 Dec.1880

My dear Sir,

In referring to my conversation with you today, I have much pleasure in informing you that the General Meeting of owners of the ship held today voted you £50 as a mark of their appreciation of your services and confidence in your skill and energy as Commander of their ship SS Active and as instructed I beg to hand you herewith cheque for £50 with best wishes for your success in life.

My dear Sir

Yours very truly

G.W.Welch

Managing Owners[14]

This was the first of many glowing testimonials Captain James was to receive in his long career.

1881 was Captain James' last year as master of the *Active* and the last of ten seasons in the employment of the Tay Whale Fishing Company. His next Command would be the *Thetis* built by Messrs Alexander Stephen & Son for themselves. A report in the 'Advertiser' of January 14th gives an account of the launch, as witnessed by a large assemblage.

The *Active* departed for the Greenland sealing on the 7th of March. A full account of her voyage was published in the 'Advertiser' the day after her return on April the 22nd. It took four days after leaving Lerwick on the 14th March to reach the ice in latitude 70.40, whereupon a terrific gale blew the ship 150 miles. It took ten days to regain the ice. The sealing conditions were difficult, the weather causing the ice field to break up into small pieces. There was evidently a close season in force, which was due to expire on the 2nd of April. About 1700 seals were eventually picked up. Captain Fairweather described the atrocious conditions:

> Throughout the fishing the weather continued very boisterous, and the sealing was carried on under great disadvantages, and often with very great risk to the men. During the season the weather was intensely cold, aggravated by biting winds, the thermometer ranging from 7 below to 3 degrees above zero. The crew suffered great hardships owing to the severity of the weather. The decks were constantly covered with ice, and at times, owing to the rapid formation of ice on the headgear, masts, and rigging, the vessel was covered to such an extent that she presented the appearance of an iceberg rather than a steamship. Occasionally the vessel was almost unmanageable owing to the weight of the ice and the steering gear becoming frozen and several men had to be constantly employed keeping the helm in working order.

The *Active* brought home 1700 seals yielding 20 tons of seal oil. Her departure from Dundee for the Davis Strait was on the 28th April. There is very little information about this year's whaling voyage, only the catch record is recorded. This amounted to:

4 Whales yielding 47 tons of oil and 45 cwts of bone.

The *Active* returned to Dundee on the 26th October. Only 48 whales were killed by the fleet of eleven ships. Captain Adams of the *Arctic* being outstanding with 13 to his credit.

The fate of the *Victor* and the *Active*:
   The Victor was crushed by ice on the 17th of July 1881, eight miles south from Elwin Inlet in the Davis Straits.[15] Basil Lubbock says that on the outbreak of war the *Active* together with the remaining ships of the Dundee fleet were taken by the Government and placed under the management of the Hudson Bay Company, who loaded them with war munitions for Russia. The result was disastrous, for these vessels were never meant to carry dead weight cargoes, and in the first gale on the voyage to the White Sea, they strained so badly that their seams opened and they gradually filled and sank. The Active was lost with all hands off the Orkneys.[16] (see Appendix V).

James and Mary Ann's third child Alexander had been born at 5 Baffin Street on Friday July 29th 1881. He was destined to die unmarried at the age of 22 from wounds sustained in the South African War.

   In a matter of weeks James had left the Tay Whale Fishing Company, for a letter of reference dated the 17th of November 1881 is addressed to Captain James Fairweather, (SS) "Thetis", Dundee. The letter reads as follows:

   Dear Sir
      I have the pleasure in stating that you have served in the Seal & Whale fishing ships, under my management, for the space of 9 years, from 1872 inclusive in several capacities through all the grades of office up to master of the (SS) 'Active" which you have commanded for the past three years, during the whole time you have given me every satisfaction as I found you always strictly sober and attentive to duty and energetic & persevering, and although I would have very much preferred that you had remained in command of the 'Active" I sincerely wish you a continuation of success in a larger ship.
         I am
               Dear Sir
                  Yours very truly
                     G W Welch[17]

   A further letter from the managers of the Tay Whaling Company dated 6 December 1898 contains the following comments, the writer having known Captain James for twenty-five years:

I have watched his career with interest. . . . and have seen with pleasure his rapid advancement to his present position in the merchant service. During the above period I have had ample opportunity of observing his conduct both publicly and privately and can testify . . .I have always found him to be a careful diligent and trustworthy man, very attentive to his duties and at all times clear headed. Temperate and honourable in his conduct.[18]

For the next seven years he would be in the employment of Alex. Stephen & Son of Dundee serving one year as master of the *Thetis* and six years as master of the *Aurora*. He was twenty-eight at the beginning of this period and thirty-five at its conclusion.

The year ends with an interesting article and diagram which appeared in the 'People's Journal'[19] of December 17th 1881 and also in the 'Dundee Year Book'. The long article contains much information about the Dundee whaling industry, its traditions and achievements. The diagram is of particular interest in that it shows the track of whalers in pursuit of their quarry. The text also reiterates the annual circuit made by the whales:

"starting from Hudson's Straits and proceeding up the west coast of Davis Straits, through Ponds Bay and Lancaster Sound, then passing down Prince Regent Inlet to escape their formidable foe the grampus, they enter Boothia Gulf, from which they emerge into Fox Channel by Fury and Hecla Straits and thereafter reach Hudson's Bay."

Captain James comments that it was the females and suckers (young whales) who pursued this course. "The large ones as a rule keep in Davis Straits until the fall of the year, if there is ice there. Then they go back to Hudson Bay the way they came out".[20] The massive slaughter in Lancaster Sound, of females and young, consequently contributed in no small measure to the near extinction of the species.

1882 In his letter to Captain James on leaving the Tay Whale Fishing Company, Mr Welch wishes him continuation of success in the larger ship.[21] The *Thetis* was certainly larger than the *Active* weighing 492 tons as against 348. This trend continues throughout the Captain's career, each ship of which he took command being bigger than the last (with the exception of the *Earl of Mar and Kellie*). It would almost certainly be ambition to achieve which led him to make this change.

Captain James's year with the *Thetis* consists of one voyage leaving Dundee on May 8th and returning home on 17th August. This was primarily a sealing voyage, the first stop being St John's, Newfoundland, arriving on the 13th April. On this leg she killed 10,598 seals. At the close of the sealing season there, she left for Greenland on 20th May. The fishing ground lying between Iceland and the east coast of Greenland was reached at the end of May and the crew succeeded in killing 3,317 old seals. Weather and ice conditions were difficult and *Thesis* proceeded northwards, the captain hoping to make a substantial addition to his cargo at the bottlenose whale fishing to the northeast of Iceland. In consequence of adverse ice conditions Thetis was obliged to steam round the south end of the island, an extra journey of nine hundred miles. By the time the vessel arrived, the fishing was almost at an end. Only eight whales were caught. As there was no hope of success the *Thetis* bore for home on August 10th arriving in Dundee on the 17th.

The *Thetis* catch was (company figure): 10,958 seals from Newfoundland yielding 106 tons of oil, and 3,317 seals from Greenland yielding 78 tons of oil; and 8 bottlenose whales yielding 9 tons of whale oil.

In his memoirs, Captain James makes a reference to his voyage with the *Thetis* during which he says "there were incidents which stand out amongst my adventures with the whalers, those with the *Active* having been uneventful as voyages to the Arctic regions go."[22] He describes describes problems with drunkenness amongst the crew both on leaving Dundee and when leaving Newfoundland. His orders were to proceed to the Hood sealing grounds between Greenland and Iceland; almost a new venture for Dundee steamers. He was anxious to get away but owing to the inebriated state of the crew, had problems with the coaling. He then goes on to describe an incident of "man overboard" which escalated into a dangerous situation:

On this voyage to the Arctic, a memorable incident occurred about a week after we left St. John's, and when we were just north of Cape Farewell. The day was dry and clear with the ship steaming head to wind. Suddenly the cry was raised that a man was overboard.

I was on the spot, and was first to see the man swimming in our wake. He was James Moncrieff, who is now a trusted assistant of the Harbour Master in Dundee. The engines were reversed, and the starboard quarter boat lowered with seven men in it (one too many).

The boat got under the counter and was smashed. Luckily the seven men were able to hold on to the ropes, and in time were brought on board.

Meanwhile the port boat was launched with six men. I asked the man who had been sent to the masthead (to keep an eye on the original cause of the trouble) where Moncrieff now was.

He replied that the second boat had got to Jimmy, but it had sunk. Ropes were thrown to the men, and they all got on board except Moncrieff, who clung to some oars that came out of the boat when it was upset.

At this stage the carpenter, without my knowledge, went over the stern with a line tied round him, thinking to swim to Jimmy, but he was soon in trouble. I attended to him by giving and taking in the line as the ship rose and fell with the sea.

Meanwhile the gangway had been unshipped and another boat launched. We had no more oars available, but that difficulty was overcome by using the bottom boards as paddles.

At last Jimmy and the carpenter were safely on board. Fortunately we had a doctor with us, and after a lot of hard 'work we got our patient round and into bed. In a day or two he was able to go forward and soon was well. It will be seen that from first to last in that incident, I had no less than twenty-one men in the water. It was almost a tragedy.[23]

The review of the Seal and whale fishing published in the 'Dundee Advertiser' showed a small increase in the Greenland seal figures but a considerable decrease in the Newfoundland figures. Adams of the *Arctic* killed 24,500 seals in Newfoundland. Captain James came next with 10,600 (press figures). Nine ships participated in the whale fishing, killing 79 whales as distinct from 48 the previous year. Captain Alexander on the *Aurora* secured 16, the biggest total.

Items of interest in the press include the report that next year (1883) the fleet will consist of fifteen vessels and that a change has been made in the command of most of them. The new appointments being generally young men. Captain James mentions this in his memoirs and comments on it to the effect that young captains are necessary to command in such demanding conditions as the Arctic presents.

Other improvements included the introduction of a steam launch for each ship for conveying men to distant fields of ice, and bringing back heavy loads previously manually done. There will be no more autumn fishing in Davis Straits, and more attention paid to hunting the bottlenose and bladdernose whale at Greenland.

1883 to 1888 The Aurora

Captain James was one of the young masters to be given a new command in 1883. *Aurora* was to be his ship for the next six years, and the vessel with which he is most closely associated.

The launch of the *Aurora* was reported in the local press on the 30th December 1876 follows:

ADDITION TO THE DUNDEE WHALING
FLEET

On Saturday an addition was made to the Dundee seal and whale fishing fleet by the launch of a fine vessel from the shipbuilding yard of Messrs Alexander Stephen & Son. The builders are the owners, and the new whaler has been built as a sister ship to the Arctic, which was launched by the same firm on the 8th March 1875. She is to be engaged with the Arctic in prosecuting the Labrador seal fishing, discharging her cargo at Newfoundland, where oil boiling premises have been secured, and afterwards proceeding to the Davis' Straits whale fishing. The ship which was named the Aurora, is barque-rigged, and is 530 tons gross register. Her dimensions are:- Length 195 feet; breadth of beam, 30 feet; and depth of hold 18 feet 9 inches. She is very strongly built, being double planked, and is specially strengthened at the bow to enable her to pass through the ice in the Arctic seas. The Aurora has been fitted up with all the most approved mechanical appliances. Her propeller, brackets, &c., have been made of malleable cast iron, and can be taken on deck when there is the slightest danger to be apprehended from coming in contact with ice. The engines are to be surface condensing, on the compound principle, and can be wrought at a high rate of speed with small consumption of coal. They are 98-horse power nominal, or 500 indicated. The Aurora is to be commanded by Captain Bannerman, and will be got ready with all possible despatch, in order to proceed in February, in company with the Arctic, to the American seal fishing.[1]

After the loss of his ship *Our Queen* in 1879, Captain Alexander was master of the *Aurora* for three seasons. In 1883, however, Captain James succeeded him on *Aurora*, whilst Alexander took over James' last command, the *Thetis*, and subsequently was master of the *Terra Nova*, and finally the *Balaena*.

The era of photography had begun and there are photographs of Aurora from this time on. David Moore Lindsay who sailed as ship's surgeon on the 1884 voyage, wrote a book about his experiences entitled *A Voyage to the*

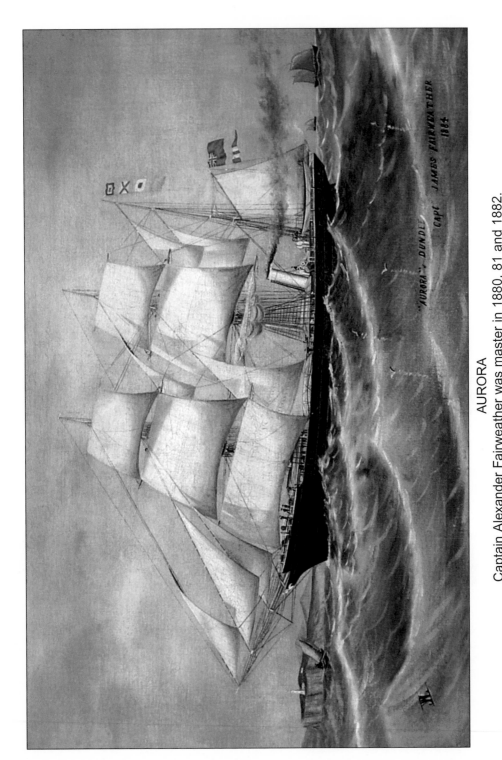

AURORA
Captain Alexander Fairweather was master in 1880, 81 and 1882.
Captain James Fairweather was master in 1883, 84, 85, 86, 87 and 1888.

St. John's Harbour in Spring.

The *Aurora* in St. John's Harbour.

Arctic in the Whaler Aurora' (1911). It is well supplied with both photographs and illustrations. In addition my cousin Jim Fairweather of Australia owns a splendid painting showing *Aurora* entering the Firth of Tay after a successful season in 1884. 'She is under full sail with flags flying and smoke is streaming leewards from the funnel."[2] The painting is inscribed: AURORA DUNDEE Capt James Fairweather 1884.

There is an excellent description of *Aurora* in D.M.L's book:

> "Having fixed terms and other details I went on board the ship which was to be my home for some months to come. She was a pretty auxiliary barque of 386 tons registered. Her engines were about a hundred horse power. She had a top-gallant forecastle and a raised poop. Running forward from the poop was the engine room skylight, which ended at the funnel casing, and steps led from the poop to the main deck on each side of it. The funnel was painted buff, the ship outside was black, and the bulwarks inside white and blue. The bridge was across the engine room skylight and in front of the mizzenmast, an iron railing around the poop, offering no protection from the weather, while a companion opened aft in front of our two wheels. The pretty little cabin was furnished in pitch pine and leather. The Captain's room occupied the starboard side, while mine was on the port, both opening into the cabin. Forward of my room was that occupied by the first and second mates, and this looked into the passage at the foot of the stairs. Forward of the passage was the pantry and also the engineer's room. A locker in which things were stowed occupied the stern and opened into the cabin. Forward of the cabin table was a stove in which there was a cheerful fire, and in the square skylight hung a bird's cage and a garland, also some plants."[3]

She sounds smart, comfortable and homely. A further description of life on board bears out the observation made by Captain James about the comfort of life aboard a whaler compared to other ships:

> "There was a wonderful amount of life on board a whaler, on account of the crew being so large. In the 'tween-decks, one generally found a number of men at work, picking oakum, spinning rope yarn, or other yarns, and weaving sennet. The carpenter and his assistant were found at work in one place, the cooper busy in another, while the sailmaker sat and sewed. On the deck, in some sheltered corner, one found the blacksmith at work, and there were always jobs being done in the engine room. But it was easy work, none of the dog's life one saw on other ships."[4] D.M.L. also states:

"Life on board a whaler is much more pleasant than other sorts of merchantman because the ships are well found and the crews very large so that except when actually sealing or whaling they have an easy enough time."

He also observes that the captains in the trade were very humane men, many of them scientific, and they treated their crews well."[5]

One must qualify these glowing comments by noting that in 1884 when engaged on the first sealing voyage of the season, from March 20-22, the ship took on board, as was customary, about 300 Newfoundland men in addition to the Scottish crew of 65 men. Conditions for the "sweilers or seal hunters, were primitive and it seems astonishing that the ship could carry so many men. Of the Scottish crew (including 16 from Shetland), some were occupied as follows: six belonged to the engine room, eight were harpooners, two carpenters, a cooper, a blacksmith, a sailmaker, and the chief harpooner — the 'specksioneer'.

The information regarding *Aurora's* voyages in 1883, 85, 86, 87 and 88 comes from the following sources:

> Captain Fairweather's memoirs
> Company Records
> The 'Dundee Year Book'
> Accounts in the Press
> *Arctic Whalers* by Basil Lubbock

1884 is covered by David Moore Lindsay's book *A Voyage to the Arctic in the Whaler Aurora*.

As was to be expected, certain difficulties have arisen in reconciling the various accounts. There are two problem areas, firstly the number of seals, and to a lesser extent whales taken varies considerably, but not excessively from account to account; variations in catches may in some cases be explained by the custom of whalers returning to port carrying the catch of another ship. Secondly there is a certain amount of confusion as to which incidents took place in which years. This has required a great deal of unravelling, and in consequence we have had to take some liberties with Captain James' chronology. Once again the back up information from the press, the 'Dundee Year Book' and company accounts has been useful.

1883 *Aurora's* destinations in 1883 were Newfoundland, Greenland and the Davis Straits. She left Dundee on the 6th February, and instead of steaming straight to St John's, she captured 11,000 seals on the way, arriving with a full load on the 9th April. Having refitted she left St John's for her second trip on the 15th April, and returned with 538 old seals; the total of 11,538 seals yielding 137 tons of oil. The Company and the Year Book figures however, give a total of 12,821 seals.

Aurora left Newfoundland for the Greenland seal and whale fishing on the 14th May and succeeded in finding the seals early in June. The crew of the *Aurora* managed to capture in the region of 2450 seals, and the fishing afterwards proving unsuccessful Captain James steered in a northerly direction in search of bottle-nose whales. He managed to catch nine, but as no more were seen the *Aurora* bore up for home, and experienced fine weather on her homeward voyage; she arrived in Dundee on the 11th August. The seals and whales yielded 74 tons of oil.

In the Year Book, figures are given for the Davis Straits whaling which indicate that the season was a poor one, only 17 whales being killed. However it is indicated that white whales and porpoises were caught. Basil Lubbock in his book *Arctic Whalers* bears this out. He states that with the scarcity of whales, captains sought for other forms of remuneration, thus 2736 white whales were caught in Baffin Bay and 535 bottlenose in Greenland waters by the fleet in 1883.[6] In addition Captain James gives a good account in his memoirs of the procedure for hunting white whales and of *Aurora's* success in 1883.

Elwin Bay in Lancaster Sound, and Knigawa in Cumberland Gulf are mentioned by him, and Prince Regent's Inlet by D.M.Lindsay[7] confirming this catch in 1883. As described by Captain James, a pair of steamers work together to drive these small whales ashore where they are killed and skinned by the crew:

> Although it is not common to get white whales in Davis Straits, it is not because they are scarce, for, like their cousins the narwhal, they are there by the thousand; but certain conditions have to exist before they can be caught in numbers worth trying for. First, the ice has to be off the land, and a bay with a flat bottom at the head of it, which dries or nearly dries at low water, must be found in the track of the whales' migrations. To the best of my knowledge there are only two such bays in the Straits, one at Knigawa in Cumberland Gulf, which can be worked without any risk by one steamer with a whaling crew, as it is at the head of a long narrow arm of the Gulf, and I think the white whales that go there in the spring remain until driven out again in the fall by the young ice. The second is Elwin Bay in Lancaster Sound. Left to themselves, the white whales would pass the mouth of the Elwin Bay, but they are so timid that they can be driven in by two steamers. Therefore, the modus operandi was this. Two masters agreed to work together and share the proceeds. Arrangements were made that one steamer went the one way along the land, the other the opposite way for an agreed-upon distance. Then both lay quiet for a while and started back for the bay again in time

to meet each other at high water there. Each steamer zigzagged and made all the noise possible, by occasionally opening the boiler blowdown cock for a moment—hammering on the anvil—or making a noise in any way possible. When, the two steamers met there was generally a great commotion, the fish jumping almost out of the water. The steamers had then to herd them into the bay. When one went in then they all followed, which was just what was wanted. The steamers then followed as far as the depth of water would allow them, then stopped and lowered eight boats each. These boats spread from side to side of the bay and continued to make a noise while the tide was ebbing. At low water the fish were aground and were easily killed. Next high water they were towed to the beach and hauled above high-water mark.

The spoil was then divided by the two chief officers, and each crew skinned which was their own share and towed them to the steamer, which was about two miles from them.

The last drive I had was in 1883 when in the "Aurora." My companion was the whaler "Esquimaux." We each got roughly four hundred white whales, and as each half-skin counted one to us, that was, say, eight hundred skins, and about one hundred tons of oil, we got for a week's very hard work and no little risk, as the ice might have come in at any hour and cut the men off from the steamer. But that was just one of the risks we had to take to make a pay-day at the end of the trip.

The white whale is peculiar in having no dorsal fin, and their yellowish-white colour makes them rather conspicuous. The skin in those days was not of so much value. Nowadays they are tanned and they make the best of leather, bringing a high price on the market as porpoise bootlaces, which are sold at one shilling per pair.

During the drive described above, when the whales were finding themselves in very shallow water, there was a great commotion amongst them that was somewhat dangerous.

One boat got hit, which caused it to heel over so far that the Doctor (who was one of that boat's crew) fell out of it into the water. When he was got out, they at once brought him to the steamer. On arrival there, he was seen to be much in need of first aid, and it was promptly given. When he had quite recovered, I said to him, "Well, Doctor, you are properly initiated into the mysteries of the Arctic regions now." With a twinkle in his eye, he replied, "Yes, Captain. At my initiation I was taught to be careful. I see it applies here also." Nuff sed. We both understood each other at once.[8]

The returns for the Fleet confirm that there was an increase in the seal catch at both Newfoundland and Greenland. Only six vessels engaged in the Davis Straits whaling, killing 17 whales. As already indicated, white whales and porpoises were caught, and two ships caught 101 bottle-nose whales in Greenland waters.

A report in the 'Advertiser' for Wednesday the 3rd October announces the return of Captain Alexander in the *Thetis*. Her catch was six whales and 700 porpoises calculated to yield 170 tons of oil and five tons of bone. At the Newfoundland sealing she captured 22,000 old and young seals. Unfortunately a boat capsized in the chase for a bottle-nose whale and two men, the carpenter and the steerman were drowned. Captain Alexander brought home two live bears.

Home from the Sea

Upon the arrival of the *Aurora* back in Dundee, Captain James returned home to find in his absence there had been an addition to his family; his fourth child and third son — Charles Craik Fairweather had been born on Friday, May the 4th at 255am at 5, Baffin Street. Charles became Main's Superintendent for the Carlisle City Electricity Board, overseeing the installation of mains electricity for the first time to Carlisle and to the surrounding North Cumberland area. He married Eva Hughes in 1912 and had three daughters Evelyn, Helen (Ella) and Diana. In Carlisle they were known as 'the Fairweather girls' and to us as the 'Carlisle cousins'. Charles died in August 1960.

The Aurora Voyage of 1884
The dates given are from D.M.Lindsay's diary account

The Aurora voyage of 1884 is spectacularly recorded by David Moore Lindsay in his book, *A Voyage to the Arctic in the Whaler Aurora*, published in 1911, which is in the form of a diary starting on January 30th and finishing on September 22nd. An account in the 'Dundee Advertiser' of the arrival of *Aurora* back in Dundee is reproduced at the end of this section.

In addition Captain James mentions this voyage in his memoirs, and there is a detailed account of the season's activities in Basil Lubbock's *Arctic Whalers*.[9] This season is particularly interesting in that the whalers were involved in rescuing Lieutenant Greely U.S.A. Army, and the six survivors of his 25-man party. Briefly, the United States were to establish two circumpolar stations, one at Point Barrow at the Behring Sea side of northern Canada, and the other at Lady Franklin Bay on the Davis Straits side. This was decided at a scientific conference held in Europe. Lieutenant Greely was in charge of the expedition to the east, and he left St John's in 1881 with supplies for three years. By 1884 two relief expeditions had failed to find him, and a third was mounted by the United States Navy in 1884. This was unknown to Captain James when he left Dundee in January.

Moore Lindsay, an enthusiastic young student of Edinburgh University, was determined to travel to the Arctic in search of adventure and was directed to Captain Fairweather's home in Baffin Street, where he awaited the captain, in a room strewn with polar bear rugs. He was taken on as *Aurora's* surgeon, to sail in January. His description of *Aurora* has already been quoted. Moore Lindsay mentions that on the day before she sailed, January 30th, he met my grandmother and Uncle Alexander on board; Alexander was to command the *Thetis*. The voyage to Newfoundland was rough and they landed on February the 25th. The first view of the New World was of Cape Bonavista, and it is interesting to note that this is the name given by the Fairweathers to their final home in East Newport.

David Moore Lindsay tells us that Newfoundland was discovered by John Cabot in 1484 and was our (British) first possession overseas. The sea round the coast soon became valuable fishing grounds for the ships of many nations. The town of St John's developed as a result of it's harbour which was the focus of the thriving fishing industry. In the 1880s when Captain James was a frequent visitor, St John's must have been a hive of activity though the town itself would be underdeveloped by European standards. D.M.L. gives us the following description: "St John's harbour is entered through the narrows. On the left, going in, there is the lighthouse; and on the right, or north side, the signal station. On this side is the city, lying at the foot of low hills, its principal street, Water Street, being parallel with the shore. From it run side streets down to the wharves and up the hill to the residences and churches. The Dundee ships lay on the south side, our yard being nearest to the narrows. From it a path led out to the lighthouse point. A hundred yards from the ship one was on the hillside and without the pale of everything."[10]

Captain James became quite familiar with St John's over the years, and I have a photograph of him taken at 'S H Parson's photographic studio and fine art emporium, 310 Water Street, St John's, Newfoundland'. He is wearing a high buttoned jacket, in this head and shoulders portrait, with revers trimmed with braid and a narrow ribboned bow tie. He sports a beard, the eyes are piercing and probably blue, and his expression kindly and intelligent. This photograph would probably have been taken about the time of the 1884 voyage when Captain James was aged thirty one years old. There is an earlier portrait done by A.Watt in Dundee and also a carte de visite photograph by A Wanlas of 28 Princess Street Dundee, which is not identified, but which bears such a strong resemblance to my cousin Jim that I feel certain it is a portrait of grandpa aged about twelve.

Ice had been a problem before arriving at St John's, the ship having been beset 220 miles out. Now the harbour was completely frozen over, and the rest of the voyage would take place in ice bound conditions, amongst dangerous bergs, the ship either breaking through the ice or following 'leads' narrow bands of open water amidst the floes or near land. D.M.L. tells us:

"The day after our arrival our ship began discharging cargo, that is to say, taking off our whale-boats and launch, and taking out all supplies for the whaling voyage. Then they began sheathing the deck and bulwarks — even the floor of the cabin was covered with plank. Bunks were erected for the men in the 'tween decks, all stores removed from the quarter hatch and bunks put in there for the quartermasters, and the crow's-nest was hoisted up and made fast to the main mast, a few feet below the truck. The crow's nest or barrel was a most comfortable place. One entered through a trap door in the bottom, and when this was closed there was no draught. Around the edge of the barrel and sticking out some distance there was an iron rail upon which the glass could rest, the latter being kept in a canvas bag or pocket inside. From there the ship was navigated, a wire going to the engine room and ringing the bell, but orders to the man at the wheel were called down.

The *Aurora* having been converted into a sealer, and having taken on board her supplies and having exchanged her beautiful whale boats for a number of very crude looking punts, moved over to the north side of the harbour, and waited for sailing day to take her crew on board.

Towards the end of February, the sweilers, as they are called, began to arrive in St John's looking for berths. As the steamers afforded better opportunities, the able men got them, while the older ones took the sailing craft, where life was not so strenuous. These men were dressed very much alike and were most athletic; some of them were perfectly wonderful in the way they jumped from pan to pan, barely touching some of the smaller ones in passage. The owners did not overfeed the men on these trips, providing them with sea biscuits and pinnacle tea chiefly, pork and duff being served only three days a week and salt fish on Fridays. The water from which tea was brewed was obtained by thawing pinnacles of ice. When a ship was amongst the white coats, as the young seals were called, the crew lived well, as they ate the liver, hearts and flippers of the seals. The men carried a supply of livers and hearts in their belts and ate them frozen or cooked as opportunity afforded.It is easy to see how little cooking can be done for a crew of three hundred men on a small ship. I have often seen a man tie a cord to a liver and drop it into a pot of tea sitting on the galley stove, drawing it out when warmed up or when the owner of the pot came for his tea."[11]

Three hundred Newfoundlanders came on board and Captain James already knew that there were six trouble makers amongst them. One man confessed to the Captain that he was in fear of his life. There followed the 'duff' incident which is described by both Captain James and by D.M.Lindsay. During dinner a terrible noise of men's feet was heard overhead. The mate was sent to find out what was happening, and found the deck and rigging full of men and the top of the skylight covered with 'duffs' (the men's dinner). There followed a confrontation between the leader of the men and the Captain, which terminated with grandpa (a man of action) planting a blow between the eyes of the ring leader, who was complaining about the food. Captain James then asked if the flour was bad, the answer was no, whereupon the Captain answered "Well do you want me to cook it for you?" In reply one of them said "Three cheers for the little Captain,' and three cheers were given in force. Captain James said, "from that day I never had trouble from a Newfoundland crew."[12]   The sealing (a revolting and bloody business) was very successful, and *Aurora* was the first ship back to St John's on March the 22nd, having set off on the 10th, and having killed about 28,000 seals.

On April the 2nd Aurora sailed again with a smaller crew, for the Labrador sealing during which the seals were shot. The ship observed Sundays and fed well on the sides of Angus beef hung from the rigging in the natural refrigerator, accompanied by onions, and tinned carrots from Carnoustie. This menu it appears was for cabin use. The ship arrived back at St John's on April the 19th. They cannot have added much to the tally of seals, for the combined catch for the two trips is 28,150.

There was great news awaiting on their arrival. The *Thetis* (which had been captained by Alexander) had been sold to the American government, and *Aurora* was ordered to take her place in the whaling fleet, and proceed to the Davis Strait. There they were to keep their eyes open for the lost Greely expedition, as a reward had been offered for any whaler picking him up, by the United States Government. The ship was then prepared for whaling. D.M.L. tells us that:

> "On board, great changes took place. All the sheathing was torn off and the ship cleaned inside and out. Her overhauling was complete. The rigging was set up, the masts were scraped and oiled and the ship painted. The punts were cleared away and our beautiful whale-boats took their place.
>
> The *Aurora* was peculiar in having two boats, one above the other, on each quarter. We fished ten boats altogether, four down each side and two upper quarter boats.
>
> The crew of a whale-boat is six, a harpooner, a boat-steerer and four men pulling. The harpooner rows until ordered by the boat-steerer to stand by his gun. In the bow the harpoon-gun is mounted on a swivel, and fast to the harpoon is the "foregoer." This is very pliable, untarred rope, about two and a half inches in circumference and eighteen fathoms long. It is

The *Thetis* and the *Bear* during the Greely relief expedition of 1884.
The *Thetis*, previously captained by Alexander Fairweather,
was sold to the American Government for the rescue voyage;
her place in the whaling fleet was taken by *Aurora* captained by James.

coiled in a tub, sitting on the port bow of the boat, while on the starboard side, in a convenient rest, lies the hand-harpoon.

The bollard head, around which a turn of the line is taken, is an important structure; it stands in the bow next to the gun. Many a boat has gone down through the line fouling the bollard head.

To the "foregoer" or "foreganger," is attached the whale line. The term "line" means, generally, one rope 120 fathoms long, and there are five of these carried in each boat, one and a half being stowed amidships and the rest aft. They are 2½-inch ropes, and tarred. The greatest care must be observed in coiling these lines, and by the line manager in the boat as the line runs out."[13]

The fleet sailed between May the 4th and 8th. Captain James had purchased a quantity of coloured handkerchiefs which the men could purchase from the slop-chest for purposes of barter with the eskimos.

It was generally believed that Greely would now be at Cape York, or the Cary Islands off the north west coast of Greenland. The two American relief boats were the *Thetis* and the *Bear,* accompanied by ten whalers. *Aurora* sailed on May the 8th for the Labrador whaling, killing one bottle-nosed whale en route for the Davis Straits.

By May the 17th *Aurora* was off Greenland and encountered eskimos in their kayaks. They were taken on board together with their kayaks, and the ship anchored at Holstenborg, a village on the west coast just inside the Arctic Circle. Besides being an eskimo settlement, Holstenborg was a Danish administrative centre where the Governor lived. Captain James and D.M.Lindsay spent a pleasant evening with the Governor and his deputy, and listened to the deputy's wife play the piano.

In the meantime a ball was taking place 'tween-decks', the eskimo girls dancing with the crew to the music of fiddles and concertinas. These instruments were played by whalers and eskimos equally well, and they knew the same airs.

The interaction between the Scots and the Eskimos had commenced in the days of the sailing ships. Later in the voyage *Aurora*, steaming up Lancaster Sound, the eastern entrance to the North West Passage, was to be regaled by the sound of 'Bonnie Laddie Highland Laddie' sung by an eskimo on the ice edge. An article in the 'Dundee Courier' and 'Advertiser' of the 1st of April 1999 by Norman Watson, based partly on an article in the Courier of June 1935, describes the impact, sometimes unfortunate, of the seamen on the Inuit people, by introducing firearms and alcohol. More than once however, Inuit people had rescued sailors in difficulty, and had taught them the skills of hunting, navigating, and driving dogs. Also in the legacy, the Inuit enjoy Scottish reels and have developed a taste for tea. The article concludes by relating that villagers in Pond Inlet, Baffin Island have porridge for breakfast, and consider mince and tatties as a local delicacy.

A considerable amount of barter took place at Holstenborg, the eskimos desiring bread in return for slippers, tobacco pouches and pretty down quilts. On departure the crew were presented with quaint ivories made by the natives from walrus tusks - such as brooches, pipes, paper knives etc., many of which would find their way into Dundee homes. As I write, a pair of walrus tusks is on the wall to my right, a souvenir amongst many from those far off times.

Captain James does not state the year the following encounter took place, but I include it here for interest and as an example of a bargain fulfilled with integrity:

My third whaling command was the "Aurora." An incident on one of my voyages on that steamer I thought very interesting. It concerned a native with whom I entered into a pact. He came on board with two bear skins and in exchange for them he wanted a rifle. The two skins were less in value than the rifle, so I wanted a better bargain, and explained to the man as best as I could that before he could have the rifle he must bring me two more skins.

He shook his head sadly and seemed so disappointed that I decided to let him have the rifle if he would promise to let me have the other two skins when I returned next season. I explained to him that he must give me some sort of a written promise that he would give me the skins the following year, and to this he agreed. I took him into the cabin, and set pen, ink and paper before him.

Without hesitation the Eskimo drew up his solemn promise to me, not in written words, but in the language of signs. On the paper he drew a series of sketches representing the arrival of the "Aurora"; the "Aurora" with himself and I aboard; the "Aurora's" departure and his own; the "Aurora's" return a year later; and, last of all, his meeting with me and giving me the skins.

That done, I handed him his rifle, and he went off satisfied. When I returned the next year I met him again, and he honoured his promise by handing over the two skins.[14]

On May the 19th *Aurora* sailed up the west coast of Greenland as far as Disco Island. They did not stop at Godhaven, and met heavy ice and tremendous bergs; they killed a bear. They sailed past Nugsuak Peninsula and the entrance to Umanak Fiord, gradually they met up with others in the fleet, including the Bear of the Greely Relief Expedition. *Thetis* joined the fleet and socialising took place. They passed Cape Shackleton and the ships all became stuck in the ice or anchored to it. Later the ships competed for getting ahead, they found a crack in the ice leading to the Duck Islands, and worked North, but ice forced them to return. They were on the threshold of the notorious Melville Bay still working up the Greenland coast, making for Cape York and struck open water. Cape York at the north of Melville Bay was reached without incident, *Aurora* and the *Bear* having won the race from St John's to Cape York.

Shortly after, the *Aurora* was in the greatest danger of being lost, being nipped between the points of two great floes. Boats were provisioned and arrangements made to abandon ship. However she righted herself and slipped up above the crunching ice; photographs were taken. A crack opened in the night releasing the ship, after which they steamed north, arriving at the Carey Islands. Here, Captain James decided to go to the whaling ground and leave the Greely part of it to the expedition ships. They picked up Greely within twenty-four hours at Cape Sabine; of his men, only six out of the original twenty-five were alive.

At the risk of repeating myself, there follows Captain James' account of the whalers involvement with the Greely rescue, starting from the vessels meeting again before crossing Melville Bay:

The season of 1884 was severe in Melville Bay, but I had seen it worse. In fact, I have failed to get through it at all, and so lost the spring fishing

When the "Thetis" met the "Bear," they, of course, kept together. Commander W. S. Schly had command of the Flagship "Thetis," and Lieut. W. H. Emory was in command of the "Bear." We had a lot of hard work to get as far as the Duck Islands at the entrance to Melville Bay, where the hard work was supposed to commence, and the Americans were beginning to see what they were up against.

The commander did just what I myself would have done under like circumstances. He kept in company with the three most powerful whalers there, the "Arctic," the "Aurora," and the "Wolf." These three steamers were equal in power to the "Thetis" and "Bear," so we were well matched.

On the way up to the Duck Islands, the "Bear" struck a sunken rock and commenced to leak badly, which rather disconcerted them. I was asked to look at the damage, so took our water-glass with me and discovered that a bit of the forefoot was away. I assured them that it did not matter very much, as there was plenty of wood at the back of what was left, and I advised them to stop the leak.

I told them to give her "a feed," as we often had to do. They were amazed and asked what I meant. I explained, and told them to get some chopped-up hemp rope yarn, to put it in a tub, fix the tub on a pole with a slip cover on it, and then to sink the tub till it was over the damaged part, and pull the cover off. The suction would draw the rope yarn in, and so stop the leak to a great extent. This they could repeat when necessary, and it was done with a great measure of success. When opportunity occurred, we proceeded, and, as I have already said, reached the Duck Islands.

Some little moves were made by various steamers, but nothing of importance happened for a few days. Then a more general move was made and five of the whalers ventured in to the pack, leaving the "Arctic," "Wolf," and "Aurora," along with the "Thetis" and "Bear" still made fast to the land ice.

"Thetis" was next to the "Aurora," and I could see the commander was in a dilemma. Finally he asked me if I thought the steamers would get away. I did not like the question, but said that, if I had thought they could, I would have been with them. Then, fortunately for the commander's peace of mind, it came down thick fog and remained so till next afternoon. When it cleared away and we saw the five whalers beset in the pack and driving away to the west and south, I could not then help giving the commander a 'Roland,' so I asked him how he would like to be with them now, and I was pleased to hear him say, "I guess you were right."

Very little is sometimes a turning-point, and that was the turning-point in favour of the Americans, including, as it afterwards turned out, Lieut. Greely and what was left of his party, as the Americans did not meet the five whalers again till they were on the way home, some weeks later, with Lieut. Greely and the few survivors of his party on board. When our chance came to leave the Duck Islands we made good use of it, but on no occasion was one of the American vessels on the lead, nor could we expect them to be, as they were new to the job, and we were only too happy to think that we were leading them to the rescue. In the book, "The Rescue of Greely," they published, they write as if they always considered us as rivals racing with them or trying to get ahead of them, instead of friends assisting them.

That is very apparent at the stage when we were nearing Cape York, for there they say the "Bear" was the first to touch the ice at Cape York, the "Aurora" being then a mile to the rear. No wonder I was a mile to the rear, for as soon as I saw the block ahead, I slowed down, and the engines were stopped when the "Bear" passed. I not only saw the block ahead, but I thought I saw a chance of crossing over to the west side from there, as I could see no ice to the west, and the sky looked watery in that direction.

The straits had been crossed there before, but later in the season, and there was always the chance of seeing whales so far north, so I stopped to wait for the "Arctic" and "Wolf" coming up. They had been held up for a bit in the last lot of ice we had come through. When they did come up we had a confab, and agreed to try a crossing there, and off we went. But, to our surprise, the "Thetis" and "Bear" kept following us. The master of the "Arctic" from his mast head advised me to go and tell them that we were now making for the west side. Considering the mission of life-saving these vessels were on, I was easily advised, so stopped, lowered a boat, went on board the "Thetis," and tried to advise the commander to go back to the block we were at in the morning. I told him that very possibly I would have to come back myself. I also told him that he might get through it that night or he might be detained indefinitely, but, in any case, be it as it may, it was their only course. I saw suspicion all around me, and was sure of it when he asked me if I was not just going west to get around the pack to the north. I was more than amazed at the question, as it was a sheer impossibility to do so at that early date. I had done what I thought was my duty. I could do no more, so went back to my own ship and started for the west again.

It was soon apparent that I had done some good, as the commander had compromised, he himself with the "Thetis" going back, and the "Bear" was sent on with us. We had only gone about fifty miles when, we came against a wall of ice, which plainly said to us — "no road this way." Back we had to go, and found that the "Thetis" had got through and away. The "Bear" kept with me till the Carey Islands were reached. There we parted in open water. My course was now west and south, theirs north, and Greely was found at Cape Sabine the next day. There were only seven of the party left alive, and these were just alive and no more. Their tent had blown down and they were unable to put it up again, but it is a sad, sad story, and can all be found in the book I have referred to.

I am far from saying that the "Thetis" and "Bear" would never have got north without our experience and co-operation, but I do say without fear that, left to themselves, they would not have got there in time that season to save those who were saved. So that is our reward. It is true that the commander in his book gives us a pat on the back here and there, and that may be his way of thanking us, but he nullifies that again by saying — "The one great advantage possessed by the whalers was in their experience. It is a question, however whether the importance of this quality in such work as the expedition had on hand, may not be over-estimated. The purpose of the voyage was to make a dash for" — etc. As far as I can remember, we did all the dashing — that is, by knowing the right openings to take. I appreciate the moral he tried to make out. It is on the same principle as "burned bairns dreed the fire," but in this case it was misapplied, as the three masters who helped them through were all young men then and without fear in their own work. In point of fact, the whaleship owners of Scotland had found out that moral for themselves in the late sixties! Before that, one had to be an old experienced man before getting command of a whaler. After that they could not get them young enough.[15]

Aurora now steamed westward towards Ponds Bay and Lancaster Sound where the serious business of whaling was to take place. They were nearing the Magnetic Pole. It was here that they encountered the singing eskimo who came on board, and the captain had a long interview with him on the subject of whales. He seemed to understand maps well and was able to point out where he had seen fish, - a good number had been in the Sound.

On July the 10th the first whale was caught followed by nine more, the last being killed on August the 10th. It had not been possible to go up Barrow Strait or visit Beechy Island because the Sound was frozen over higher up.

It was now getting wintry in Lancaster Sound and they set off for the south west fishing. They sailed south, fishing for salmon off Baffin Island. They met many eskimos and the Captain ordered that coffee and biscuits be provided for the children who came on board. Some barter took place and a live fox was purchased, "it was young and blue, and spent the rest of the voyage walking about the funnel casing where its home was in a lime juice box."[16]

On September the 8th they set off for home, everyone was happy; the voyage had been a success and there had not been a serious accident. On September 20th they sailed by St Kilda and steamed north of the Orkneys crossing the Moray Firth on the 22nd. Coming close to the Aberdeen coast, a fishing boat from Fraserburgh was hailed and they had fish for breakfast. The first question that was asked "was England at war?" the answer "no" was pleasing to those in the Naval Reserve; shortly afterwards they were at home. The following day notice of arrival of *Aurora* was noted in the 'Dundee Advertiser' with a full account of the voyage:

Davis Straits Whale Fishing - Arrival of Aurora.

The steamer *Aurora*, belonging to Messrs. Alex. Stephen & Sons, arrived at Dundee yesterday afternoon from the Davis Straits whale fishing. The *Aurora,* commanded by Capt. Jas. Fairweather, has had a very successful voyage. At Newfoundland 28,150 seals were secured during the two trips, the *Aurora* being the only one of the Dundee fleet which was fortunate in securing a good catch. On the 8th May she left St. John's for Davis Straits, and on reaching Disco fell in with the *Thetis* and *Bear*, on their way north in search of the Greely Expedition. The three ships thereafter kept in company until they reached the north water, when Capt. Fairweather steamed across to Lancaster Sound. An impenetrable barrier of ice blocked the Sound, a circumstance which told in favour of the fishing, as a large number of whales were secured at the edge of the ice. The crew were successful in capturing ten, and also three bottle noses, which will yield 105 tons of oil and about 5 tons of whalebone. As the season advanced the fishing was prosecuted along the west coast of Davis Straits, but without success, owing to the immense quantities of ice, which seemed never to have been driven out of the Straits this year. The frost came on unusually early and very severe, 12 to 14 degrees being registered in August. Capt. Fairweather bore up for home on the 8th of September and experienced a good deal of foggy weather in crossing the Atlantic. He confirms the news previously received of the catches of the fleet, and mentions that the *Polynia* is the only vessel which has added to her cargo, which now consists of 6 whales, equal to 60 tons of oil.

The *Triune* sailed for home on the 6th Sept. Capt. Fairweather has brought home a fine specimen of the Sabine gull, a bird rarely to be met with in Davis Straits. It ought to be mentioned that the crew of the *Aurora*, after receiving the news of the *Chieftain* disaster from the pilot at the mouth of the river, subscribed the sum of £20 18s. to the fund.

The *Chieftain* disaster occurred on May 26th when four of her boats in pursuit of a whale were lost in the fog. Three boats eventually found their way to Iceland with only one casualty; the Captain being in charge of one of the boats. The seamen in the fourth boat perished with the exception of one, who had to have both legs amputated.

Whalers sailing from Dundee in 1884:

Ship	Captain	Tons Reg.	Seals	Whales	Bottle Nose	Tons Seal	Tons Whale
Active	Brown	267	4,258		11	61	
Arctic	Guy	522	101	13	17	1	112
Aurora	Fairweather	386	28,153	10	3	283	97
Cornwallis	Nichol	394		2			21
Esquimaux	Milne	466	1,830	11	24	25	115
Intrepid	Davidson	326	940		8	29	
Jan Mayen	Deuchars	319	3,750	8		57	80
Maud	Watson	276	191		56	5	
Narwhal	Phillips	362	2,759	10		40	90
Nova Zembla	Kilgour	255	160	8	7		88
Polynia	Walker	359	991	6		13	58
Polar Star	Robertson	216	3,508		10	93	
Resolute	Jackman	424	4,722		3	102	
Star	Salmon	229	46		45		
Triune	Soutar	382		11			92
Chieftain	Gellatley	169			3		

1884 ended with the launch of the Terra Nova on December 30th. She was the last of the steam whalers to be built by Alexander Stephen & Sons; Captain Alexander Fairweather was to be her master for at least the next four years.

Launch of a Whaler
as reported in the 'Advertiser'
of Wednesday December 31, 1884.
The new whaler Terra Nova was launched from Messrs. Alexander Stephen & Sons' yard, Dundee, yesterday afternoon in the presence of a large assemblage. As the vessel began to

slip off the ways she was christened by Miss Stephen, of Douglas Terrace, Broughty Ferry and hearty cheers were given when the ship took the water and sailed out to mid-stream. A tug was in attendance, and the Terra Nova was brought to Victoria Dock to receive her engines and boilers, and be equipped for sea. She was berthed alongside the 70 ton crane, and within three hours her masts and bowsprit were set and the lower and topsail yards fitted up. On the invitation of Mr. Stephen a company of ladies and gentlemen assembled in the drawing-loft immediately after the launch and were entertained to cake and wine. Mr. William Stephen presided, and among those present were Mr. David Bruce, Mr. R.A. Miller, Mr. W.G. Thomson, Mr. Joseph Gibson, Mr. James Gilroy, Captains J. Fairweather, Guy & Jackman, etc. Various toasts were then given including one to the captain of the Terra Nova viz. Captain Alexander Fairweather.

As previously stated, the Terra Nova is 750 tons gross, and will have engines of 120 horse-power. She will be barque rigged, and her bowsprit or 'horn' will be of one piece, an innovation which is certain to be advantageous, as the jibbooms are often carried away while crossing the Atlantic during the month of February. It is expected that the Terra Nova will be ready to start for St. John's about the 10th February.

Home from the sea

Grandpa came home to see for the first time his fifth child and fourth son. William Craik Fairweather had been born on Tuesday the 19th of June 1884, at 8.15 pm. He was my mother's favourite brother and was to die tragically of tuberculosis at the age of 21. He was a writer; his stories and sketches were published in the 'People's Friend' as well as forming the second part of grandpa's memoirs under the title 'Rotation of Stories'. The place of his birth is. however, very significant.

The Fairweathers had moved across the Tay from Dundee to the more refined small town of Newport-on-Tay. Not only was this a great improvement in the environment from the dirty and unattractive city, but it placed them in a different social milieu, a signal that they were rising in the world. The move probably took place in the autumn of 1883, and they rented a house in Tay Terrace - a substantial semi-detached building now known as Derby House. They were to spend the rest of their long lives in Newport.

Captain Alexander's family also moved to Newport, and it appears from the ages and birthplaces of his children in the 1891 census that they did so about the same time. In 1891 they were living at 3 Wellpark Terrace, West Newport, whereas granny and grandpa were the 'Faireys East'.

1885 Aurora

From comparisons between the various accounts it seems likely that the dramatic events ascribed by Captain James to this year in fact took place in 1886. According to press and company accounts the voyages of 1885 were by arctic standards fairly straightforward with the exception of the loss of the Cornwallis.

Aurora left Dundee on the 3rd of February and arrived at St John's on the 16th. The following press report was published on her return:

DAVIS' STRAITS WHALE FISHING.
LOSS OF THE CORNWALLIS.

The steamer Aurora, belonging to Messrs Alex. Stephen & Sons, arrived at Dundee yesterday from the Davis Straits whale fishing, and has brought Captain Nicholl and six men of the Dundee whaler Cornwallis, which was crushed by the ice off Cape Kater, on 21st August, the crew, fortunately, being saved. The catch of the Aurora is one whale, which will yield 15 tons of oil and three-quarters of a ton of whale bone. The Aurora, which is commanded by Captain James Fairweather, was employed at the Newfoundland seal fishing in the spring, and landed 12,300 seals. She left St John's at the beginning of May for Davis Straits, and encountered heavy westerly gales on the passage. This season there was comparatively little ice on the East side of Davis Strait, a succession of easterly gales having packed it up against the West side, so that the passage northward was accomplished with the greatest ease. Melville Bay, which is generally so difficult to navigate, was free of ice, and it was crossed without stopping, a most unusual occurrence, weeks being often spent by the ships in forcing a passage through it. Proceeding through Lancaster Sound, the fishing was prosecuted at Prince Regent Inlet, but without success, and the Aurora steamed down the Sound to Pond's Bay, where one fish was caught. A number of whales were seen, and Captain Fairweather was hopeful of making up a cargo, but the fish were scared away by the presence of a shoal of grampus. The remainder of the season was spent along the West coast, but no whales were to be seen, and very stormy weather was encountered. The ship was several times beset, and ran narrow escapes. On the 13th September the Aurora bore up, and arrived yesterday afternoon after a fine passage of twelve days.

The Year Book states that 12,030 seals were killed by *Aurora*, whilst the Company records put the figure at 12,458. Basil Lubbock says 12,345.

The fleet returns show an increase of 39,061 on the previous year's sealing at Newfoundland, whereas there was a decrease of 6369 at Greenland. Only ten whales were caught at Davis Straits against 30 in 1884. However considerable numbers of narwhals, white whales, bottlenose and walrus improved the yield. Walrus skins were by this time sold at 1/6 a pound to make bicycle seats; the slaughter duly increased. *Aurora* returned to Dundee on the 22nd of September after an absence of over seven months.

Basil Lubbock states that in 1885 a good number of white bears were brought home. It seems that some may have been captured alive. Norman Watson in his book *The Dundee Whalers* gives the following account:

Perhaps the first live polar bear returned to Scotland was the cub captured by Captain Sturrock of the Dundee whaler *Alexander* in 1846. Her crew had seen two adult bears and the cub on an ice floe, and the larger male was eventually dispatched after 17 shots. (The crossfire also accounted for Captain Sturrock's son, who was fatally wounded.) The cub was roped, taken on board and 'cooped up in a cask'. It was subsequently transported by the Gourlay-built passenger vessel *Britannia* to Edinburgh where it 'became a tenant in the zoological gardens'. Polar bears became major attractions in subsequent years and it was rare sport catching them, according to the experienced whale man James 'Toshie' McIntosh: 'A lasso was thrown round their necks, and then they were dragged to the ship. and the rope reeved in a tackle on the yard-arm, we hoisted them on board. A big strong barrel was got ready on deck, and 'bruin' was lowered into the cask stern foremost. The cooper was standing by with a cover made of strong iron hoops, and as soon as the bear was fairly caged, he covered him up and secured him tight'. An advertising flyer of February 1886 provides an impression of the excitement the polar visitors offered on arrival in port:

Last week of the bears!
Positively Closing on Saturday 6th February
TO BE SEEN ALIVE
AT COMMERCIAL STREET (Top of Seagate)
The 3 Largest Polar Bears
EVER IMPORTED from the ARCTIC REGIONS

These Beautiful Animals, which are as White as the driven Snow, were brought to Dundee by the Brothers Captains Fairweather, in the whale ships 'Arctic' and 'Terra Nova', and will be Exhibited here for a few day only, previously to being sent to the Zoological Gardens, Dublin. Mr Woods, wishing the inhabitants of Dundee to have an opportunity of seeing them, has decided to make the Price of Admission merely nominal. ONLY 2d. On view from 9am to 10pm.[17]

It would seem that if these bears were exhibited in February 1886, they must have been captured in 1885. At this time Captain Alexander was master of the *Terra Nova*, but Captain James was in command of *Aurora*; the Arctic was under Captain Guy.

1886 *Aurora*

There are two major accounts of this year's eventful voyage which Captain James states to have taken place in 1885. One is from the Captain's memoirs, the other a long account from the 'Dundee Advertiser' of September 3rd, written on the return of *Aurora* to Dundee. Basil Lubbock also describes the voyage, which he places in 1886. However his account is probably taken from Captain James' memoirs.

The Captain writes that the season of 1885 was not so successful as that of '84 and from the very beginning of the voyage bad luck followed them. They left Dundee in February in the face of a south-east wind. When crossing the bar the helmsman got thrown over the wheel and was laid up for the rest of the passage with a broken rib. Shortly after, three men were hurt when a heavy sea was shipped, one sustained a broken leg. Water got down below resulting in the stoke-hole plates being washed up and the loose coal choked the pumps.

Two days were spent at Longhope in the Orkneys putting the ship to rights. They had to fight every mile of the passage to St John's against westerly winds, but arrived long overdue on the 9th of March. They had to work hard to be ready to sail with the sealing fleet the following day; that same night the engine broke down and the ship was helpless amongst the pack ice. There was difficulty with the 240 Newfoundlanders aboard as they wanted to put their tea kettles on the blacksmith's fire whilst he was doing repairs, and a guard of their own officers had to be put round the forge.

In a crippled state they managed to secure just over 3000 seals but were then beset. They then struck an iceberg and all hands were ordered on the ice. When the Captain realised that the berg was aground on the Haypook's Shoal and therefore stationary, the ship was for the moment safe but the pack ice had broken most of the starboard bulwark. The crew were ordered on board again. I leave it to Captain James to finish the story:

> I discovered then that the pack-ice was passing us going south and west at rate of about two or three miles an hour. It was only the best of the men that could keep pace with that on ice and get on board. The weaker ones were, so to speak, as if they were on a treadmill, and could not gain enough to get on

board the steamer. Seeing that, I asked two of my Newfoundland officers to go out again and encourage them on, and if they could not catch up to the steamer to make for the land in an organised manner. The chances were about equal then that we would all have to walk to the land, or something worse. The men who had got on board were set at work to clear the decks of the ice that had been forced over the bulwarks. When daylight came in, no men could be seen on the ice. So the roll was called, and I found that we were short of sixty men.

I leave my readers to imagine the state of my mind, as I did not know whether those men had reached the land or been carried away South and lost. There were still about two hundred and forty of us on board. The steamer was packed tight against the face of the berg, and, looking upwards from any part of the deck, it appeared as if the upper part of the berg would fall on us.

We had to keep very still and quiet, to lessen the chance of an avalanche, and could only venture to go down below deck for a few moments at a time. Fortunately that state of matters did not last long, although, in our anxiety, it appeared long to us. About three p.m. another berg, considerably smaller than the one we were on, was seen drifting in the pack towards us from the North. We feared that if it did strike our berg, the "Aurora" would be between them. When it was seen that the berg was sure to collide with us, we were at our wits' end and quite helpless, but when the contact came, it was on the Western side of the spur of pack-ice already referred to, which loosened it from the berg we were on, and pushed it round the corner to the East. We were thus clear before the bergs met. The collision did not seem to disturb the original berg very much, as the pack-ice between them acted like a buffer. The oncoming berg swung round to the East of the big one and drifted way. The "Aurora" was now clear of the berg, but well up out of the water with the ice that was underneath her. Bit by bit we got her clear and again water-borne. Meantime the fires were set away, and when steam was ready it was found that with the ice pressure on the propeller, the tail-end shaft had been bent, and we could only steam slowly. The steamer was also found to be making a lot of water at the stern tube. As soon as possible, I got her into Catalina Harbour and set the telegraph working along the coast, both North and South, and in a few days I had fifty-nine of the sixty of the lost crew on board again. The other man had to be reported as missing, as no one seemed to know anything about him.

Thus ended our sealing trip for that season, as with the repairs we lost the second trip, and so had no further chance of adding to our catch of three thousand young seals. The only comfort I had out of the whole mess was that my crew stuck to me to a man, as was evident the next season when they set out with me again.[18]

The account in the 'Dundee Advertiser' is worth quoting in full and reads as follows:

THE DUNDEE ADVERTISER, FRIDAY, SEPTEMBER 3, 1886
PERILOUS VOYAGE OF THE WHALER AURORA.

The whaler Aurora, belonging to Messrs Alexander Stephen & Sons, and under the command of Captain James Fairweather, arrived at Dundee yesterday morning, and was berthed in Victoria Dock. The Aurora has been absent from Dundee since early in the year, and has had a most eventful voyage. She left Dundee for St John's on 4th February and arrived at her destination on Friday, the 26th, after a stormy passage, through which she safely passed. On 10th March she, along with the vessels of the Newfoundland sealing fleet, steamed out of St John's for the sealing ground, and was so fortunate as to strike the Eastern pack four days later, At that time a hard gale was blowing from the Northward, accompanied by a thick and blinding snow storm. On nearing the sealing ground two or three of the men got on the ice, and every one was elated at the prospect of securing a full cargo, but unfortunately a gale broke out, and by its force and that of the currents the Aurora by next morning had been driven back fully 40 miles, having in its course passed within three miles of the Ireland rocks on Fogo Island, upon which the Dundee whaler Resolute was lost twelve days later. The ice upon which the seals were congregated had been rapidly altering its position at the same time as the vessel, but ultimately touched at the Berwicks of Fogo, while the Aurora was carried helplessly past. The gale continued, and veered from the North to the North-East, but not losing in impetuosity until Friday, the 19th, by which time the Aurora had been driven back more than 100 miles. During the whole time the Aurora was drifting she was enveloped in impenetrable clouds of snow, the scene to those on board being of the most melancholy and dreary description. On the Friday the vessel was seen to be rapidly approaching a towering iceberg lying aground on Haypook's Shoal, off Cape Bonavista. The strong current which carried the Aurora along was divided into two portions, one of which flowed past each side of the berg at the rate of between four and five miles an hour. While rapidly nearing the berg the greatest excitement prevailed on board, a disaster being imminent. It was about eleven o'clock at night, and the dismal scene was dimly illuminated by the feeble light of the moon. The conduct of Captain Fairweather during the trying ordeal through which he passed is spoken of in high terms of praise and commendation by his men, it being by his example of coolness and the exertions of himself and his officers that a panic was avoided. The Aurora soon afterwards collided with the iceberg, which rose to a height of more than 100 feet. A huge mass of ice hung above the ship threatening every minute to fall, and in order to avoid what looked like an impending disaster Captain Fairweather ordered all hands to leave the vessel and seek safety on the drifting ice. A number of the men had time to carry a portion of their clothes off the ship, which, however, they in most cases afterwards lost. After the men on the ice had spent thirteen hours the ship showed signs of moving, and all the men again went on board. A second iceberg soon thereafter loomed in the distance, and moving forward caught the Aurora, holding her fast across the face of the first iceberg. The second iceberg moved slowly round carrying the ship along with it to the leeward. Considerable damage was done to the fittings of the vessel by the twisting and by the falling ice. A boat was lost, and for a time she was in a most perilous position. Those on board scarcely expected that she would escape from the danger, but gradually she was carried into a place of comparative safety. Strange to say, little damage had been done to the hull, although the vessel was leaking considerably. The men, who had spent a miserable time on the ice, many having had narrow escapes from losing their lives, were all able to return to the ship with the exception of William Whyte, 42 years of age, a native of Bo'ness, and residing with his wife and family in Dundee. Far a period hopes were entertained that the unfortunate man would be discovered, but these had to be abandoned as the time wore on and no trace of him could he found. The Aurora then proceeded to Carolina Harbour, which was the nearest port. On Sunday, 4th April, Captain Fairweather was forced reluctantly to return to St. John's, as the greater part of the crew had lost their clothes. St John's was reached on Monday, and the Aurora left on a second sealing trip on the following day. On that occasion 642 old seals were captured. After refitting at St. John's the vessel left on 13th May for the Greenland seal and whale fishing, which, as already reported, proved a failure in consequence of the stormy weather.

The similarity between the two accounts make it certain that the same voyage is being described. The differences are that Captain James states that he caught 3,000 seals before encountering the iceberg and that as a result of damage and repairs *Aurora* was unable to make the second sealing trip from St John's. The 'Advertiser' account makes no mention of the 3,000 seals, but says *Aurora* caught 642 old seals on a second voyage. Captain James' account of losing sixty men overnight and his fears for their safety has the ring of complete authenticity.

Lubbock states that the Greenland seal fishing, owing to bad weather and the breaking up of the ice, was very poor, only three Scottish vessels getting amongst the young seals. The *Erik, Hope* and the *Earl of Mar* and *Kellie* then captured 4,500. Up Davis Straits bad weather made the season a disastrous one, several ships were lost: the *Jan Mayen* sank, the *Star* was lost in Cumberland Gulf and the Catherine of Peterhead ran ashore and was abandoned. Altogether 19 whales were killed. The season was slightly better at Greenland, 14 whales many quite small, were caught, together with 1033 white whales, 23 bottlenose and 320 walrus being killed by Scottish ships.[19]

> The 'Dundee Year Book' puts the figures at:
> Newfoundland sealing
>   5 steamers caught 41,880 seals
> Greenland seal and whale
>   2 steamers: *Aurora* 'clean'
>   *Polar Star* 1 whale,   610 seals
> Davis Straits whale fishing
>   8 steamers caught 15 whales plus a large number of
>   white, black and bottlenose whales; 100 walrus,
>   some seals, 27 narwhals and a rorgual.

The number of seals caught was half that of 1885, but only six steamers took part as compared to eleven the previous year.

Aurora returned to Dundee on the first or second of September.

Home from the Sea

A month before, a new member of Captain James' family had arrived: a girl called Mary Ann Craik Fairweather was born at 5pm on the first of August, at 4 Prospect Terrace. 'Tan' or 'Tannie' as she was called by her brothers was to become a nurse and midwife, and marry Stuart Bolton M.D. F.R.C.S. Ed. Their children are Alastair Stuart Graham Bolton born in Lerwick on April 24th 1920, and Nancy Mary Rycroft born in Halifax on January 13th 1930. 'Tan' was the sixth child and second daughter of James and Mary Ann.

It seems appropriate to note here that James was at sea when most of his children were born. Helen (Aunt Ella) born in October was the only one of eight not born between late March and mid-September.

The family had moved from Tay Terrace to 4 Prospect Terrace in late 1885 or the first half of 1886. The house looks deceptively small from the outside, being the westernmost dwelling of a stone built semi-detached house. The appearance is of a bungalow with dormer windows, but a description given to me by William Owen of the Tay Valley Family History Society is as follows:

> "Room layout is: upstairs two bedrooms with a bathroom between them; downstairs: lounge to the front (North West), dining room to the front, double bedroom to the rear, small bedroom to rear below the stairs. Living room to rear, kitchenette to the West side. There is a low walled garden at the rear, which was backed by open fields until 1950." He adds: "I know all this because I lived next door for over 30 years!" The house has now been renumbered Number 10.[20]

At the time of the 1891 census there were twelve people in residence, three of them being visitors - a shipmaster, his wife and little girl.

1891 Census of Forgan Parish, Book 4, Schedule: 312 (Ref: 43120)

Prospect Terrace	Rooms: 8	(House: 756)				
James Fairweather	H	M M	37	Shipmaster		For Dundee
Mary Fairweather	W	M F	39			For Kirriemuir
Elizabeth Fairweather	D	U F	11	Scholar		For Dundee
Alexander Fairweather	S	U M	8	Scholar		For Dundee
Charles Fairweather	S	U M	7	Scholar		For Dundee
William Fairweather	S	U M	6	Scholar		Fif Newport
Mary A Fairweather	D	U F	4			Fif Newport
David Fairweather	S	U M	2			Fif Newport
Lewis S Lewis	Vis	M M	42	Shipmaster		WLS
Margaret Lewis	Vis	M F	43	Shipmaster's wife	WLS
Jeanette Lewis	Vis	U F	3			WLS
Sarah Moore	Ser	U F	16	Dom Serv		IRL

There are two points to note here. Firstly James and Mary Ann's eldest son James is not at home; he would be about 15 years old and may well have started his career at sea. Secondly, the Fairweathers now have a 16 year old Irish girl as a domestic servant.

The family were to live at 4, Prospect Terrace until in 1900 grandpa became an owner occupier by purchasing 15, Norwood, a stone built semi-detached house; he called number 15 'Bonavista'. All three houses had excellent views across the Tay estuary, and 'Bonavista' would have a special meaning for an arctic sailor.

1887 *Aurora*

At the beginning of Part III of his memoirs Captain James makes some general observations about whaling, distinguishing between the finner whale (as caught by the Norwegians in the Arctic and in the Antarctic) and the Greenland (right) whale. It was the latter that was hunted by the Dundee whalers. Lancaster Sound was first penetrated by Captain William Adams Snr in 1868. It was now known that the whales wintered in Hudson's Bay and in the early spring enter the Davis Straits. The larger ones, predominately male, return to Hudson's Bay in the autumn, but the smaller ones and the mothers enter Lancaster Sound and return to Hudson's bay via Fury and Hecla Straits. Intensive whaling in Lancaster Sound therefore killed not only the whales but the whaling trade.

Captain James explains that the ice in Davis Straits tends to the West, therefore the steamers have to make their passage up the West coast of Greenland to Disco Island. After that they have to take the pack westwards to reach Lancaster Sound. However in the early part of the year the area from Resolution Island (latitude 61 North) to Disco is all considered good whaling ground. Resolution Island being on the north side of the entrance to the Hudson Strait and considerably further South than Disco Island.

He then relates an incident which took place in 1887 concerning the behaviour of a mother and baby whale. When hunting a mother and her young (sucker) the rule is to fasten the mother first and then the sucker will soon be got. If the sucker is taken, the mother makes off and shows absolutely no fight for her young. On this occasion it appeared that the mother (observed by the Captain from the 'barrel' or 'crow's nest') was lying low and sending her youngster repeatedly to the surface. Both were caught but Captain James says "I have nothing to build on when I accuse this mother whale of being a coward in sending her young one up first before she would venture herself; but it certainly looked like it."[21]

Both Captain James and David Moore Lindsay vividly describe the hunting, harpooning, killing and flensing of the whale. They also portray the dangers consequent upon the pursuit in small boats leading to many mishaps, although meticulously organised. Moore Lindsay describes Captain James with an 'irregular crew' killing a whale himself by lancing.[22] He also describes the careful recording of the catch, with the circumstances of the kill (illustrated by stylised drawings) the size and weight of each whale, and the amount of oil extracted.

The fishing year began for *Aurora* when she left Dundee for St John's on the 20th of February. There she was moderately successful in the sealing, landing 3,250 on the first trip and 2,000 on the second. However she was vastly out fished by Captain Alexander in the *Terra Nova*: various totals of between 25 and 26,000 are given for him.

After the usual refitting in Newfoundland *Aurora* set off for the Davis Straits on the 24th of May. Melville Bay was blocked with huge floes of ice, and she had to steam almost to the entrance of Smith Sound before getting a clear passage to the West coast. This occupied several weeks with the result that the best month of the fishing season was past before *Aurora* and the rest of the Dundee fleet got through Lancaster Sound to Prince Rupert Inlet where Aurora secured three black (Right) whales. As no more whales were to be seen, Captain James steamed to the white whale fishing grounds and was successful in capturing about 200.

After visiting all the fishing grounds on the West coast without sighting any whales the *Aurora* bore up for home on the 22nd of October. The press report says "Captain Fairweather states that the frost set in about the middle of September and prevailed with great intensity, so that the vessel had to steam through hundreds of miles of young ice before she got into clear water. The passage home was very stormy." *Aurora* arrived back in Dundee on Friday the 11th of November and brought with her three black whales and 200 white whales which will yield about 46 tons of oil, and one ton of bone. She also brought home a live bear,

Once again Captain Alexander excelled, *Terra Nova* producing 115 tons of oil against *Aurora's* 46. However *Aurora's* catch provided one ton of bone against Terra Nova's ½ ton.

The 'Dundee Year Book' states that in 1887 five steamers were engaged in the Newfoundland sealing, landing 51,650 old and young seals. This catch yielded 690 tons of oil. One vessel went to Greenland and two to Labrador where only 400 seals were caught. The total seal catch was up by 14,110 from the previous year 1886.

The Davis Straits whale fishing yielded 496 tons of oil, but this was largely made up by the capture of white whales and walrus. "The amount of whale bone on which the success of the fishing is dependent being limited to seven tons".

1888 *Aurora*

This was Captain James' last whaling voyage in the *Aurora*. From his memoirs we know that he was aware that overwhaling had killed 'the hen that laid the golden egg'. However there were other reasons for the decline. In a newspaper article of December 1926 he states of the decline "the causes were various, the oil had been in great demand as a dressing in jute batching, but its place was taken by cheaper substitutes. Then gas came into general use for lighting and that killed the demand for fish oil used as lamp oil; and now there is no demand for imitation ostrich feathers that were made out of whale bone." Surprisingly, in contradiction he continues, "If only some demand could be found for the products, the whaling industry could flourish again."[23]

This was to be Captain James' most successful sealing voyage. Aurora left Dundee on the 6th of February. There was to be only one sealing voyage from St John's this year as the sealing had to close on the 26th of April following an Act passed by the legislature of Nova Scotia "to prevent the exhaustion of such valuable fishing."[24]

Aurora left St John's on the 10th of March, and there are two accounts of what happened, one in Captain James' memoirs, and one in the 'Advertiser' of the 22nd of May. The main discrepancy is in the date of the voyage, which Captain James places in 1886. There is no doubt however, that it actually took place in 1888 as reported in the newspaper.

For this year, I feel I cannot do better than quote in full my grandfather's account of the seal fishing. My first thoughts are that the aura is so different from modern times. There was little or no technology, as Captain James himself comments. The success or failure of the voyage, apart from the weather conditions, depends on the experience, skill and personality of the captain to an awesome extent in the face of such dangers. It is up to the captain to keep the ship safe, find the seals, ascertain the latitude with "two soup bowls and molasses", negotiate with the locals and oversee the whole enterprise. This surely requires exceptional qualities in a man.

The season of 1886 at the seal fishing on the coast of Newfoundland was very severe, owing to persistent north-east winds with snow, the wind sometimes reaching gale force, which caused the ice to pack on the land. After leaving St. John's on the 10th March, it was of the first importance to the masters of the steamers to keep their vessels free, for to be beset means to get frozen in the pack with no prospect of getting free again till the wind changed to westward, and possibly not until the pack got far enough off the land to allow the swell to get through it and break it up. But keeping the vessel free was not getting her near to where we expected the seals would be.

In those days, each master had to form his own opinion as to where he thought seals might be. It was not like going to a fixed-on port for a cargo. It was more like a game of blind-man's buff. We had to look for our own cargo. I have got the seals about one hundred miles north-east of Belle Isle. I also have got them off Cape Bonavista, and have heard of them being just outside of St. John's Harbour. These positions are roughly about three hundred miles apart. It was generally agreed on that the seals whelped near Belle Island (an island at the eastern entrance of the strait of that name) on or about the end of February or the beginning of March. The seals whelped on new ice, so that they could break through it to their young. Should the ice pack as I have described, my method of trying to place them was to keep a record of the winds and their force, from an early date in February (the Arctic current was a known quantity to us), then work the whole up day by day — add experience — and so fix on a spot which might be near the mark, and I never was very far out. I understand that the masters nowadays are free of all that worry and anxiety, as a seaplane is sent out from the land when weather permits, and when the seals are spotted the position and information is sent to the masters, the steamers being all fitted out with wireless sets.

On this occasion I kept working out and north until the outside edge of the ice was in plain view from the masthead. As it was not advisable to get out of the pack into a heavy sea with so many men on board, the engines were stopped, and in a short time we were beset and lay quite still, although we could see the sea breaking outside us. After the gale took off, a very thick fog set in, but towards noon the following day it cleared up overhead and the sun came out. I then had a very vague idea as to how far north I was, and as I was most anxious to find out, I asked the Dundee mate to get his sextant, and two soup plates with some molasses in each, for artificial horizons, while I went for my own. With so many men on deck tramping about, I found it almost impossible to take the observation on board, so got two men to carry the plates and went on the ice. The bulk of the Newfoundland men were at a loss to know what I was to do, and many a quaint remark was heard.

That was a break in the monotony for the men, and I got the latitude we were in, which was satisfactory to me, so we were all happy. But I was very anxious, as time was passing on, and we were for the time being firmly beset.

The young seals, as a rule, commence to cast their white coats and take to the water when they are just over three weeks old, but in the then state of the ice, they could not get into the water. But they were growing, and as soon as the ice opened out they would take to the water at once, leaving us no time to look for them. I had made up my mind to make for White Bay as soon as I possibly could, as the most likely place to find them. In a few days the weather cleared up and we saw the land and made it out to be the big Horse Island, just to the eastward of White Bay, and about five miles distant from us. But we were still held fast. Next afternoon, two men were seen coming to us from the island over the ice. I have already said that in these days we had no seaplane or wireless to help us, but we had a system, such as it was, although, as it happened, it was never of any use to me.

We had paid observers here and there along the coast where their homes were. Their function was to give the steamers of our company all the information they could, to help them to find the seals. I was supplied with a list of the men's names and where they could be found, also with the countersign for the season, and I knew we had two of these men on the big Horse Island. When the coming of the two men towards us from the shore was reported to me, I concluded that they were our own secret service men.

As they drew near I went to the cabin, leaving orders with the St. John's mate to bring them down to me. When they got seated and had a drink, I asked their names. The names given did not correspond with the names given on my list. I then tried them with the countersign, but drew a blank. I then asked them straight, what they came out for. They said to see if I could give them some medicine. On being asked what they wanted the medicine for, they looked at each other and seemed to be very uncomfortable. I then asked them if they had seen any seals that spring. They both said no, at once. Then, pointing to some blood on their clothing, I asked them where they got that. Again they looked confused, and the elder one said they killed a young hood seal when coming out. I then told them that, no matter what they said, I was to go in as soon as ever I could, so if they wanted to make anything out of their trip, they had better tell me the truth, and I would pay them well in kind for it.

After some hesitation and another refresher, out it came. The seals were just on the west side of the Horse Islands, and from there to Partridge Point in White Bay. When I asked their reason for coming off to us, I was told that when they saw us yesterday it was agreed amongst them that they would go out and try to stop me from coming in with my three hundred men, while their neighbours were hauling the seals ashore. At once all was bustle aboard the "Aurora," and my men wanted off at once, but, as night was coming on, I would not let them go, but gave orders for an early breakfast and a start at daylight. But they were so keen that I could not keep them back, so they were away before dawn, which was a mistake, for with floundering on the ice in the dark, quite a lot of them had to return with sprains, etc. The Dundee crew was kept back to work the ship in.

The arrangements were all made the night before, and the men took with them what stores and gear they could carry. It was a big stunt, and they had to a great extent a free hand to take what was necessary. The Newfoundland crew, of say two hundred and fifty men, were divided up into four watches, each in charge of a master watch and quarter master, with the second hand or Newfoundland mate in charge of all.

They left the steamer in watches. The first to leave had to work on the left of all, the next on their right, and so on. They also carried with them the pan flags. These were numbered, the left-hand master watch getting from one to twenty-five, his quarter master from twenty-six to fifty, the highest numbers being on the extreme right. These precautions were taken in case of thick fog or snow when I was looking for them. Say, for instance, I came on flag number ninety-seven, I would then know that I was about the middle of my men, and that they bore right and left from me. The flags bore the letters A.R.O. in white on a dark blue ground, and were attached to a staff and planted in the middle of a pan or bing of seal pelts. The flag claimed the pelts for the steamer whose flags were on them. Although I had over fifty men on board after the Newfoundlanders went away, the steamer had a very deserted-like appearance, and it was three days before we could attempt to break out and get a move on. These three days I will never forget. I was only content when at the mast-head in the day-time. Night to me was then a horror.

Meantime the wind was coming from the westward and freshening. The next day the ice commenced to ease and we got to work. It was hard and slow at first, but in time we got in the wake of the Horse Islands and got close up to them, and I discharged my obligations to my two visitors.

I had told the second-hand to carry our men far enough away from the islanders to give them fair play, and he must have carried out my orders, as the islanders thanked me for it. The next night I had all my crew aboard, after being away on the ice for five days. They reported having panned thirty thousand young seal pelts, but a lot of them were lost when the ice broke up. The second-hand reported that all had gone fairly well with them. They built snow houses and covered them with poles (which they carried from the steamer with them) and seal pelts, but they had enough of it for a time, and were glad to have the steamer under their feet again. The knowledge that they could have gone ashore on the islands at any time before the break-up of the ice was a great help both to them and to me. In my opinion none but Newfoundlanders could have done it. Their sang-froid carried them through.

Next day we got the steamer among the pans and com-menced loading. I saw for myself then that some of the heavy pans had broken and the pelts lost. But we collected over twenty-five thousand, then went after the beaters— that is, the young seals after they have taken to the water. For a few days they only go for a short distance, when they come up again on the ice to rest—and made our cargo up to about twenty-six thousand three hundred, far more than I expected, as the seals were ready to take to the water as soon as the ice broke up. In this case the ice came off the land in one unbroken sheet, and, had it not been for the icebergs that were aground in the vicinity, it would have remained so until a swell got through it. But the bergs split it up sufficiently to let us work.

On arrival at St. John's with our catch I was reminded of something I had read about a skipper's woes. It went on to say: -

Alas! poor skipper, if at sea you have trouble,
Perhaps in port you may have double.

This was my case now, for my crew, on the strength of the good trip, got out of hand, and some of them took French leave.[25]

One item of particular interest in the above account is the flavour of espionage arising from the company's action in paying observers to provide information to help the whalers locate the seals, to the extent of the use of an annual 'countersign' or password. There must have been a degree of competitive ill feeling between the locals, and the incomers from far off Scotland, who made money from the produce of their shores. And Captain James was careful to treat the locals fairly.

The 'Dundee Advertiser' of the 9th of April noted that telegrams had been received from Newfoundland reporting that several of the steamers which had been prosecuting the seal fishing at Newfoundland were lying beset amongst the ice off Twillingate, about two days passage from St John's. One of these was the *Aurora* and a telegram from Captain James reported his catch to be 25,000 seals. It was hoped that a favourable change of wind would soon liberate the imprisoned steamers and allow them to reach St John's.

Aurora's return is reported in the 'Advertiser' of Tuesday the 22nd of May, 1888, and is worth including as a comparison with Captain James' account:

ARRIVAL FROM NEWFOUNDLAND. The Steamer Aurora, Captain James Fairweather, which was the most successful of the Dundee fleet at Newfoundland this year. arrived at Dundee yesterday morning, and was berthed in Victoria Dock. Captain Fairweather reports that he left St John's on the 10th March, and after a deal of hard cutting through the ice, during which the vessel was closely beset for three days, he arrived at the entrance to White Bay, where the main pack of seals lay. About 1000 seals were got on board on the 22d March. Three days later, on account of the impossibility of getting nearer the seals in consequence of the heavy ice floes, the men were sent away from the ship, and walked a distance of seventeen miles before they reached the pack. About 13,000 were killed and panned. Two days afterwards the ship forced a passage nearer the seals, and the men were again sent out, and secured 11,000, making up a total of 25,000. The time occupied in getting this cargo was less than twenty hours, but much time was necessarily occupied in traversing the distance between the ship and the seals. In addition to her own cargo, the Aurora has brought home the sealskins of the Terra Nova and about 60 tons of oil. The passage homeward was tempestuous.

There are reports of the seal and whale fishing for 1888 in the 'Dundee Year Book' and an account in the 'Courier 'of 2nd November. Considerable detail is gone into about the amount and value of the catches. By far the most successful area was the Newfoundland sealing where four vessels killed approximately 66,900 seals whereas in 1887 five vessels had killed 51,500. The Greenland sealing had been disappointing as had the whaling in the Davis Straits, where only six or eight black whales, two of them small were caught. The seven ships engaged (which did not include Aurora), also brought back a few bottlenose whales, supplemented by over 1,000 white whales and a miscellany of seals, walrus and narwhals. There is a certain discrepancy between the figures given by the Year Book and the newspaper.

Emphasis is placed on the amount of whalebone produced, which is described as by far the most valuable production of the whale fishing; in 1888 barely three tons of bone was secured, compared to seven tons in 1887. The account in the 'Courier' concludes, "but for the fact that two of the vessels caught a large number of white whale, not one of the vessels prosecuting the fishing in Davis Straits would have realised sufficient to cover her expenses."

The total financial aggregate for the year was £33,000 compared to £54,804 in 1887.

Despite his success at Newfoundland in sealing it seems that Captain James realised that the 'writing was on the wall'. His first step was to relinquish Aurora and leave the company of Alex Stephen & Son, after an association of seven years.

Captain James' references from Alex Stephen & Sons are dated 1898 when he must have been considering a job application which is not apparently obvious. However the comments of the writer bear testimony to the high esteem in which he was held by his whaling employers. Phrases used include "a competent master, sober, steady and attentive to his duties;" "I shall always be pleased to hear of his success in life." "So far as my observation goes I have always found him to be a careful, diligent and trustworthy man, very attentive to his duties and at all times clear headed, temperate and honourable in his conduct." These comments were to be exceeded in future testimonials.[26]

Aurora remained in the Dundee whaling fleet until 1894. She next appears as 'a sealer from Newfoundland' bought by Douglas Mawson for his 1911 to 1914 Australasian Antarctic Expedition.[27] In 1914 Ernest Shackleton bought her from Mawson for £3,200.[28] *Aurora* was to convey the Ross Sea party of Shackleton's Imperial Trans-Antarctic Expedition to their base and act as a support vessel. Unfortunately after landing the party, *Aurora* was beset and had to return to Hobart, leaving the expedition members stranded for over two years. In January 1917 Shackleton rescued the survivors in Aurora.[29] Almost immediately *Aurora* was sold to an American firm for £10,000.[30]

There is an air of mystery about the fate of the *Aurora*. Captain Hector writing in *Sea Breezes* (undated) quotes J.K.Davis in *With the Aurora in the Antarctic* as follows: "A sailor cannot but regard with affection the good ship which has carried her living freights in perfect safety, over many miles of tempestuous ocean, and through the berg-strewn seas of the Southern Ocean. After five voyages the *Aurora* though somewhat scarred and weather-beaten was still sound and serviceable in February 1914." Adams continues: "since then the ship sailed from Sydney, N.S.W., on June 20th, 1917, bound for Iquique, Chili (sic), but failed to arrive. She was carrying coal, and finally posted as "Missing" at Lloyd's on January 2nd, 1918."[31] However, in Captain James' scrapbook an undated press cutting from the 'Daily Mail' states:

FATE OF SHACKLETON'S
RELIEF SHIP.
Aurora Believed Lost
With All Hands.

From news received in Britain it is feared that the relief ship Aurora, which rescued the members of Sir Ernest Shackleton's South Polar Expedition, who were marooned for nearly two years at the Ross Sea base, has been lost with all hands on the homeward journey to Britain.

Last Wednesday Lloyd's was notified that the Aurora was considerably overdue. The vessel had been overhauled at Wellington, New Zealand, and on Sir Ernest Shackleton's returning to Britain he gave the ship over to Captain R. J. Reeves to bring home.

The Aurora, it is believed, left Wellington in June last with a crew of about 22, but no tidings of the ship have been received since.

Vessels sent by Mr George Scales, shipowner, of Wellington, to search the islands of the South Pacific found no trace of the crew, but a floating lifebuoy and wreckage bearing the name Aurora were found. Daily Mail.[32]

1889 *Earl of Mar and Kellie*

It is not clear why Captain James left *Aurora* and Alex Stephen to be captain of the *Earl of Mar and Kellie* (owned by Mr Duthie) particularly as she was a smaller ship, which was contrary to his usual pattern. *The Earl of Mar and Kellie* was originally a Peterhead vessel and was only in the Dundee fleet for three years 1888 to 1890.[33]

This one season he captained her cannot be regarded as successful and no doubt the poor result confirmed his decision to make a career change.

The Earl of Mar and Kellie left Dundee on the 7th of March; after making up her crew at Lerwick she proceeded to the Greenland waters. Owing to foggy weather she was unable to find the main seal pack, and the fishing was a failure, only 360 seals being picked up.

Afterwards Captain James went in search of whales and was successful in capturing two, one large and one small one on the 26th of May. He was unable to get near the few other fish he sighted. and after unsuccessfully visiting the old sealing grounds he bore up for home on the 5th of August, and arrived back in Dundee on the 7th of August. There is a slight discrepancy in the accounts of the catch ranging between 13 to 16 cwt of bone and 23½ to 25 tons of oil.

The fleet accounts in the 'Dundee Year Book' show that the Newfoundland sealing was still buoyant, four vessels catching 76,286 seals, nearly 10,000 more than in 1888. Only three vessels pursued the Davis Straits whale fishing and their efforts only produced 125 tons of oil compared with 308 tons in 1888. However the amount of whalebone increased from 2 tons 2cwt in '88, to 5 tons 5cwt in '89. The three steamers that proceeded to Greenland (of which the *Earl of Mar and Kellie* was one) did better than in '88, producing 196 tons of oil and 3 tons 3cwt of whale bone, as against 95 tons of oil in 1888.

Home from the sea

Shortly after Captain James' departure for Greenland there was a further addition to his family. David Fraser Fairweather was born on Tuesday the 26th of March 1889 at 4, Prospect Terrace, Newport. He was the seventh child and fifth son of James and Mary Ann. David was to marry Johan Ingles and emigrate to Australia. where he spent the rest of his life, mainly in Mount Isa. He had a distinguished record in the First World War serving with the *Queensland Light Horse*, the *4th ANZAC Camel Battalion* and *The 15th Light Horse Regiment* in Mesopotamia. He had no children (for a narrative of David's life see *David Fraser Fairweather* 1889-1968 by his nephew James Fairweather).

As a tailpiece to the whaling years of Captain James' career here is a whaling folk song from *Songs and Ballads of Dundee* by Nigel Gatherer, 1986:

THE OLD POLINA
Sung to the tune of 'The Balaena'

Chorus:
Ooooh! The wind was on her quarter,
and the engines working free;
There's not another whaler
That sails the Arctic Sea
Can beat the Old 'Polina',
You needn't try; my sons,
For we challenged all, both great and small,
From Dundee to Saint John's.

There's a noble fleet of whalers, a-sailing from Dundee,
Manned by Scottish sailors, to take 'em o'er the sea,
On a western ocean passage, we started on the trip,
And we flew along just like a song, on our gallant whaling ship.

'Twas the second Sunday morning just after leaving port
We met a heavy sou'west gale that washed away our boat;
It swept away our quarterdeck, our stanchions went as well,
An' the whole she-bang went floating in the waves and in the gale.

Art Jackson set his canvas, Fairweather got up steam,
And Captain Guy, the daring b'y, came plunging through the stream;
And Mullins in the 'Husky' tried to beat the bloody lot,
But to beat the old 'Polina' was something he could not.

There's the noble 'Terra Nova', a model without a doubt,
The 'Arctic' and 'Aurora' they talk so much about,
Art Jackman's flying mail-boat, the terror of the sea,
Tried to beat the old 'Polina' on a passage from Dundee.

We're back again in old St John's where rum and beer are cheap.
An' we'll drink a health to Captain Guy who brought us o'er the deep;
A health to all the girls out here and to our wives so fair,
 No other ship could make the trip with 'Polina' I declare.

1889-1890   The State of Alabama

The only indication of the next stage of Captain James' career apart from his memoirs is contained in a reference, which states that "His reason for leaving the whaling was the apparent declining state of the trade at that time and he preferred to push (sic) his way in the general Mercantile Marine."[1]   Captain James says in his memoirs that he had to seek employment in the general trade, and was appointed master of the State of Alabama.[2]   It is possible to work out that he remained with this ship from late 1889 or 1890 until he became captain of the SS Kentigern in March 1893, approximately three years or over. The State of Alabama was owned by the State Line and was engaged in general trade between America and 'this country'.[3]   There is an anecdote in Captain James' memoirs about this ship concerning an incident which was "the nearest that I came to a shipwreck." At the time they were en route from Philadelphia U.S. for Havannah, Cuba.

Some time ago we were hearing of a steamer on her beam ends in the Atlantic, with an American liner standing by to save the crew before the steamer foundered. It was an epic of the sea.

It was my misfortune at one time to be in the same position as that steamer.

When in command of the "State of Alabama" I loaded a cargo of anthracite coal at Philadelphia, U.S., for Havannah, Cuba. We were put under the tips right away at 9 p.m., and loading commenced at once. When daylight came in, I saw that the coal we were loading was almost like a cargo of billiard balls. The steamer had two iron decks under the main deck, and it occurred to me that if the steamer were not full, the cargo would be liable to shift. But it was too late to fit up shifting boards.

Shortly after we got out of the Delaware, we steamed into a gale from the south-east, which in the course of two days veered through south to west and then round to north-west. The steamer was more or less head on to it with no bad effects till we were south of Cape Hatteras. Then the wind, still at gale force, got more on the starboard side, and one unusually heavy sea struck her, and she went over till the port rail was in the water. The engines were stopped, as the wing fires had to be drawn. All hands were called and sent below to trim her up.

It was about 8 p.m. when she first went over. By 6 p.m. things looked very bad. By 8 p.m. they looked worse. All the rooms in the port alleyway, including those of the first, second, third and fourth engineers, the mess-room and lamplocker, were gutted out. The port boats were almost in the water, and were of no use to us then. The chief engineer, about 9 p.m., again came to me and said, "Do you know the ship is sinking?" I said: "Yes, I know she is sinking, and if you have come to me for consolation, all I can say is that the water is nice and warm." (We were in the Gulf Stream then.) But I was thinking harder than ever then, and asked the chief if he could get the engines to go for, say, a quarter of an hour. He said: "I will try." I told him he must say "Yes" or "No." He said "Yes," but that he would need a short time to get ready.

I then explained that, as a last chance, I was to turn her over the wind in the hope that a sea might strike her on the high side and square her up. I told him to go down and ring up when he was ready. When I rang off, he was to shut everything off and come to the bridge-deck with his men, and take his chance with the rest of us.

Meantime, I had sent for all the men that were down trimming the cargo, to come to the bridge-deck at once. When they were all mustered, I explained the position to them, and sent them to unhook the boats' tackles, and swing the davits clear of both starboard boats: and I impressed on them the necessity of keeping the boats upright if the steamer went down, then one man could be helped in and in turn he could help the others.

When the telegraph rang ready, I put her on full ahead and she came up better than I had thought she would. After she was well over the wind and sea, I stopped the engines and rang off, and all hands came on the bridge-deck to await events. Both boats were the same size, so half the crew were at each. The mate was to take the after one and I the forward one, as it was nearest me.

The men were all again instructed that every effort must be made to keep the boats upright till they floated out of the chocks. The outer halves were turned down.

The steamer fell off very wide, almost bringing the wind on the quarter. Then she came to a bit and brought it on the beam. When the steamer was in that position it beats me to describe the scene. The weather bulwarks were right in the water; I cannot say how many degrees she was over, as I had no clinometer. In about twenty minutes from the time she came over the wind, I saw the sea coming and sang out to the men to stand steady—that 'kill or cure' was coming. With that, the sea struck her on the high side of both main decks and more than squared her up. She was left with a slight list to starboard. I rushed the engineers below again, and got her head to wind. I remember saying to the mate, "this is Hogmanay, and if it is next Hogmanay till the gale takes off, keep her head to the wind." I also remember the feeling that I had through it all. My mouth and throat felt dry and parched, but that might have been with the salt water, otherwise I felt quite normal. That was the nearest that I ever came to a shipwreck, but it was pretty near.

I had a patent medicine in which I had a great belief, and it was good for most sailors' troubles.

When leaving St. John's, Newfoundland, with a large whaling crew, we had to satisfy the authorities that we had so many bottles of that medicine on board, before we got our clearance, and I had such a good opinion of it that I carried the idea with me to the general trade.

One afternoon, a sailor came to me complaining of spasms. I gave him a teaspoonful of the mixture with water. He then went forward on the main deck, while I was going forward on the bridge deck. When I reached the end of it, I heard voices under me. One said: "What did the old man give you, Jim?"

"Why, he gave me yon hot stuff."

Then I heard the first voice saying—"He gave me dat to rub my leg with this morning."

I had a laugh to myself, but it was good for both.[4]

Apart from this, nothing further is known of these years. Eventually, presumably in 1893, the ship became obsolete and was laid up.

The early 1890s proved a sad time for James and Mary Ann. Janet, James' mother, died on December the 17th 1890 aged sixty six. At the time she was still married to Benjamin Forbes, her second husband, and they were living at 8, Baffin Street Dundee. The informant however, was her son Captain Alexander, and it is interesting that he describes his deceased father James Fairweather as cabinet maker (master). Both sons show evidence of regard for their late father, despite his unexplained departure to Australia.

Charles Craik was the next to pass away. He died on June the 20th 1891 aged eighty three. His wife Eliza died the following year on May the 4th 1892 aged seventy nine. Eliza died at the home of her daughter Mary Ann, at 4 Prospect Terrace, East Newport; this ran true to the nineteenth century pattern, that an elderly couple managed, until one of them died (usually the man), after which the survivor was cared for in the home of one of their children. The modern culture of residential or nursing home care was not an option.

A happier event occurred five months later. Helen Mitchell Fairweather (Aunt Ella) was born on Monday, October the 10th 1892 at 4 Prospect Terrace, Newport. She was the third daughter and eighth and last child of James and Mary Ann.

1893 to 1898   The Kentigern

For four years Captain James was master of the *Kentigern* and subsequently master of the *Vortigern*.   Both ships seem to have been owned by the company Arch'd McMillan & Sons Ltd. Shipbuilders of Dumbarton.   However most of the extant references are written by E.P.Babtie, Ship & Insurance broker of 111 Union Street Glasgow, their manager. The *Kentigern* was then in the Atlantic trade.[1]

There is one anecdote relating to the *Kentigern* in Captain James' memoirs. I make no apology for including it in full, for to me it shows so many of the qualities which made up his character.   Excitement and optimism at going through the Suez Canal for the first time, his fondness and feeling for animals (despite his whaling past), his conscientiousness in identifying and solving a problem, and using his initiative in the interest of his employers, and completing a difficult task to his own and the owner's satisfaction.

When the whaling industry gave out, I had to seek employment in the general trade, and was appointed Master of the S.S. "State of Alabama." In time she became obsolete, and was laid up, and I joined the S.S. "Kentigern." She was then in the Atlantic trade. On one passage from New York to Glasgow we got rather badly broken up by a heavy sea, and had to put in to St. Michaels, Azores, with a broken bridge, steering gear out of order, hatch covers torn, and so on. The owner had fixed the steamer to load a general cargo for the Malabar and Coromandel coasts of India. He knew when he fixed the steamer that he was tight enough for time to get her to Malabar Coast and away again before the S.W. Monsoon broke. When he heard that the steamer would lose some time at St. Michaels, repairing, he became very anxious indeed, and when we arrived at Glasgow he came at once to see me. I saw the charter, and ignorance of the conditions of the Indian Coast made me very optimistic and I managed in some way to convey a part of my optimism to him.

At least he seemed to go away less anxious and better pleased. What I now think was at the back of my optimism was that I was going through the Suez Canal to India for the first time in my life. That thought I think elated me and made me see things through rosy glasses.

As a boy, I had been across the Equator and as far south as Bahia on the Brazilian Coast, and up the Mediterranean as far as Alexandria, in the Dundee Brig, "Wycliffe."

To digress a little, the "Wycliffe" had a history. When she was barque-rigged she carried one half of the second party of

The Fairweather Family, circa. 1895
Elizabeth (Lizzie), James jnr, William, Alexander, David.
Charles, James, Helen (Ella), Mary Ann, Mary Ann Craik (Tan)

Scotsmen that up to that time had settled in New Zealand. They were in charge of a Mr. Cargill. There were two large wooden mooring bitts on the poop of the "Wycliffe," one on each side, and they were known to us as "Cargill's Chairs."

I understand that a son of Gilbert Burns, the elder brother of our National Poet, was in charge of the other half of the party. They were, of course, in another vessel, but they all landed safely.

When I am on the subject of my apprenticeship, I would like to refer to another education I got then. One day when I was at the wheel, the cook, who also acted as steward, came to the Master, who was alone on the poop. The cook had a box of red herrings with him. I heard him tell the Captain that the herrings were going bad and asked if he would give them to the men. The Captain said, "Certainly not, if you do they will throw them at you. Put the box somewhere where they can steal them." That was done and they must have turned into flying fish, as they all disappeared in a short time. That Master knew sailors.

After the steamer was discharged and dry-docked at Glasgow, we left for London to load for the Malabar Coast. On arrival at (I think) Victoria Dock, loading commenced and ominous clouds commenced to appear in the distance, when we were told that some fifty pieces of bridge-work of about four and three-quarters of a ton each had to be taken in for Calicut. I had put out heavier lifts than that, but smooth water was required and one could hardly expect smooth water on the Malabar Coast during the S.W. Monsoons.

There was no definite time named in the charter for discharging, nor was there any saving clause for bad weather, so it looked as if we might have to wait for some months for fine weather. Meantime we could do nothing but take in the cargo as presented to us and hope for the best. So the loading went on until she was full under hatches. Some acids were put on the deck as deck cargo and, last but not least, a pack of foxhounds, as passengers, for the North Indian Hunt. The pack consisted of twelve hounds and one Irish terrier, all most beautiful animals and well supplied with everything necessary for them during the passage. They were to be landed at Calicut. The hounds were made fast to the iron stanchions on the starboard side of the bridge deck, about six feet apart.

When we were leaving, the steamer was backed out of her berth and headed for locks with a swing bridge over them. The pilot, to get the bridge open, pulled the lanyard of the steam whistle and with the very first toot, each of the hounds made one simultaneous jump over the rail, and they were suspended by their collars and chains over the side. One half of the crew were forward and the other half aft at the time, but they rushed to the rescue, and in time we got the dogs on board again, none the worse of their adventure. They were all very docile, except one that was rather morose and continued so all the passage. I took charge of the dogs myself and loved the job. The terrier used to walk round the decks with me and reminded me of Landseer's "Dignity and Impudence." The hounds had the dignity all right, and most certainly the terrier had the impudence to think he could fight them all.

When we reached Port Said it was a new world to me and a long cry from the ice and snow of Greenland that I had been accustomed to. The canal passage, with its slow steaming and occasional stops, was rather trying when I kept thinking of the possibility of the S.W. Monsoons breaking before I reached India.

By some means or other I had got into my head the idea that the Red Sea was some sort of a glorified lake, but it took the "Kentigern" six days to steam through it, then, another day more, and we were past Aden. A few days later we reached and anchored off Calicut, with no doubt about the Monsoon being on or off. It was on and rather much of it for discharging heavy cargo. A boat came off and took me ashore, where I met the agent who explained to me that all the cargo lighters had left three days ago for Beypore, a small port a few miles south of Calicut, where lighters could get shelter when necessary. After some talk, it was agreed that they would take delivery of the cargo at Beypore and that I would shift the steamer to a position just off Beypore and as close in as possible, which I did do, and discharging commenced, the dogs being the first to be landed.

For a short time all went fairly well, but the heavy things were always in the background and the time came at last when we were up against them. The lighters were all of the sailing-craft type. One mast and beam about one-third from the bow, which left very little open space for the bridge-work lifts. At last all the cargo but the heavy lifts was discharged.

I saw by that time that, given an open lighter big enough to lower the lift right in without any attempt at stowing it, I could manage. The receivers and agents, of course, were not troubling themselves much about it. It was up to me to give them the cargo, and they were in no hurry; but I remembered my promises to the owner and had to do something. At night-fall, the two lighters went ashore without any cargo.

After thinking hard over the position, somewhere about midnight I called the chief officer, an old school-fellow of my own, and explained the position to him. I also gave him orders that when the two lighters came off in the morning, he was to get the crews (four men in each) out of them on some pretence or another, then to take the mast and sailing beams out of them and then make them as open lighters. I had found out that there were thirty lighters available, so, if it was a success, they could take the masts out of fifteen and use the other fifteen for towing purposes.

In due course the lighters came off in the morning, and my ideas were carried out successfully. By noon we had one bridge-butt strap in each of the two lighters, and the code flags, meaning — send more lighters for my cargo — flying. I afterwards learned that ashore they could not understand the position, owing to the masts being out of the two lighters. Even with their glasses they could not see them from the land, and had concluded they were sunk. All the lighters belonged to native owners, and they would not give the receivers any more. So a pulling boat came off with my agent and the receivers' representative. They saw for themselves now that I could give them the cargo if they would give me open lighters. I pointed out that they had thirty lighters, they could take the masts out of fifteen of them and use the other fifteen for towing. In short, the boot was on the other foot now, and I could afford to laugh, but instead of doing so I let them know that I had learned that the bridge-work I had was for a bridge on the line between Beypore and Madras, and I offered to carry it freight free and put it out with the Madras cargo when we reached that port. But the steamer would now have to be considered on demurrage.[2] They had no authority to accept the offer, but said they would cable to London. On the following day my offer was accepted, and we proceeded to Cochin, our next port.

Before leaving London, I was empowered by the owner to get the steamer off the Malabar Coast as soon as possible, even at some expense. So he was somewhat surprised when he received a draft for demurrage, etc., at Beypore, instead of having to pay anything out.

At Cochin, the sea was so rough that it was not possible to discharge even ordinary general cargo there, so we shifted to Narakel, about five miles north of Cochin, where, owing to a mud flat extending off the place and breaking the force of the ocean swell, the usual sea existing in an open roadstead is barely felt in a depth of five fathoms, and under three fathoms the water is perfectly smooth. In consequence of the total absence of surf on the beach, a free and easy communication with the shore can be maintained at all periods of the year and in all weathers, by boats of any description, and Cochin can be communicated with either by land or back water in less than two hours. So we discharged the Cochin portion of our cargo there by back water.

After the Cochin cargo was all out, we took our various other ports in turn and finally finished discharging at Madras, including the heavy weights, which were all landed without any trouble.

It was quite a relief to me to get clear of the cargo I had just finished landing, and a pleasure to hear the owner say (when we next met) that he was highly satisfied with the result.[3]

In a letter dated the 9th of December 1896, Mr R.M. McMillan the owner of the *Kentigern* states his appreciation of Captain James' services "You are a man with his head on right and we all know how scarce that is. I never have any trouble or anxiety with your ship." And in contrast with the problems he has with other shipmasters he makes the amusing observation, "I wish you had been made in duplicate and that I had the other man too!" Mr McMillan also expresses regret that Captain James has had to be away from home so long and says that he will "endeavour to bring the *Kentigern* to this side this time." As a postscript he tells Captain James "we are very busy at the building of ships just now and have eight in hand."[4]

It is not clear exactly when Captain James left the *Kentigern* and became master of the *Vortigern*. On the 29th of September 1897, Mr E.P.Babtie, the company manager, wrote to him as follows: "You have at all times, and often in very trying and difficult circumstances, given the utmost satisfaction not only in the navigation of the steamer but also in the way you have handled all the many business matters a ship master has necessarily to attend to. Your energy, tact, sobriety and strict integrity combined with your shrewd common sense have all contributed to make your services exceedingly valuable."[5]   This letter gives the impression that some change was imminent, an impression strengthened by two references from Alex Stephen & Son written on the 26th and 28th of November, 1887. However papers held by my cousin Jim Fairweather indicate that Captain James' son, James Jnr served as chief officer on the *Vortigern* from the 1st of January to the 9th of September, 1898 under Captain W.M. Deuchars. If so, Captain James cannot have assumed command of the *Vortigern* before late 1898 or 1899.

James Jnr followed in his father's footsteps, obtaining his masters certificate in 1898 and his extra masters certificate in 1901. He was second mate on the *Kentigern* under his father from the 2nd of May, 1895 to the 26th of May, 1896. There is an anecdote that during his service on the *Vortigern*, James Jnr met his father by chance in a bar in Japan. At that time Captain James would have been captain of the *Kentigern*.[6]

Captain Alexander Fairweather

Captain Alexander is worthy of a biography of his own, and I regret that it has not been possible to include a full account of his outstanding career in this book. Fortunately, obituaries in the 1890s were long and packed with information about the lamented deceased. Alexander's obituary was no exception and is included in the appendix.

An important event in Fairweather family history took place about this time as a consequence of the decline in Arctic whaling. A company of Dundee gentlemen organised an Antarctic Expedition to search for whales in the Southern Ocean. About fifty years previously Sir James Clark Ross had described on his return from the Antarctic having seen "great numbers of the largest sized black whales . . . and that numbers of ships might procure a cargo of oil in a short time."[1] It was on the strength of this that the Dundee South Atlantic Expedition was mounted.

On the 9th of September 1892, four whaling barques - the *Balaena,* the *Active*, the *Diana* and the *Polar Star* set out from Dundee. Alexander was master of the *Balaena*, and William Speirs Bruce the Scottish explorer and scientist, and W. G. Burn-Murdoch the writer and artist, were on board. It was during this voyage that W. G. Burn-Murdoch painted the portrait of Alexander, which was presented to the Royal Scottish Geographical Society by Sir James Wordie (Shackleton's geologist) in 1945. This portrait was amongst the exhibits at the Royal Museum of Scotland 'Scotia' exhibition during the summer of 2003 in Edinburgh. W. G. Burn-Murdoch subsequently wrote and illustrated a book about the voyage entitled *From Edinburgh to the Antarctic.*[2]

From the tone of the book it appears that Burn-Murdoch and Captain Alexander did not think highly of each other. Alexander regarded the scientists as rather an encumbrance, and was impatient with their trawling and examination of small objects from the sea. To him the voyage was essentially a business venture. In turn, Burn- Murdoch regarded Alexander as a philistine interested only in a good material outcome. Ironically, in view of the two men's relationship, their families were to become connected by marriage, for William Burn-Murdoch's nephew John Burch married Priscilla (Peggy) Duncan, a first cousin twice removed of Captain Alexander, in Keith Mackay's branch of the family.

The Dundee South Atlantic Expedition was not a success as far as whales were concerned. Sir James Clark Ross was proved wrong in this respect and they returned to Dundee about nine months later without a single whale. However they brought back 3,700 Seals and 150 tons of Oil, and some useful scientific observations were taken.[3]

Alexander persisted in the whaling trade a few years longer than James but in 1896 the unexpected news reached Dundee that he had died suddenly on board the *Balaena*, in which he had a financial interest, on May the 31st, off Spitzbergen; his age was given as 48. The Dundee papers were full of long obituaries and he was sincerely mourned.

His body was brought to Newport and was ferried across the Tay to be buried in the Eastern Necropolis after a funeral service at his home, Wellpark Terrace; as was usual in those days there were no women at the funeral. Tom and Alexander, his sons were chief mourners. Also present were three of his nephews, Captain James' sons James, Alexander and Charles Fairweather. Captain James must have been away, on the *Kentigern* at the time.[4] It seems appropriate here to quote from a letter sent to Miss Kathleen Duncan by her uncle Lyon Duncan of Dey, Duncan & Muirhead Ltd of London, Exporters & Importers, dated August 23, 1937. Firstly I would like to pay tribute to Kathleen. She was sister to Peggy Burch (see Duncan family tree) and in the 1930s became extremely interested in family history. Her efforts to gain information about the Fairweather brothers, to whom she was related, are extremely touching. Without the aid of photocopiers and fiches she wrote letters pleading for any scrap of knowledge, seeking in vain a copy of grandpa's memoirs. She died unmarried in 1990 without I fear knowing what has been uncovered since that time.

Lyon's letter to Kathleen, after reassuring her she is not mad because she is interested in family history, as her father told her she was, contains an eye witness description of Alexander, and reads as follows: "It was Captain Alec Fairweather whom I knew the better of the two, and I have been on his ship often when I was in Dundee, home from the whaling. He was a real buccaneer, and looked it. He was a quiet man on shore, but at sea something of a desperado, and he had to be. In addition to a crew of able-bodied seamen picked not only for seamanship, but also for their fighting qualities, the Dundee whalers carried about four hundred of the scum of the earth, picked up at ports on their way to the whaling fields, and they never had a voyage without a good deal of revolver practice."[5] I think we must make allowance for some exaggeration here, though Lyon was probably referring to the sealing crews picked up at Newfoundland which were notoriously rowdy and undisciplined.

Captain Alexander Fairweather,
portrait by W. G. Burn-Murdoch painted during
the Dundee South Atlantic Expedition, 1892-93.

1899 to September 1904   The Vortigern

It is probable that in late 1898 or 1899 Captain James left the *Kentigern* and took command of her sister ship the *Vortigern* until September 1904 when he left the employment of Arch'd Macmillan & Sons. From 1900, James was on a three years time charter to carry coal from Calcutta to the Indian ports.[1] His movements between 1897 and 1900 however cannot be specifically identified. During these years one must assume that the ship was in the general trade. Presumably it was at this time that he travelled widely, which would also have been the case during some part of his time as master of the *Drumgeith* later. My late cousin Ethel Burton, another grand-daughter, who knew Captain James very well and in fact spent several years of her girlhood at 'Bonavista', has written "I remember my grandfather saying that he very much regretted never having seen the west coast of America. He had sailed to every coast but not to this one. I'm sure he went to China, for he spoke of an event ashore. He brought home two enormous Ali Baba sized jars which stood either side of the drawing room window at 'Bonavista' blue and white china, with white dragons climbing round them, and a very large blue and white china plate."[2] There is also mention in a press cutting of the many times he had called at the Port of Durban, the first being in August 1896 and the last in about 1911.[3]

The only thing I remember my mother telling about her father was that he sometimes took one or other of his children on his voyages. I believe she herself had been to one of the north German ports, and also to Canada; this was not unusual in the Merchant Navy. Mother said that it was the naughty children who enjoyed the privilege, presumably to ease the lot of their overburdened mother. However as my mother possessed an angelic temperament and has been described to me by a fellow Scot as 'couthie' i.e., the opposite of uncouth, I wonder how she ever came to be one of the chosen!

On this theme, in the introduction to William Craik Fairweather's posthumous *Rotation of Stories* grandpa writes, "I took him with me to Calcutta and back" (for the sake of his health).

India

Once again the story is best told in Captain James' own words. His account of his Indian experiences from 1900 to 1903 comprises the last five pages of his memoirs:

> Reference has been made to the fact that I had sailed far and wide before it was my lot to get to India. But when the way was once found, I got a good share of it.
>
> In 1900 when I reached a home port with the "Vortigern," I learned that she was fixed on a three years' time charter to carry coal from Calcutta to Indian Ports.

VORTIGERN

Captain James Fairweather was master from 1897 to 1904, four of these - 1900 - 1904 - in the Indian Ocean

The trade at that time was possibly not more than a decade or so old, as far as the exporting of it was concerned, and speaking from experience, the coal we got for bunkers was of a poor quality indeed, and proved to be too much for the European firemen, for they could not keep the steam high enough with it, and the deck hands had to be put on to heave the ashes up and dump them.

We had no steam ash-hoist then, so it had all to be done by hand. It was an endless job and only ceased some time after our port was reached, so it goes without saying that there was trouble with the European crew. They all wanted to be paid off.

I had no authority to pay their fares for a passage home, and the shipping master would not allow them to be paid off unless they were sent home or other equivalent employment found for them. so we had to get on as well as we could by engaging two or three Indians for each white man that left the steamer. That took some time to do, so as far as the crews were concerned, it was somewhat of a mix-up for the first year. After that the coal seemed to get better, or the Indians could handle it more easily, and improvements were made on the ash-hoist, and to a great extent the position improved as we adapted ourselves to the business.

We worked the steamer out to India by carrying a full cargo of Welsh coal to Colombo. From there we went to Calcutta. On arrival, I found that most of the locally-owned steamers had been taken up by the home Government in connection with the Boer War, and that outside steamers had been chartered to do their work.

I also found that my steamer had been sub-chartered to the British India Steamship Co. for six months, as I was ordered by them to take in a full general cargo for Colombo. That was the only general cargo I carried in the three years I was on the coast, all the others being coal. With one exception, we always returned in water ballast to Calcutta.

When going down the River Hooghly with the first cargo, we found out what we were up against with the bad bunker coal. By the time we had reached Budge-Budge, just on the outskirts of Calcutta, and met the flood-tide, what with that and the want of steam, we were just creeping past any stationary object.

Some of my friends hailed me from the pier at Budge-Budge and asked me to come ashore for a drink, adding that I would have plenty of time to catch her at the other end of the compound.

But time brings all things to an end. The tide eased up and

the engineer was trying other methods with the coal, but at its best it was a heart-breaking time. However, we were most fortunate in having the N.E. Monsoon then, with fine weather which lasted until we returned to Calcutta and commenced loading a full cargo of coal.

The system of loading then was by hand with small baskets. The coal was dumped on the ground out of the wagons, then carried by coolies, male and female, from the dump to the steamer in baskets.

When they passed a certain point they got a token, and when they had, I think, eight tokens, they gave them back for one anna. There are sixteen annas in one rupee, and a rupee is one and fourpence sterling. The coolies had no regular working hours then; they just came and went when they liked, and when they had earned four annas they generally stopped, as that was all they required to keep them for the day. As a rule, after they had earned the four annas, they made straight for a bustie (mud-house) where toddy was sold. When there, they all sat with their legs hunched under them, heads well up, mouth wide open, till the supplier came with his can of toddy. The can had a long tapering spout, and I have seen him go along a row of about 20 open mouths and fill each one with the greatest dexterity, and without spilling a drop, just like an oiler oiling the spindles of a spinning frame. The supplier seemed to do a good trade, but it was crude in the extreme.

During the second year that I was on the coast, the "Vorti-gern" had the honour of taking in the first cargo of coal loaded by the first mechanical appliance used in Calcutta for loading coal. There was a big turnout of the powers that were, and I had the "Vortigern" dressed for the opening ceremony.

When in Calcutta on this occasion I was at a dinner party, and during the evening I was explaining some problem referring to the sea. Just as I finished speaking, a grey parrot that I did not know was in the room, said, "Rats!"

Whether it caused any doubts on my remarks I do not know, and can only console myself with the fact that my opinion was asked for later on.

On one occasion we took a cargo of coal to Aden and brought back a cargo of salt, which was the exception I referred to when I said that I only brought back one cargo. The salt pans of Aden are well worth seeing. They are all filled automatically from the sea, and dried by evaporation, the highest pan being on a level with high tide. All the others are on a lower level—as they go back on the neck of land between Aden and the coast.

Our next cargo was for Rangoon. When there what interested me most was seeing the elephants at work. One big one was piling teakwood logs. Some he would get into place by lifting first one end and then the other, others he would get up by rolling. After they were in place, he would slowly go to the end of the pile and if the last one he had just put up was not flush, he would, if it were sticking out, push it in till flush with the others. If it was too far in, he would walk to the other end and flush it from there, and all off his own bat. A mahout was in the howdah all the time, but never had to say a word. Yet they told me that the elephant would not work if the mahout was not in his place.

Another that interested me very much was a smaller one, presumably a female. Her duties were apparently to drag away the slabs from the saw pit. When she was drawing away one slab, it split in the middle, and the lower point caught under an iron bar that was across the pit. When she found it would not come she came back and saw what was holding it. She lifted it up clear of the bar, then resumed her position, and hauled it away to the pile, then came back for another, and so on. Whenever the whistle was sounded to cease work, she stopped at once and downed tools, so to speak. The operations were well worth seeing.

When in Calcutta I was very comfortably housed in the Shipmasters' Club, but always had the feeling that my officers were not so comfortably placed, so set to work to remove that evil, and in the course of time had the pleasure of seeing my work bear fruit in the erection and naming of "Fairweather House."

During the three years that I was on the Indian coast, I was, as far as a man can be that is away from his own home for so long, fairly happy. I had no worry with cargoes or latterly with crews, and when at Calcutta the Club was my home, where I met many genial companions, and when together we were just like a lot of schoolboys let loose. Happy memories of these days crowd in on me as I write. Then I had many friends to spend the week-ends with, both up and down the river, where I was always made welcome.

After the three years expired, the steamer was chartered to carry a general cargo from Calcutta to Hamburg. The lascar crew was paid off, much to my regret, and Europeans taken in their stead, which brought all the fireman's trouble back again.

It was towards the end of December when we reached the River Elbe, and found it all frozen over, which brought some of my Arctic experiences back again to me. We all took very bad with the cold after being so long in India. But now that it is a thing of the past, and with nothing else to do now but sit in my chair at the fireside and think of the past, forget all about the colds and all other past troubles, and, may I whisper, would like to do it all over again.[4]

The way into Calcutta is up the Hooghly to the west of the Ganges Estuary. Grandfather became very familiar with this route over the years, but the river is treacherous and it required the services of a pilot to negotiate it safely. Once again we must be grateful to Kathleen Duncan for tracking down and finally corresponding with M.H. Beattie, who wrote a book entitled *On the Hooghly*, the reminiscences of a River Hooghly Pilot.'[5] Mr Beattie piloted the *Vortigern* on several occasions, and an extract from his book gives a lively description of grandfather including the usual, in this case literally 'hair raising' anecdote:

Among the first steamers which came on time-charter to carry coal on the coast I recollect the JUPITER and VORTIGERN, which fell to my lot on several occasions to take up and down the river. The VORTIGERN was commanded by Captain James Fairweather, who had been for many years in the whaling trade, sailing out of Dundee, and I found his stories of life in the Arctic most interesting. He had been close to the spot where the members of the ill-fated Greely expedition had wintered, and from his description one was able to form some idea of what winter in the Arctic really meant.

He had one rather grisly anecdote about a man of his crew who in heavy weather had been washed off the forecastle head, swept along the foredeck, and jammed under a winch. When extricated, the man's head appeared as a red ball with no trace of any features, but Captain Fairweather discovered a tuft of hair in the place where his chin ought to be, and by careful manipulation gradually uncovered the features. The scalp had been severed at the back of the neck and turned inside out over the man's face. It was satisfactory to know that he made a good recovery, and was none the worse for his misadventure.

It was with tales such as this that Captain Fairweather beguiled the time and relieved the monotony of a long day on the bridge. He was a great many years on the coast, and naturally acquired some knowledge of the river. This tempted him on one occasion, when there was a shortage of pilots at the Sandheads, to attempt the journey up by himself. He got as far as Diamond Harbour, but then thought better of it, and remained at anchor there until a pilot was sent down to bring the vessel up.[6]

Mr Beattie lived to a great age in retirement at Eastbourne, and in March and April 1938, in correspondence with Kathleen, gave the following description of grandpa: "He was a small man, about 5' 6" or 5' 7" in height; strongly built with a very florid red complexion. His hair was black and so were his keen active eyes. He had a strong determined expression and looked what he was - a smart tough seaman - he was very Scotch. I took him down the Hooghly several times and we were good friends. Your kinsman was a very religious man, with a keen sense of duty; he also had a sense of humour. He was very much respected and I was always glad to meet him."

April 23, "I did not pilot the *Drumgeith* but recalled meeting Captain Fairweather in Calcutta when he was in command of her . . . he was a man of great personality and much energy . . . "[7]

During his frequent visits to Calcutta, Captain James was comfortably accommodated at the International Shipmasters' Club at 2, Mangoe Lane. It is characteristic of him that he was aware that his officers were not suitably housed, and set about remedying this deficiency with his usual energy.[8] Prior to this initiative he states in a newspaper article there were moral dangers due to lack of provision, and also "sleeping in stuffy cabins amongst the coal dust, mosquitoes and heat was ruining the health and spirits of the officers, making them physically unfit for their duties. Indeed this habit caused much illness and discontent, and many officers had to go to hospital while others were sent home . . . I aired my views to many. They agreed it was a good idea, but passed on; so I had to tackle the job myself."

"After more than two years of agitation (my work was made more difficult by the fact that I was only touching at Calcutta for a few days every month. I succeeded in persuading the port authorities to build a club for officers and engineers only. In recognition of the part I had taken in the work the building was called The Fairweather House. There is now another club for stewardesses and both are highly appreciated and extremely useful." There follows the usual Fairweather humorous story to the effect that his colleague in the enterprise was one Captain Andrew Work, whose wife had pointed out that if the club had been named after her husband it would have been called the Work House, which she said would be rather against its success.[9] A further cutting in Captain James' scrapbook on the subject is headed:

FAIRWEATHER HOUSE, KIDDERPORE. About 1903 it was pointed out by captains and engineers of steamers visiting this port that it would be a great relief to the officers and engineers of all steamers loading in the Kidderpore Docks, especially the coal boats, if a building could be provided outside the Docks where the officers and engineers could go and obtain at a reasonable cost, meals, refreshments and a bed, and so get away from the heat and discomfort of the ship. Captain J. Fairweather of the Steamer *Vortigern* was the prime mover of

Fairweather House, Calcutta.

the scheme and became spokesman for the captains on the coal trade, and through his push and zeal the Port Commissioners decided to build a suitable house. This house is now an accomplished fact and was opened on Saturday last, although the internal fittings were not quite complete. The house is appropriately called "Fairweather House" after the genial skipper of that name, and it is pleasant to hear that the comfortable beds, good meals and refreshments are much appreciated, and the house is well patronized. The building has been constructed at a cost of over Rs. 32,000 and is two-storied; there are 16 beds upstairs, each in a separate cubicle, and 4 nice large bathrooms. On the ground floor is a fine billiard-room, dining-room and a reading room, all nicely furnished. Captain Eaton W. Petley, R. N., C.I.E., is the President of the House and Mr. W. R. C. Jewell, the Honorary Secretary, and they were chosen on account of the experience they possess in the working of the International Shipmaster' Club, 2, Mangoe Lane.[10]

An extract from the book *Clipper Ships to Ocean Greyhounds* by H.C. De Mierre gives a vivid picture of Calcutta in the early twentieth century and the benefit the writer gained from Fairweather House. He first describes the beautiful city Calcutta was, in contrast to the dusty conditions the crew endured whilst coaling. It was like a brief period in purgatory and the only escape, when not on duty was to go to the nearby Fairweather House - "a sort of hostel for ship's officers where one could enjoy cool drinks, sitting under a large fan, and where for a moderate charge one could stifle on a cot under a mosquito net, in relatively clean air!" However he did receive an offer of a different kind, which he states none of the officers took advantage of to his knowledge! This was a billet-doux as follows: "Dear Mr Third Officer, so hot and dusty in the Docks - my bungalow - so cool and so clean - Fairweather House such a beastly bore man. Come and have a jolly time . . . with pretty young widow."[11]

During a business visit to India in April 2005, Keith had the pleasure of visiting Fairweather House on two occasions and meeting the present officials. The following is his account of this memorable experience.

Fairweather House
One hundred years old and thriving!

Fairweather House is located at 58 Circular Garden Reach Road, Kidderpore, or as it has now been named, 58 Karl Marx Sarani. The exact date for the opening of the House has not yet been established, having been lost in the mists of time. Although it is believed to have been circ. 1905/06.

The property owned by the Kolkata Port Trust, was built by the Port Commissioners and renamed The Fairweather Institute in 1930. It continues today as a Club for the Officers of the Port Authority. The President of The Fairweather Institute is Mr. M. A. Bhaskarachar (also Deputy Chairman of the Calcutta Port Trust) and the Honorary General Secretary is Mr. S.K. Dey. During my visit I also met Mr. A.K. Sur (ex General Secretary of the Institute), and Dr. S.S. Saha (ex President and Historian).

Over the years, the building has undergone many structural changes, however, one can still see and visualize the design and layout of the original building. At some point, the original building was reversed in its layout, in that you now enter from the rear. The front door has been closed up. The square windows of today were originally large arched windows and to the rear, there would have been an arched verandah at first floor level; the front of the house being the same, but with a substantial portico and large front door which entered into a spacious entrance hall with a wide sweeping staircase to the first floor.

Upon entering the House today, you come into a large central reception hall from which all the principal reception rooms lead off. To the right is a spacious lounge with bar to the rear. To the left is the Secretary's Office and also the original Billiard room with original billiard table dating back to the opening of the House. (The Club also retains the original piano). Leading through from the central hall one enters what was the original entrance hall with suspended staircase. To the left of this hallway are the library and other offices, to the right is the bar. At first floor level are the bedrooms and to the rear, a very large Ballroom which runs the entire length of the building.

It is most likely that in the original layout, this grand room would have opened out on to a long verandah overlooking the rear gardens of the Club; there are a series of arched double doors which run the entire length of the

Fairweather House, Calcutta,
the present frontage, May 2005.

Fairweather House, Calcutta,
the original frontage, May 2005.

room. The verandah has now been blocked in and turned into a number of small rooms which include a gym.

Externally, the grounds have now been laid to grass and car parking areas and there is no indication of what the original gardens would have looked like. There are two badminton courts and a tennis court within the grounds. In 1992 there was talk of constructing a swimming pool, however that has not appeared.

Sadly and as is the case with many institutions in India, all the early records have been lost or destroyed and no-one has any recollection of the Club in it's heyday. In fact the President of the Club, Mr. M.A. Bhaskarachar and other Members of the Committee were unaware of its existence prior to 1930! According to Mr. Manik Jain of Calcutta, prior to 1930 the Club was used exactly for the purposes it was established for to provide accommodation and facilities for Officers visiting Calcutta. As with many places in Calcutta, being known as a Chummery (lodging house for single men).

2005 marks the 75th anniversary of the opening of the Fairweather Institute and the Club is holding a number of events throughout the year to celebrate this achievement.

The Club remains an important part of the history of the Calcutta Port Trust and is very popular and well used by its members; being regarded as the "Premier Institute" amongst the other Officers Clubs and Institutes of the Port Authority. The Members are very proud to have the benefits of such a club and its facilities.

The President of the Club has decided to have one of the photographs of Captain Fairweather enlarged to full portrait size, in order that it may hang in the House in memory of the Founder of the original Club. It may well be that the Members of the Fairweather Institute will have to celebrate its Centenary in the very near future.

There are two more press cuttings in Captain James' scrapbook relating to the Indian years. One concerns Kidderpore Dock and the installation of mechanical appliances for loading coal, which Captain James refers to in his memoirs: "His Honour Sir John Woodburn K.C.S.J. Lieutenant Governor of Bengal opened the new berth and started the crane at 8am (on an unspecified date). It was the *Vortigern* which was being loaded and His Honour was received on board and conducted round the steamer by her genial commander Captain J. Fairweather M.S.G. who took pains to explain everything to his Honour, and had his steamer dressed with flags for the occasion"[12]

Amongst the guests at the opening was Mr R. Duncan, Keith Mackay's great grandfather. Richard Duncan was James' second cousin, and spent much of his working life in India. He was senior partner in Andrew Yule & Co, owners of jute, coal and tea companies, and managing agents for many others.

In Captain James' memoirs, he mentions going down the Hooghly River for the first time. He was hailed by friends from the pier at Budge-Budge who asked him to come ashore for a drink. Keith believes these friends were probably the Duncans, who lived there.[13]

Two undated cuttings refer to the annual dinner of the Merchant Service Guild. One is of the third annual dinner, held at the Italian Restaurant in Calcutta. In both cases Captain J. Fairweather was in the chair and about 35 guildsmen were present.

The guild seems to have been an association for masters and officers in the Merchant Service with the object of bettering the merchant service on a purely self supporting basis without the help of the owners. Speeches to this effect were made and after a number of toasts and 'capital songs' the proceedings closed with the whole company singing 'Auld Lang Syne' and the National Anthem.[14]

Captain James' inventive turn of mind is clearly seen in his production of a booklet entitled *Fairweather's System of Signals Utilizing the New International Code of Signals during the Night*. This pamphlet is dated SS *Vortigern* Friday 31 January 1902. James' chief facilitator in promoting his system was Sir John Leng (the local newspaper baron), and in the scrap book there are three undated cuttings relating to the subject. The first entitled 'A Dundee Invention' is an account of a question in the House of Commons by Mr Leng to the President of the Board of Trade, asking whether his attention has been drawn to the ingenious invention of Captain James Fairweather, of Dundee; Mr Mundella replied that he had been advised against the system because the Washington Maritime Conference was averse to the use of coloured lights at sea at night. This exchange may have taken place in March 1893. The second cutting describes the system in detail and is headed 'Signalling at Night, Dundee Shipmaster's System'. The third cutting is of a letter written by Captain James to (now) Sir John Leng, headed 'Night Signalling at Sea' and dated S.S. *Vortigern*, Cuddalore, May 30 1902. In it he observes "that the answer he got from the Board of Trade was the same in substance as he received to nearly the same question in March 1893 more than nine years ago. Since then nothing has been done to meet the want." However he continues at length to promote his scheme expressing puzzlement as to why the Board of Trade will not adopt it.[15] The pamphlet itself consists of a decorated frontispiece and three pages of explanation and a page of diagrams, indicating the arrangements of the lights to represent the letters of the alphabet.

From the dating of the relevant letters it appears that Captain James left the Indian coal trade after two years eight months, though he carried on in the employment of McMillan as captain of the *Vortigern* until the 30th of September 1904.

The first letter is dated the 9th of August 1902 from Madura Co, Ltd.

Negapatam and is in the form of a testimonial. However it commences "Captain Fairweather having informed us that this will probably be his last voyage to Negapatam . . . she (the *Vortigern*) has discharged eight cargoes here, during the past two years."

The second dated Calcutta the 6th of October 1902 is also a testimonial from Turner Morrison & Co., Calcutta & Bombay, the steamer's agents in Calcutta. The writer had known Captain James of the SS *Vortigern* for some years, and more intimately since February 1900 when this steamer (the *Vortigern*) began running on time charter in the coasting trade. This comment indicates that Captain James had visited Calcutta for some years before the coal contract commenced. In both cases the signatures are indecipherable. The third letter, from the Secretary of the International Shipmasters' Club, is dated 12th October 1902 and reads as follows:

> To Captain Fairweather
> from the present members of the above club on the
> occasion of his going home from the Indian Coast,
> as an appreciation of his good fellowship by his
> brother shipmasters and officers. We wish him a pleasant
> voyage home and a happy reunion with
> his family.[16]

It seems difficult from a modern perspective, to imagine that a man can be away from his family for nearly three years in time of peace, and how a large and growing family managed in his absence. However, this seems to have been the lot of seafaring men since the days of Nelson and Captain Cook.

As James set off for home to the colder northern climes, one wonders if he already knew that his son Alexander had been seriously wounded in the Boer War, which had just come to an end.

Our knowledge of Alexander's war service comes almost entirely from his obituaries, for he died of wounds after a long illness on August the 2nd 1903 at the age of twenty-two. My mother nursed him at home until the end. There are two newspaper cuttings, one headed 'Death of Mr Alexander Fairweather' and the other 'Funeral of Trooper Fairweather'.[17]

Evidently Alexander had enlisted in the Scottish Horse and was one of the band of young men that Newport sent to the front in the South African campaign. He took part in several of the actions in which his regiment was engaged. In the course of one of the many hot skirmishes with the enemy he was struck on the thigh by an expanding bullet, which inflicted a dreadful wound. For long he lay in hospital where he was subjected to several operations. Many months later, a cripple for life, he was brought home to his parents' house. His health declined thereafter until he died. There was a large attendance at his funeral and he was buried at Vicarsford Cemetery, Forgan, the first of the Fairweathers to be buried there. He was lowered to

Memorial Stone at Vicarsford Cemetary, Forgan

his last resting place by two of his brothers Charles and David; his father was evidently not present. Family legend has it that he was hit by a 'dumdum' bullet which expands on entering the body; and that he lay on the veldt all night.

An impressive grey granite memorial was erected, topped by a draped funeral urn, and the first inscription was engraved:

ERECTED
By JAMES FAIRWEATHER
And his Wife MARY ANN CRAIK
IN LOVING MEMORY OF THEIR SON
ALEXANDER
WHO DIED AT NEWPORT
2nd AUGUST 1903 aged 22 years

At the base of the monument in large letters is carved:
Thy Will be Done

On a happier note the first Fairweather marriage took place on March the 9th 1904, Elizabeth (Lizzie), James and Mary Ann's eldest daughter married James Corr of Dundee Scots/Irish origin, but whose address is given as Gourepore, Bengal. They were to spend most of their married life in India.

There are three accounts of the wedding, one entitled 'Pretty Wedding at Newport (by Annette)' in the 'Dundee Courier' of March 10, 1904 and another, 'Wedding Bells, a springtime wedding in Newport' from the 'Evening Telegraph' of March 9th. A third cutting (by our lady correspondent) is almost identical to the second (Capt James' scrapbook). The account in the 'Dundee Courier' is so excellent that I quote it verbatim below. Captain James was away in New York at the time and there is a slight discrepancy in the accounts as to who gave Lizzie away. 'Annette' says that in the unavoidable absence of her father when she entered the church she was accompanied by Mr R. Kinnes; 'our lady correspondent' says she was given away by her mother. Probably both are true. It was not unknown for a bride to be given away by a female. Charlotte Bronte was given away by her friend and old head mistress Miss Wooler when the Rev. Patrick refused to attend the ceremony.

PRETTY WEDDING AT NEWPORT
(BY ANNETTE)

The brilliant sunshine of a perfect spring day added to the brightness of the pretty wedding which took place yesterday in Trinity U.F. Church, Newport, where Miss Lizzie C. Fairweather, daughter of Captain James Fairweather, Newport, was married to Mr James Corr, Gourepore, Bengal, the son of the late Mr W. T.Corr, Dundee.

The church, which had been nicely decorated by Mr Grossart, was well filled with guests and onlookers, and while these assembled an organ voluntary was played by Miss Maggie Scott. During the singing of a wedding hymn the bridal party entered the church, Miss Fairweather being accompanied (in the unavoidable absence of her father) by P. Kinnes. The officiating clergymen were the Rev. J. Scotland and the Rev. James Wilson, and at the close of the service an interesting little ceremony took place, Mrs Corr being presented with a Bible in recognition of the fact that hers was the first wedding to be solemnized in Trinity U.F. Church. The Bible, which was bound in white ivory, was encased in a dainty white satin bag, the work of Miss Janet Scott.

THE BRIDAL PARTY.

The bride looked very sweet and graceful in her lovely wedding gown of cream satin and chiffon. A spray of orange blossom kept in place the long tulle veil, and knots of the same flower appeared here and there on the prettily-made gown. The first bridesmaid was Miss Belle Corr, whose dainty gown was of biscuit-coloured voile, touched with blue. With this was worn a white tulle Victorian bonnet, trimmed with pale blue ribbon and pink button roses. The other two bridesmaids were the bride's sisters — Misses Mary and Ella Fairweather —both of whom wore pretty white frocks and large white hats. To the two first bridesmaids the bridegroom gave a gold curb bangle, while Miss Ella Fairweather received a gold necklet and pendant. Mr T.J. Robertson, Cupar Fife, acted as best man.

From the church the guests went on to the Smaller Blyth Hall, where a reception was held by Mrs Fairweather, and luncheon served. Among the many congratulatory telegrams received by Mr and Mrs Jas. Corr was one from Captain Fairweather, sent from New York. When later in the afternoon the bride and bridegroom started on their wedding journey Mrs Corr was wearing a smart costume of dark blue and white, with hat to match.

Among those present at the wedding were — Mrs Corr and the Misses Corr, Mrs and the Misses Fairweather, Mrs Baker, Mr and Mrs P. Dickson, Mrs Rogers, Mr and Mrs Cherry, Miss Birrell, Mr and Mrs Kinnes, Mrs James Wilson, Mr and Mrs William Scrimgeour, &c.

MARRIAGES

Corr — Fairweather. — At Trinity U.F. Church, Newport, Fife, on the 9th inst. by Rev. James Scotland, assisted by Rev. James Wilson, Dudhope Crescent Church, Dundee, James

Corr, third son of the late W.T. Corr, to Lizzie, eldest daughter of Capt. James Fairweather, Bona Vista, Newport, Fife.

Lizzie and Jim were to have three children: James b. 9/10 June, 1905, Calcutta; Ethel Mary b. 23 August, 1911, India and William Duncan b. 2 January 1918 India.

On the 30th of September, 1904, Captain James finally left the employment of Arch'd McMillan & Son Ltd after a period of eleven and a half years. In January 1903 he had received a special bonus of £176 in recognition of Mr McMillan's high appreciation of the very able manner in which he (Captain Fairweather) had managed his steamer and conducted the important business which was entrusted to him while engaged in the Indian Coastal Trade during the previous three years. In October 1904 he departed with the usual glowing references stating him to be "a first class navigator, business man and diplomat . . . at all times strictly sober energetic and careful of the vessels he commanded . . . his character has been irreproachable." The letters also state that he has resigned his position on his own accord, and that "he leaves our service now to take command of a larger steamer"[18]

Captain James' next command was the SS *Drumgeith*, built and owned by R.A. & J.H. Mudie of Maritime Buildings, Dock Street, Dundee. In a newspaper article of December 15, 1926, Captain Fairweather says he supervised the building of the ship and subsequently sailed her between this country and India. From a reference dated 30 May 1911 we know that he commanded this ship for six years.

Though Captain James gives the impression that the Drumgeith shuttled between the UK and India, he indicates a much wider range in his memoirs. He describes voyaging between Philadelphia and the Far East, and good-natured competition with a fellow shipmaster regarding the best routes between various far distant ports. The extract also displays his interest in navigation and sea conditions:

> Once, when loading case-oil in the "Drumgeith," at Phila-delphia, the steamer "Lennox" of Leith was loading the same kind of cargo for China. She was also going via the Cape of Good Hope, so our route was the same as far as Java Head. The then Master of the "Lennox" was a young man who, after being some years in the company as an officer, had just been appointed Master, and was very anxious to learn. One day he asked me what route I took after leaving Durban. I told him that I went via the Mozambique Channel, north of the Seychelles, then straight for Java Head. He said that he would follow that route also. I asked him what was the regular route of the company. He said they had always gone south of Madagascar.

"Well," I replied, "You take my advice, and go that way till you get liberty from your owners to deviate."

But for the private information of both, we agreed to exchange abstracts of our logs from Durban to Java Head.

He left Philadelphia one day after me, and Durban one day before me, which was as I expected, as the "Lennox" was both bigger and faster than the "Drumgeith." He left a letter at Durban reminding me of our agreement, and repeated that he was to go south of Madagascar. I left Durban on the 5th of January 1911, and went by the Mozambique Channel, then north of the Seychelles and straight for Java Head, and got there in twenty days, and to my first port of discharge, Krang Antoe, the same day. It is just round Java Head to the north-east. After getting east of the Seychelles, we went half speed for a few days to save coal, while we were in the easterly-going current. When I got my friend's abstract, it showed that the "Lennox" went south of Madagascar, and had nothing but strong south-east trades and high seas nearly all the way, and was twenty-three days from Durban to Java Head.

The comparison was very interesting to me, as I had been making a study of the trade winds and currents of the South Atlantic, Indian Ocean, and out east generally.

Another comparison I made was during the South-West Monsoons. I left Colombo in company with the large four-masted steamer "City of Edinburgh." We were both homeward bound from Rangoon. She went straight across, while I went south to the 1½% channel and crossed in latitude 1 North. We met again and compared notes in the smooth water of the Gulf of Aden. He had experienced strong monsoons and high seas all the way, while I had nothing but light winds and smooth seas till we were between Socotra and the African coast. Then the wind was fair and the sea following.

I was doing my best when the "City of Edinburgh" passed me in the smooth water of the Gulf, yet she went away ahead and was in Perim and out again before I got in.

During the South-West Monsoons in the Bay of Bengal, I never went straight for the Basses from the sand heads. After landing the Calcutta pilot, I steered as if I was going to Madras, just keeping a good berth off the land till I had the longitude of the Basses, then went straight for them, and I scored every time. For three years I was up and down the Bay of Bengal once a month and was forced to learn.[19]

There is also an extract from a letter from Wm. Crosby & Co. Melbourne, dated 29 July, 1908, "We should just like to express to you our appreciation of Captain Fairweather who from first to last, while protecting his owner's interests to the utmost, was all that we could wish a captain to be. It is seldom in our chartering business that we come across a Captain who is so fair and strictly upright in all his dealings as we were glad to find Captain Fairweather was, and although he was not at all in good health, he left nothing to chance but had the business of the ship at all times under his supervision. We may say also that our Agents in Africa write very nicely about him."

This is interesting in two respects, firstly it tells us that Captain James had by this time visited Australia as well as Africa, and secondly that we have an adverse reference to his health. He would be just fifty-five at the time.

At home health, or rather ill health, had been a major preoccupation at 'Bonavista' for some years. William Craik Fairweather, my mother's favourite brother, just two years older than her, had been delicate from boyhood. In his introduction to Rotation of Stories by Willie, the second part of grandpa's book, the father writes "The writer's fourth son, William Craik Fairweather, when quite a lad, turned ill. The doctor said he had been overdoing it at football. I took him with me to Calcutta and back. The voyage seemed to do him good, so it was arranged for him to go to Natal, but in time he grew homesick, and a friend of mine brought him home via South America. He was then a confirmed invalid but able to read and write. Fortunately he had been taking notes during his travels, and was able to produce the work appearing in the following pages." Willie died six weeks before his twenty-second birthday.

It seems clear that Willie died of tuberculosis and the account of his travels and illness bear resemblance to that of his grandfather James senior, who died in Australia in 1857, probably also of tuberculosis.

There is no account of Willie's funeral in the scrapbook but there are two news items, the first reads: "Today's 'People's Friend' contains a capital short story entitled '*Stealing a Tombstone*', an adventure on the Canton River by Mr William C. Fairweather of Newport. Mr Fairweather tells his weird story remarkably well, and his contribution is sure to be read with interest." The second: "We regret to record the death of a young contributor to the 'People's Friend' . . . Mr Fairweather was only 22 (sic) years of age, but had travelled widely in South Africa and South America. In spite of the restrictions imposed by a severe illness lasting over several years, he was full of plans for work and enjoyed nothing so much as writing the stories and sketches which from time to time have appeared in the 'People's Friend'. By his untimely death there is no doubt that a most promising career has been cut short."[20]

In a separate scrapbook possibly started by Willie shortly before his death, are pasted various articles written by him. The last article includes an editorial note that reads, "Since the above paper was written, the author Mr W.C. Fairweather has passed away. Though an invalid, he was, as this sketch shows, exceedingly cheerful and greatly interested in all that was going on around him. He was fortunate in having his residence in the beautiful little town of Newport, Fifeshire, and in his last years he enjoyed the loving care of his devoted mother and sisters."

Tuberculosis is now known to be caused by an infection, many talented literary figures are recorded as dying from it until the advent of penicillin during the Second World War; George Orwell being one of the last.

So a second inscription was added to the memorial stone at Vicarsford Cemetery; it reads:

also their son
WILLIAM CRAIK
who died at Newport
9th April 1906 aged 21 years

It is hard to over estimate the effect on my mother and her young sister Ella, of nursing their two brothers to the end, at home. My mother was just 17 and Ella 11 when Alexander died. By 1906 when Willie died after a long illness, Mother was 19 and Ella 13, Willie was two years older than Mother and her favourite brother. From the photograph he looks to be a handsome, debonair and we know him to be a talented young man. It is now my opinion that my mother never really recovered from her traumatic teenage years, despite a progressive Scottish education at Dundee High School and membership of the local tennis club. In 1910 she entered the Royal Infirmary of Edinburgh School of Nursing, a privilege which my grandfather would in those days have to pay for, and qualified as a nurse in March 1914 and afterwards as a midwife. It was at the Infirmary that she met my father; newly qualified, in a traditional doctor nurse romance!

In the meantime however, Mary and Ella were daughters at home, and Mother told me that Granny Fairweather would go upstairs for her afternoon rest followed by one daughter carrying her book and another her spectacles.

There are excellent photographs of all the Fairweather youngsters in their teens as well as a group portrait of the whole family taken in about 1899. Three studio portraits of the daughters taken when they were aged about twenty five, eighteen and fifteen are particularly striking. Lizzie wears a high necked day dress with a short train and a large hat decorated with plumes; she wears a wedding ring so must have been newly married. My mother looks a dream in a heavily embroidered full length sashed dress, and Aunt Ella very much the charming modern miss, seated in a simpler but elegant dress. Mother's photo was taken by Valentine of Dundee, as were probably those of her sisters. The outfits are so lavish one feels they must have been ordered for a very special occasion; they do not however correspond with the description of the dresses for Lizzie's wedding.

One obvious thought looking at these photographs is how far James and Mary Ann had progressed up the ladder of prosperity since their marriage.

It was a far cry from 3 Crescent Street to 'Bonavista' and three beautifully attired and leisured daughters.

In 1909 James and Mary Ann in effect lost a third son - David. After an apprenticeship as a shepherd at Ballinbriech, Flisk, he married at the age of 20, Johan Ingles aged 19 of Perth. The same year the young couple emigrated to Australia, and his parents never saw David again. His father however is known to have kept in touch with him.

We now come to the last years of Captain Fairweather's career as a Merchant Marine Master. There are three letters dated 1911. The first dated 30th May is from his employers R.A. & J.M. Mudie, and is a testimonial stating that he has been in command of SS *Drumgeith* for the past six years and comes home now at his own desire which they greatly regret. He is a good businessman and first-rate master who devoted his whole time and thought to the care of his ship and the discharge of his duty. "We consider him a man of exceptional ability, energy and resource." The second letter dated 5th September is also from Mudie. It states that while in command of the *Drumgeith*, Captain James took entire charge of repairs at Savannah and Newport News consequent on serious damage sustained in the Atlantic and put steamer through her No. 1 Survey. The work occupied about ten days and he attended to the whole matter, held surveys, prepared specifications, superintended repairs, agreed accounts and arranged payment all in the most satisfactory manner. He also handled with great discretion a very difficult position that arose in Australia when, owing to time charters having loaded inferior explosives, which the authorities reported as dangerous, but would not condemn for shipment, the crew refused to proceed.

Both these letters are in the nature of testimonials, as is the third from our old friend E.P. Babtie, who gave his usual glowing reference.[21]

In the fourth and last of his articles for the 'Evening Telegraph" dated 16 December 1926, Captain James gives an account of his career from leaving the *Drumgeith,* until the *Morning* voyage of Spring 1914. Confusingly he states that he was on the Drumgeith for about eight years, although the Mudie letter is probably correct in giving the figure of six years; the article continues: ". . . I retired from continuous command, but at the request of my friends in Glasgow took command of various large steamers in a sort of relieving capacity." One deduces that this fills the years 1911 – 1913, in which year his obituary in the 'Dundee Advertiser' of 24th March 1933 states that he retired from the Merchant Navy.

At home, 'Tannie' (my mother) had been at Edinburgh nursing school for five months leaving Mary Ann and Ella, not quite 19 years old, alone. However, their lives were shortly to be greatly affected by the arrival of James (Jimmy) Corr, their seven-year-old grandson sent home from India to be educated. He would probably arrive in 1912 and his sister Ethel states that they looked after him for seven years.

Mary Ann Craik 1851 - 1934
m James Fairweather

Elizabeth (Lizzie)

Mary Ann (Tan)

Helen (Ella)

1914 The Morning

Captain James' obituaries tell us that in the spring of 1914 he came out of retirement and at the owners' request made a final voyage to the Arctic in the *Morning*. His obituary in the 'Dundee Advertiser' says that the purpose of the voyage was to investigate the possibilities of new fishing grounds. Lloyds says the purpose was to see what could be done in the way of rearranging trading stations. There is a splendid account of the departure in the 'Dundee Advertiser' of 10 June 1914, the ship having sailed the day before. I was unaware that two ships took part in the expedition until I read this cutting. Neither did I realise that Captain James like many a sailor was superstitious.

The Morning in 1914.

OFF TO THE ARCTIC
DEPARTURE OF DUNDEE WHALERS

The departure of the two whaling steamers, the Active and the Morning, from Dundee for the fishing grounds of the Far North caused quite unusual interest at the Harbour yesterday afternoon, and the scenes on the quays were reminiscent of the strong excitement of former days, when the whaling industry immediately affected a much wider circle.

During the forenoon large crowds visited both vessels, and the work of loading the stores was productive of considerable amusement. In this department the steward of the Morning was a zealous worker in white sleeves and apron, with a towel round his waist, and his dexterity in dealing with the different packages was a source of amazement to the watching crowd.

In the early part of the afternoon a spirit of conviviality made itself apparent, and the men's quarters were transformed into temporary concert halls, sweethearts and wives, along with the crew, spending a happy hour together, singing the latest chorus and generally creating an atmosphere of hilarity. Captain Murray, who had succeeded his brother as skipper of the Active, told a Dundee Advertiser reporter that he felt confident that the forthcoming season would be a success. "It is my heart's desire to see the whaling industry restored in Dundee," said Captain Fairweather, of the Morning. "I am leaving," he continued, "under favourable auspices, and for the sake of my men, I strongly hope for a prosperous season. When I say I am leaving under favourable auspices I mean that I have taken every care, some of them even superstitious, to invite success – for example, I would not engage men on Friday." Later it was discovered that Captain Fairweather had torn the thirteenth order sheet from his store book, while visitors to his own cabin might even have seen a bunch of red herrings strung up by the tails with a blue ribbon.

The Morning, which had been previously booked to sail at half-past one, was taken in tow at three o'clock by the tug Conqueror, and drawn towards the Camperdown Dock, where she set off under her own steam. As she passed through the locks, red herrings, oranges, bananas, and coins were exchanged between the crew and the onlookers on the pier head. When about 100 yards from the gates, the crew, with heads bared, mustered at the bulwarks, and led by Captain Fairweather, gave three loud cheers. The Union Jack at the stern was lowered, and the farewell signal was given.

Similar scenes attended the departure of the Active, although one little incident added zest to the proceedings. Two of the ship's company arrived too late at the Victoria Dock, where the whalers have been berthed, and one of them, the carpenter - probably thinking his services indispensable – raced down the pier to Camperdown Dock, and boarded the vessel as he passed through the lock. His companion, however did not show the same determination, and finally decided to stay at home.

The Active is going on a fishing expedition in the Cumberland Gulf and Davis Strait direction, while the Morning is taking stores to the Hudson Bay stations. Most of the crews are Dundonians.

Whereas the departure cutting states that the *Active* was going on a fishing expedition in the Cumberland Gulf and the *Morning* to take stores to the Hudson Bay stations, the homecoming cutting tells a different story. The *Morning* was to fish in the Cumberland Gulf neighbourhood where Captain James also proposed to make arrangements for the institution of stations to facilitate trade. In his 'Evening Telegraph' article of 16 December 1926 Captain James writes:

> I then made my last trip to the Arctic in 1914 on the whaler Morning to see what could be done in the way of re-arranging the trading stations.
>
> When I left I took with me everything that could possibly help us to win the good will of the natives. I knew that the two chief complaints from which they suffer are a form of bronchitis and bad eyes, and part of my equipment was a quantity of cough elixir and a supply of boracio powder.
>
> When we reached Cumberland Gulf my fame as a sort of witch doctor was not long in spreading among the Esquimeaux, and ever morning there was a regular queue outside the cabin door waiting for treatment.

Eskimos on Baffin Island

> None of them had ever been treated with such medicine before for either their colds or their eye ailments, and the cough elixir and boric acid had almost an immediate effect.
>
> He concludes: I am very sorry that the war spoilt that voyage, for I saw great possibilities in it.

In my brother's family there survives a series of photographs of the voyage.[1] I believe these to be of the *Morning* rather than the *Active*. The photographs have been examined by Dr W Gillies Ross of Quebec, who is an expert in nineteenth century whaling in the Davis Strait.

He is of the opinion that most of the photographs were taken in the vicinity of Cumberland Gulf, probably at Blacklead Island, Kekerten, and Niantelik (near Blacklead Island). Eskimos with their children and dogs, figure large in the photography, either on board or in groups on shore. There is an eskimo house, drying whale lines, and a series showing whaleboats lashed together and apart. There are two photographs of the whaling station on the island of Kekerten which looks new and clean, and another of sailors' graves. Two others show an elderly white man in shirtsleeves apparently addressing a group of eskimos on board. The scenery in these photographs looks bleak and unappealing with traces of snow on the barren slopes of the hills and stony uneven foreground.[2]

To what extent the voyage was a success is uncertain. I believe no whales were caught, but the return account in the newspaper states that cargo was brought home. Whether the proposed stations were established is not known. What is known however is that "the outbreak of war put a stop to any thought of reviving the whaling trade".[3] The *Morning* returned to Dundee on the 26th of September 1914.

DUNDEE WHALER'S RETURN
LATE NEWS OF THE WAR

After a successful three-months visit to the Far North, the Dundee whaler Morning, commanded by Captain Fairweather, returned to port yesterday.

The Morning left Dundee early in June, and the captain's intention was to prosecute the fishing in the neighbourhood of Cumberland Gulf, where he proposed to make arrangements for the institution of a number of stations with the purpose of facilitating trade. Up in the icy regions, however, very rough weather was experienced, and the vessel's rudder was damaged, while large ice fields also interfered considerably with the crew's operations. Despite these difficulties, however, Captain Fairweather has been successful in bringing to port a fair cargo of oils, skins, and other products of the Arctic.

It is a somewhat remarkable fact that the crew of the whaler were unaware that war had broken out between Britain and Germany until the day before yesterday. They were passing the Shetlands when they were hailed by some fishermen, who supplied them with the latest news regarding the campaign.

The *Morning* was lost on the same voyage as her sister ship the *Active* transporting war munitions to Russia in 1915. She went down off the Faroes and there were only two survivors - Captain Smith and his second mate. "They managed to keep alive in a stove-in whale boat (which was only kept afloat by her tanks) for four days in the dead of winter, and were then picked up by one of the cruisers of the Northern Squadron."[4]

1914 to 1919   War Service

Captain James tells us in his article:

> War had just broken out when I returned from my voyage on the Morning. I got as many of my men as I could to join the R.N.R., and then joined myself. At first I was told I was beyond the age, but the fact I suppose that I had been a trained man in the R.N.R. in my younger days counted in my favour.
>
> Be that as it may, I got my commission, dated November 11, 1914, and was appointed as Examination Officer, Tay Defences.

The situation over the next five months can only be deduced, for neither his commission nor any letter of initial appointment to the Tay Defences survives.

It seems likely that his first appointment was as Examination Officer, and that the subsequent letter and certificate refer to his promotion to Chief Examination Officer.

The letter quoted below is dated 3 April 1915 and is from Captain Laird, Brigade Major, Tay Defences. From later correspondence we know that Headquarters was at Broughty Ferry Castle, which until recently housed the Whaling Museum.

> Captain Fairweather
> Tay Examination Service
>
> I am directed to inform you that you have been appointed Chief Examination Officer.
>
> The following rate of pay has been approved: £5 (five Pounds) a week.
>
> A free issue of the Field Ration has also been approved which you will receive from the North Scottish R.G.A at Broughty Castle commencing 6 April 1915.
>
> You should arrange with the Adjutant, North Scottish R.G.A. whether you will draw the ration daily, or every two or three days.
>
> You will be informed later from whom you will receive your pay in future and that now due in addition to the £3 per week already advanced.

This rather amusing epistle tells us a great deal of trivia. I wonder what Grandmother thought of her portly husband aged sixty-one bringing home field rations to Bonavista. Perhaps they were very welcome in wartime. In fact the rations were probably in the form of meals eaten when on duty.

Captain James' undated Certificate of Appointment as Chief Examination Officer for the Port of Dundee is addressed to Lieutenant

James Fairweather R.N.V.R. and states that he is empowered to take such steps as may be necessary for the verification of the friendly character of vessels in the immediate vicinity of the port and of those desiring to enter the port. It continues:

> You have authority to issue all necessary orders under the Public Traffic Regulations for this Port for the purpose of controlling the navigation and mooring of all vessels other than H.M. ships, in the Port and the approaches thereto.
>
> Disobedience on the part of a master to orders issued by you under the above authority will constitute a Breach of the Defence of the Realm Regulations, 1914, and will render the vessel liable to be fired upon.[1]

My cousin Jim Fairweather who is an ex-naval officer tells me that Captain James' duties would be in connection with searching neutral vessels which entered the Tay estuary, to ensure that they were not carrying contraband which might be useful to the enemy.

One press cutting refers to his job as 'Inspecting Officer on the river Tay', and Ethel Burton writes that he patrolled the mouth of the River Tay.

Captain James' obituary in the 'Dundee Advertiser' says, "His work was mainly in the North Sea looking for enemy submarines and sweeping for mines." None of the family has any knowledge of this, however David Henderson tells me that the Broughty Castle Garrison was a group of Royal Engineers called Submarine Miners; that they had a small ship moored in Castle Harbour and were tasked with the laying of mines across the Tay. This may account for the above erroneous information in the 'Advertiser' obituary fifteen years after the event. However Captain James records one alarming encounter with a mine in his article:

> On one occasion the master of a steamer reported to me that he had seen something like a mine coming in with the flood tide.
>
> On examination I found it was a line mine. I first tried to sink it by rifle fire, but without immediate effect. It was close to Tayport by that time, and I could not delay further. I, therefore, got into the small boat along with two men and ran a line to the mine.
>
> When I was making the line fast I saw the mine was perforated above the waterline with rifle fire. When we commenced to tow it seaward it gradually heeled over and sank.

Captain Hector Adams, writing in 'Sea Breezes', says, "during the War he (Captain James) was in command of the Examination Vessel (off the Tay Bar) for Dundee; and barked at the Nation's Gates in good style."[2]

The question of his rank is confusing but I now believe the sequence is as follows: three newspaper cuttings state that he was given naval rank on his appointment as Examining Officer. His Certificate of Appointment to Chief Examining Officer refers to him as Lieutenant James Fairweather R.N.V.R. Lloyds's obituary states that this was as early as November 1914, and this is confirmed by Captain James himself. It seems however, that there was no clear distinction amongst the seamen between R.N.R. and R.N.V.R. The term R.N.V.R. is never used by them in common parlance in the sources read by me in the course of compiling this book, whereas the use of R.N.R. is frequent.

Ann Savours in her book *The Voyages of the Discovery*[3] states clearly that on taking command of *Discovery* he was granted a temporary commission as Lieutenant Commander, Royal Naval Reserve; whilst the surgeon Dr Gerald Martin was made an acting surgeon, R.N. There is a family legend that this was done in order that Captain James would out-rank Sir Ernest Shackleton if the two should happen to be on board together. The rank of R.N.R. was professionally senior to that of R.N.V.R. Jim Fairweather states that Shackleton was a Lieutenant R.N.R. of some seniority, and adds "if the Admiralty had only promoted Grandpa to Lieutenant Commander and left him in the R.N.V.R. it is probable that Shackleton would have ignored him in any decisions he took."[4] The rank was withdrawn after the completion of the *Discovery's* voyage, as was common in war time; however his previous rank was certainly reinstated, as there are two letters to "Lieutenant James Fairweather, Chief Examination Officer" from Captain D.S. Pithie, Staff Officer Tay Defences. One dated 21 April 1917 says: "Herewith your commission as Lieutenant Royal Naval Volunteer Reserve", and indicating that further promotion will follow shortly. The second from Tay Defences, Wednesday, indicates that Captain Pithie has just heard privately "that the Admiralty are to sanction our application. You will therefore be gazetted in due course Lieut.-Commander."[5]

An undated press cutting in Captain Fairweather's scrapbook reads as follows:

SCOTTISH COMMAND MENTIONS

The names of the under mentioned belonging to Scottish Command, have been brought to the notice of the Secretary of State for War, for valuable services rendered in connection with the War, and where applicable, an entry will be made in the records of service of officers and other ranks.

The first name is: Fairweather, Lt. J. R.N.V.R.,
followed by ten others.

Captain James' comment on this honour reads as follows:

We were demobilised in March, 1919. They were good enough to give me a Mention for valuable service rendered, which I value and look on as at least a scrap of fame I started out in my boyhood to look for.

Marriage of a Daughter

On Wednesday the 8th of September 1915, my mother Mary Ann Craik Fairweather (Tan) married Dr Stuart Bolton (Dick) at Trinity U.F. Church, Newport at 1.45. I know this because I have the pretty invitation before me. At the top is an embossed F and B intertwined. The reception afterwards was at the small Blyth Hall, and carriages were at 4pm.

Grandfather was certainly present at this event for a wedding album survives including charming groups taken on the lawn outside Bonavista. Mother and father are sitting on the grass flanked by Aunt Ella and Auntie Grace (Father's twin sister who had travelled from Oxfordshire for the occasion). They were to be the bridesmaids. Behind mother and father sit a smiling Mary Ann and James. Grandpa in his Captain's uniform, complete with white cap and blazer.

One interesting feature of the wedding groups is the presence of a kilted boy who I presume to be Jimmy Corr, who would have been ten at the time.

The Corr children were born in India, but like so many others, were 'sent home' for their schooling. I will return to this topic later.

The account of the wedding in the press is headed 'from Newport-on-Tay', and dated 23rd September 1915, and reads as follows:

> A recent pretty wedding was that which took place in Trinity United Free Church where Miss Mary Fairweather was married to Dr Stuart Bolton. Quietness was the note of the wedding, and the floral decorations of the church were distinguished by a graceful simplicity. (Not so the bridal gown and train which I remember from my play days). The bridal gown was composed of ivory satin, with a tucked skirt and corsage trimmed with iridescent lace, which also formed the Medici collar. The court train was of satin brocade lined with taffetas, covered with chiffon, and the white net veil over her dark hair was confined by a wreath of orange blossom and white heather, repeated in the trimming of the corsage. Her bouquet consisted of white roses and lily of the valley. Miss Ella Fairweather (the bride's younger sister) and Miss Grace Bolton (twin sister of the bridegroom) were the two bridesmaids, and they were gowned in shell pink satin with two scalloped flounces over a satin frill while the sleeves and corsage were of ninon over net. Their hats were of black satin with a velvet underbrim and shell pink trimming and they carried posies of shaded mauve sweet peas, toning beautifully with their gowns. A handsome toilette of black moire was worn by the bride's mother, with a plumed velvet chapeau.

Not one word about the men, or even the name of the best man!

I quote this in full because it vividly displays the elaboration of these entirely hand made outfits, which would no doubt have been stitched in the rooms of some Dundee dressmaker. The amount of work put in must have been phenomenal. I remember vestiges of such workmanship in the 1950s, before mass production became the watchword.

1916   Discovery   The Shackleton Relief Expedition

The episode in Captain James' career for which he is best known is his command of *Discovery* for the Shackleton Relief Expedition of 1916. As it turned out, this voyage was a disappointment in every way, and initially I must quote my cousin Ethel again for she rightly commented to me that far from being the high point of his long and illustrious career it was a rather sad ending for an elderly man in indifferent health. In his article[1] Captain James expresses his feelings about this episode.

> In June, 1916, I was promoted and given command of the S.S. Discovery to go to the relief of Sir E. Shackleton's men who were marooned on Elephant Island, south of Cape Horn.
>
> When that appointment came I remembered that I had started out on my career in search of fame and adventure. I had got my fill of the latter. Was I now to get the former?
>
> But that was denied me, for when I reached Montevideo I was recalled, as the object of my mission had already been accomplished.
>
> I was glad the crew had been saved, but I have not yet forgotten my disappointment at being recalled, and I never will.

The narrative which follows is drawn from three sources, firstly Ann Savour's book *The Voyages of Discovery* of 1992, also Roland Huntford's 1985 biography of Shackleton, and papers in the possession of the Bolton family.

Readers will recall that Sir Ernest Shackleton's grandly named 'Imperial Trans-Antarctic Expedition' ran into deep trouble when his ship the *Endurance* sank in pack ice before reaching the Antarctic continent. After incredible adventures the crew reached Elephant Island, a remote rocky island deep in the South Atlantic. From there Shackleton and his comrades Frank Worsley the captain, Tom Crean, Harry Macneish the carpenter, Tim Macarthy and John Vincent made the epic voyage in the *James Caird* to South Georgia. Shackleton, Worsley and Crean then crossed the mountains to reach the whaling station at Stromness. Shackleton had not been seen for two years and the world had no idea of the expedition's fate, it was the 20th of May 1916. Mcneish, Macarthy and Vincent were picked up, and Shackleton immediately sailed for Elephant Island in the steamer *Southern Sky*, but failed because of ice conditions to rescue his comrades. The three picked-up sailors were sent back to England, where they were able to brief the Admiralty about the location of the camp on Elephant Island. Shackleton then proceeded to the Falkland Islands and cabled to London on the 31 of May. By the 2nd of June the London newspapers were full of the story.

The Shackleton Relief Advisory Committee had already been set up and by the middle of May had reported and recommended that the ship *Discovery* be supplied and fitted out to search the Weddell Sea for Shackleton. The news that Shackleton was alive and his men marooned on Elephant Island caused a change of plan. The Advisory Committee reported on the 10th July that a vessel should be acquired and equipped for six months, and sent south under an experienced ice master. The Hudson Bay Company lent *Discovery* for this purpose.[2] By the 24th of July it was reported in the press that "in view of the possibility of the failure of the third attempt now being carried out by Sir Ernest Shackleton . . . the Government has now decided to dispatch a vessel from England as soon as she can be fitted out. Lieut.-Commander James Fairweather R.N.V.R., an experienced ice master has been appointed to command the vessel now fitting out at H.M. Dockyard, Devonport."[3]

Ethel recalls that Grandfather was on holiday at Kirriemuir when he was summoned by the Admiralty to take the *Discovery* across the Atlantic. The telegram was apparently delivered at dead of night by a dispatch rider on a motorbike. The news soon became public, and in grandpa's scrap book there is an unattributed press cutting with a striking photograph of Captain James in full uniform with a sword, headed 'Lieut.-Commander J. Fairweather, R.N.V.R., Commander of the Shackleton Relief Ship'.

The text commences "The news of the appointment of Lieut.-Commander James Fairweather to the command of the *Discovery* will be read with pleasure by the number of relations and friends of that esteemed officer in South Africa." There follows a resume of his career.

The 'Dundee Advertiser' reported the news and appointment on Thursday 20 July, and continued:

DUNDEE OFFICER
to Command Shackleton Relief Ship
Lieutenant James Fairweather R.N.R Newport has
been appointed to take command of the Shackleton
Expedition Relief Ship, and left Dundee last night to
take over this important duty.

A letter from Kathleen Duncan to Keith Mackay on the occasion of his 21st Birthday is full of praise for the adventurous Fairweather brothers, and also comments about grandpa's appointment "Capt James was most annoyed, Aunt Lily said, as he was some big noise in Tay Defences (First World War), also he had wanted to lift his potatoes."[4] I don't know about annoyance, and rather doubt this, but I can understand his concern for his potatoes!

I stated earlier that my mother told me only one thing about her father (taking the children on his voyages). However I now remember another, which was that he was nearly knocked down and killed by a taxi in London on his way to the Admiralty!

Captain James Fairweather, 1916

There followed a spate of telegrams between Shackleton and the Admiralty about the relationship between himself and the commander of the *Discovery*. From the start the Admiralty had been ambivalent in its attitude to Shackleton and the rescue. It was wartime, and some felt that the expedition was very much a sideshow. Members of the Relief Committee, including Mawson and Admiral Lewis Beaumont the chairman, were distinctly unsympathetic to Shackleton. On August 17 Shackleton cabled, "Your silence leads me to suppose supreme command vested in commander Discovery. Trust this is not so." The Admiralty replied, "Captain Discovery to embark you and carry out as far as possible measures you advise for rescue of men. Command of vessel and all on board and responsibility for action remains in his (Captain Fairweather's) hands."[5] In the meantime *Discovery* was fitting out at Devonport.

The family have in their possession a folder containing twenty-three miscellaneous documents relating to the voyage, some of them in duplicate. These include Captain James' sailing orders, with an enclosure for Shackleton, photographs of Elephant Island and other Antarctic islands, including a pencil drawn map of the Seal Islands done in 1821 by Robert Fildes, commander of the brig *Corvac*. There is correspondence about

Captain James Fairweather, now Lieut.-Commander R.N.R. in command of *Discovery*.
The photo shows him together with his fellow ship's officers at Devonport, he is holding the ship's cat. August 1916.

© National Maritime Museum, London

photography. Only the surgeon can take photographs and write a narrative of the voyage. A representative of the International Film Service of New York will join the ship at Montevideo. All copyright is strictly with the Admiralty. There is a memorandum about the officers and men's clothing.

The hydrographer's office conveyed to Captain Fairweather the rights of the surgeon in various matters, and it appears there was a little friction between the two. One letter in particular is amusing in that it tells grandpa that "he (the surgeon) is in entire charge of all medical stores and medical comforts of all descriptions, and the responsibility as to their use and issue rests entirely with him. I am rather specially making these remarks owing to your retention of a certain portion of the comforts which action seems undesirable." One would imagine that grandpa was reserving some 'comforts' for himself, however he was a teetotaller. I can imagine that as a merchant navy captain, accustomed to total control of his ship, he found the Royal Navy bureaucracy difficult and frustrating. He is even told that the surgeon is experienced in codes and that he must make use of his practical knowledge of this subject.

By this time McCarthy, Vincent and Macneish had arrived in England, and by far the most interesting documents in the folder are a statement by Vincent, and sketches dated 3 August 1916 by Vincent and Macneish of Elephant Island and the probable sites where the men might be found. These are forwarded with a letter from the Hydrographic Department to Admiral Parry as follows:

> Dear Admiral Parry,
>   We interviewed Mr. Vincent Boatswain, and A.B. McCarthy yesterday morning as directed. Vincent seemed fairly intelligent but we did not get much out of McCarthy. Vincent's statement is attached together with a rough sketch of the camp. Later in the day Mr. Macneish, the Carpenter, arrived and corroborated Vincent's statement, except as regards the position of the camp.
>   This difference is shewn on chart cutting which I have attached. Macneish is probably the most intelligent and I am strongly of the opinion that his position is correct and that Vincent confused the first landing place with the final position of the camp.
>   Macneish drew a rough sketch of the coast, and also a sketch of the camp, which agrees more or less with that drawn by Vincent. Both these are attached.
>   In any case Shackleton is sure to have left full details of the position at the Falkland Islands.

TO THE RESCUE OF EXPLORERS.

The Discovery leaving home waters for the Antarctic regions.

I tried to get Vincent to go to Plymouth.

He said he would do so, but I rather doubt it.

If he does turn up he will come with Northcott.

Yours sincerely,

E.V. Hardy

The sketches by the two men are in the folder, and were presumably intended to assist Captain James in his attempt to rescue Shackleton's men.

STATEMENT OF MR. VINCENT, BOATSWAIN OF "ENDURANCE"

Next morning we sighted the Island again. That night we had a strong breeze and could not make the Island until 10 o'clock in the morning. Sir Ernest Shackleton then found a small shelf just sufficient to act as a landing for that day. The next day we started to find a better landing place and found a large beach and decided to camp there (this is where the party now is) we remained there for one week fitting a boat for the passage to South Georgia. There is no difficulty in landing boats on the beach, which is sloping, with occasional rocks off it. Usually three or four days heavy surf, and a couple of days of little surf. Flag will be probably hoisted near the Cave and the Party left behind have red flare-ups for night work.

The hole where the cave is stationed is inconspicuous and cannot be seen from the sea.

The Glacier in which the cave is situated runs in a Northeasterly direction. The entrance to the cave is about 30 feet up the Glacier. There was a strong blizzard blowing the whole week we were in camp.

On leaving we came through two streams of pack ice – experiencing strong westerly and northerly winds. Sir Ernest Shackleton left orders with his second-in-command, Mr Wild that if he did not hear from him by the beginning of summer – November next – he was to send the boats through to the Whaling Station on Deception Island. Two 20 ft. boats were left with Party on Elephant Island. They had farinaceous food enough to last for a couple of months on full rations – plenty of seals, killed 14 seals, 6 sea elephants, 500 to 800 penguins – plenty of meat. 22 men left behind.

Mr Macneish states that eight days rations were left at spot marked B.[6]

By this time *Discovery* was ready to sail, and the 'Daily Mirror' of August 15 1916 has a spread showing the ship "leaving home waters for the Atlantic regions" with the crew at the bows. There is also a photograph of Captain James holding the ship's cat with the eight officers in their uniforms surrounding him, and a further photograph of the riggers, a group of men in a circle holding an enormously thick rope.

Captain James' sailing orders dated 2 August are two and a half foolscap pages long (appendix). He is to leave Devonport in tow of the collier *Polesley* and proceed to the Falkland Islands (The object of the tow was to get the slow *Discovery* across the Atlantic as quickly as possible). He is to report back to the Admiralty on arrival and to the Governor, who he is to inform of his mission. Should Shackleton be at Port Stanley, he is to confer with him about the rescue. A letter to Shackleton is enclosed. *Discovery,* under Captain Fairweather's command is placed at his disposal, to effect the rescue of the party; however, "the command of the ship and all who may be on board as well as the responsibility for the action he takes, must belong in (Captain Fairweather's) hands". There follows detailed guidance in the event of various circumstances.

There is also a copy of a secret communication from the "Admiral Superintendent Superintending transport officer" to the master of the *Polesley* "to be destroyed by fire on arrival at destination," giving detailed sailing instructions. A reference sheet from the Captain of Dockyard and deputy Superintendent Devonport to the commanding officer *Discovery* dated 10 August, reads as follows:

> Being in all respects ready, you will leave your present berth at 6pm (G.M.T.) today, and proceed to the Sound to be taken in tow by the collier ss Polesley, when you will proceed on your voyage to Port Stanley, Falkland Islands, calling at St Vincent, Cape De Verde Islands and Montevideo en route. You will be escorted by two patrol vessels for a certain distance after leaving this port . . .[7]

So on August the 10th, *Discovery*, towed by the *Polesley*, left Plymouth Sound for St Vincent in the Cape Verde Islands. From there it took them twenty days to reach Montevideo on the 11th of September. There they heard the momentous news, that Shackleton, having been given use of the *Yelcho* by the Chilean Navy, had been successful in rescuing all his men from Elephant Island on August the 30th. On September the 3rd they had landed at Punto Arenas in triumph.

One can only imagine the disappointment and frustration suffered by the Captain and crew of *Discovery*. In one moment the whole purpose of their expedition was negated. The surgeon, Dr G. M. Martin was paid off and discharged by mutual consent, as he wanted to get home. The ship was next piloted to Buenos Aires to take on a cargo of grain. Bad weather plagued them *en route* and on arrival they had to be towed into harbour on 21 September. 100 tons of coal were landed, and the holds were cleaned for cargo; the wheat was loaded in bags. On the 30th of September

Discovery departed from Buenos Aires under her own steam, homeward bound. The deck log records that on 11 October, engines were stopped 'to see how the ship would act under canvas, the breeze being satisfactory for such a purpose'. However, the trial proved a failure: 'no sooner the engine stopped than the helm had to be put Hard up'. Even with the helm hard over, 'the ship came to the wind and so remained as if Hove to and as if the helm had been Hard a lea'. Full speed was then rung. On the 16 October *Discovery* berthed at Pernambuco[8] (on the Brazilian coast) where Captain Fairweather cabled The Hydrographer, Admiralty, London; as confirmed by his letter:

```
                    S. S. "DISCOVERY"
                         PERNAMBUCO,
                              17th October, 1916
Sir,
   This will confirm my cable of this date — copy enclosed
I am very sorry at having to put in here. When leaving
the Plate, I thought with a few days of sail alone in the
S.E. Trades I would have ample coal to reach St. Vincent.
I tried her under the most favourable conditions with sail alone,
but it was a complete failure, as had to steam all the way.
But,  Oh Dear, she goes slowly — about five knots in fine
weather, and up to six and a half with the assistance of the
sails.          After consultations with the British Consul
here I have taken my supply of coal — 103. tons — from Messrs.
Wilson, Sons & Ceyl, Ltd., and have drawn on the Admiralty
to the extent of £641-9-3 ----------------------------
at three days' sight to meet the bill and disbursements at
this port.
   My reason for taking so much coal here is that I am a
little afraid by what I have seen of her that if the N.E.
Trades are strong, I may not be able to fetch St. Vincent.
If so, then I will have sufficient to reach the Azores via
the sailing route.
                    Your obedient servant,[9]
```

She berthed at St Vincent, Cape Verde Islands on the 31st of October. On the 3rd of November Captain Fairweather (in the words of the Log) "called the crew together and explained to them that he had been invalided home and that the Chief Officer would become master, and he trusted that the ship's work would go on satisfactorily to all concerned." At 1.45 he left the ship for home;[10] so ended Captain James' last command; he was sixty-three years old.

He returned to his appointment as Chief Examiner Tay Defences until the end of the war; where he was in command of the Examination Vessel (off the Tay Bar) for Dundee, and "barked at the Nation's Gates in good style".[11]

Captain James in later life

Retirement

Grandpa had fifteen years of retirement with Granny at Bonavista. The grandchildren had been arriving since 1905, and there were to be nine, four boys and five girls. The two who must have made the biggest impact on their lives were Jimmy and Ethel, the two eldest grandchildren and the elder children of Lizzie and James Corr. Jimmy arrived from India in about 1912 at the age of seven, as was customary, to be educated in England. Unfortunately in consequence of the 1914-18 War he was not to see his parents and sister again until 1919 when he was fourteen During that time he was the responsibility of his grandparents, and attended Dundee High Preparatory School followed by boarding at Glenalmond; he subsequently qualified as a doctor.

In 1919 Jim, Lizzie and one year old Duncan arrived from India with Ethel aged eight. Ethel did not return, but stayed on with her grandparents for her education. By 1921 Lizzie had gone back to India with Duncan, but returned to Scotland from time to time, renting a house near Bonavista as necessary. Ethel says in her memoirs "They (the grandparents) lived at 15, Norwood Terrace when I was young, and my home was with them for quite a long time, ten or eleven years I should think. Part of the time both my parents were in India, and part of the time only my father. When we came home from India in 1919 my grandfather had already retired from a life of 52 years at sea."

Ethel probably attended Dundee High School (as did my mother) and was at Craiglockhart Convent boarding school in Edinburgh from 1925-28. She subsequently graduated from St Andrews University. Both Jimmy and Ethel must therefore have played a large part in their grandparents' lives during quite long periods of time, roughly from 1912 to 1929.

Ethel's memories of her Bonavista days are evocative: "When I was a child my grandfather used to take me over a little hill past the end of Norwood to look at the stars in the dark. We sat on an iron seat by the road and looked over the river to Dundee and the North. He pointed out the Plough and the North Star, and I am sure many more besides, and sometimes we would watch the Aurora Borealis dancing in the sky. Sometimes we used to play cards in the evening - German whist and another game for two which I forget. I expect my grandmother was busy with her knitting. She used to knit shawls and socks, and long black stockings for me to wear with my gymslips which I didn't like at all because they were prickly, never quite long enough, for by this time skirts were getting quite short and not at all like the ones other girls had. She used to make bedjackets too and teapot stands for sales of work, and I used to have to go to D M Brown's in Dundee to buy wool for them . . . so many hanks of this and so many cuts of that. She was always very good and kind and sympathetic to me, for she was getting quite old - her seventieth birthday was in 1921 when my parents were in India, and she had raised eight children of her own, and already looked after my brother Jimmy for seven years with aunt Ella's help."

The third Corr grandchild was William Duncan, known as Duncan, who was born in India in 1918. In grandpa's scrap book there is a cutting, possibly from a church magazine, describing his christening. Uncle Jim Corr had worked in the jute industry in Calcutta in various capacities. In the cutting he and Lizzie are referred to as "of Albion Jute Mills." The christening evidently took place at home as we are told, "There was a fine gathering in the drawing room, of Mr and Mrs Corr's house at which it was pleasing to see representatives from Budge Budge, Caledonian and Lothian Jute Mills." It seems likely that the Budge Budge representatives were Keith's great grandparents Richard and Lillias Duncan, keeping up the family link.

It was probably during the 1919 visit, when Duncan was a baby, that a photograph was taken of a family group outside Bonavista including the ayah (Indian nanny) who had been brought over to look after young Duncan. She looks amazingly incongruous in her Indian clothing; grandpa is in his naval uniform, but no doubt they had a lot in common as grandpa knew India so well. Duncan's widow Pam recalls how he loved his ayah. Duncan remained with his mother, and they visited Scotland from time to time until he was of an age to go to boarding school.

My parents had moved to Halifax in 1923 when my brother Alastair was three years old. I was born in 1930 and shortly before this Duncan had been brought home from India to be educated, and in effect became one of our family at Kingston Dene and later at Invermark. The two boys were brought up together and attended New College Preparatory and Ashville College in Harrogate. Alan Denby and Jim Fairweather also went to Ashville, a remarkable family event.

In effect my parents were in loco parentis to the Corr children from the time the grandparents were too old to cope until Jimmy married Margaret Clow, and Ethel married Rupert Burton, both in 1934 in successive weeks, November 17th and 24th. I was a small bridesmaid to both couples. Ethel and Rupert were married from our house, Invermark, and I remember Ethel reading Beatrix Potter to me the night before the wedding. They were married at King Cross Methodist Church by the Rev. Bramwell Evans, 'Romany' of Children's Hour fame. My father gave Ethel away and my memory of the reception was a sea of legs as I was so small. My dress was of gold taffeta with brown velvet trim for Ethel, and pale sea green velvet for Jimmy, and I was wrapped in a shawl. Duncan remained my parents' responsibility; he and Alastair were like brothers and up to all sorts of tricks. Duncan lived up to his reputation for high spirits by joining the Royal Air Force. He became Squadron Leader W D Corr D.F.C., and was killed in action in a raid on Le Creusot armament factory in Eastern France on the 17 October 1942. He is buried at Ecuisse in France and left a widow, Pamela.

Charles Fairweather had married Eva Hughes in 1912. They lived at Carlisle and had three daughters, - Evelyn born in 1916, Helen in 1917, and Dorothy in 1920. The girls spent regular holidays with their grandparents in Newport, and Dorothy who died in May 2004, had many happy memories of their visits there. The Carlisle Fairweathers remained very close to the grandparents, and were always supportive in difficult times. Their visits lengthened as granny and grandpa became older, and needed a bit more help in various ways.

The story of grandson James (Jim) Fairweather is more complex and altogether more tragic. At the age of about thirty one, James, granny and grandpa's eldest son, who was a Merchant Navy officer, married Lilian Vicars of Liverpool at All Saints Church in Childwall, Lancashire. At that time he had been with the company, Messrs Alfred Booth & Co, for five and a half years, after having obtained his extra master's certificate in 1901. The couple went to South America, as James had joined the Amazon River Steam Navigation Company. The marriage was childless, and Lilian died shortly after their return to England in 1923. James retired from the merchant service in his late forties and commenced a pedigree pig farming business in the Midlands. It appears that grandpa used to lend a hand on his visits. My cousin Jim has a photograph of him in action, helping out, which seems absolutely typical of the man. James' smallholding was at the village of Spalford, halfway between Gainsborough and Newark. The adjoining smallholding was run by a widow, Nellie Denby, who had a small son named Alan. The press cuttings in grandpa's scrapbook must indicate the family's pleasure when James and Nellie married at Wigsley Methodist Church on April 4th 1925. To everyone's delight a son was born to the couple in January 1926.

The delight was to be short lived, as James tragically died of cancer less than two years later in October 1927, leaving Nellie with two small sons, Alan and Jim.

It is quite clear from the correspondence that Jim was a very special child to his grandparents. He was the son and namesake of their eldest son, the third of their sons to predecease them. They were also supportive of Nellie in her loss, and affectionate letters to her survive from both grandpa and granny in which they sign themselves "your affectionate mother/father". One letter from granny is a heartfelt letter of condolence to Nellie written only a week after her son James' death. It appears that grandpa attended the funeral at Glasson Dock near Lancaster, and Eva Fairweather is mentioned as accompanying Nellie on a short break to Liverpool. Granny notes in a postscript to tell Lizzie that she has sent Ethel's dressing gown away that afternoon, so Ethel must have been with her mother in attendance on Nellie. Diana Kelly tells me that her grandmother Eva looked after young Jimmy for a while when he was a baby, whilst Nellie was nursing her terminally ill husband; the family were rallying round the bereaved widow and her two young sons.

Another sad inscription was added to the memorial stone at Vicarsford Cemetery, Forgan. Engraved on one side it reads:

also of James
who died at Glasson Dock
Lancaster
11 October 1917
aged 51 years

There are two letters from Granny to Jimmy, (Jim), one dated May 22 1932 acknowledging his birthday greetings and the other of January 3 1933 thanking him for his Christmas card and letter, in which she wishes him well at his new school and hopes he will beat all his young cousins at lessons and good behaviour. A third letter to Alan reveals that the boys were at New College, Harrogate. She exhorts Alan to look after Jimmy and not let the big boys bully him! She signs off to Alan just as she does to Jimmy 'I remain dear Alan, your loving Grandma M A Fairweather. I have already referred to the letter from grandpa to Jimmy on the occasion of his fourth birthday, but make no apology for reproducing it, for it conveys to the full his understanding and affection for his grandson and ability to communicate compassionately with a very young person. It also displays his sense of continuity within the family from his own grandfather to himself leading on to his grandson. Also his patriotism is marked, as has been seen in other letters in which he speaks of himself and his sons, Alexander and David having "done our bit for the good of our country", going on to explain that his mother's father served under Wellington at Waterloo.

14/1/30

My Dear grandson

        Just a wee letter to your own dear self, to wish you a very happy birthday and that you may see many more of them is the prayer of your grandmother and myself. Now I am to tell you a little story. You know or will learn as you grow up, that I held a naval commission during all the Great War, at the end of the War I never applied for a medal. About two months ago, I saw in the newspapers that they had a lot of medals as yet unclaimed so I wrote asking if my name was amongst them, and got back a form to fill up and last Friday I got my medal (War 1914 – 1918). I am very proud of it, and I will then be able to say and prove that your Grand Father played his part in the Great War. My Grand Father

on my Mother's side was in the Battle of Waterloo,
and I remember as a boy I was very proud of the fact
when I came to understand it. So that you can now
say that your Grandfather was in the Great War, and
that his Grandfather was at Waterloo. But I hope
that we are all done with Wars now as they are not
nice. We hope that now, and at all times – you will
be good to your Dear Mother for she has done a great
deal for you and that both you and Alan will do all you
can to help her. Trusting that you will enjoy yourself at your
birthday party, and Grandma joins me in wishing that God's
blessing will be with you now, and at all times is the
Prayer of your

Ever loving

Grandfather

James Fairweather

Of the grandchildren, it only remains to mention my brother and myself. Alastair was born in Lerwick in the Shetland Islands in 1920. My father had been running the Gilbert Bain Memorial Hospital there since shortly after his marriage to Tan in 1915. In 1923 my father entered a practice in Halifax, West Yorkshire, where I was born in 1930. Consequently we did not see our Fairweather grandparents very often, though my parents did drive from Halifax to Dundee from time to time, and spent family holidays at Lundin Links with Duncan, and probably Ethel who was at University nearby. There exist charming photographs of Grandpa in a flat white cap holding Alastair aged about two.

Altogether James and Mary Ann seem to have been ideal grandparents, affectionate supportive and practical, and one hopes that they received in return the love and respect they so richly deserved.

Family life is made up of happy and traumatic events. The permanent departure of Aunt Ella from Dundee certainly falls into the latter category. Ella was always strong willed and a complex character. Not for her the lot of the youngest unmarried daughter to stay at home to look after elderly parents. At some time in the twenties she took the road south, qualified as a secretary and took a good job as secretary to the Principal of Royal Holloway College University of London. She never lived in Scotland again, but successively at Egham, London and Little Common on the Sussex coast in retirement with her close friend Kathleen Underhill. The consequences of this I will explain later.

Much of the family information included in this narrative is derived from grandpa's scrapbook, which is in the possession of my cousin Jim Fairweather. Jim's description is as follows. "This book appears to have been bought as a scrapbook by or for William Fairweather, since his name appears on the flyleaf together with the date, - January 1906 . . . The scrapbook may have been continued by grandma and was certainly continued by grandpa. It includes many items that do not relate directly to the family, they are included in the list to show the range of grandpa's interests".

Apart from the family events described above, these interests include poems, most of a sentimental nature, sport (racing and cricket), cuttings about Mary Slessor, the Dundee missionary who went to Calabar (also a heroine to my mother), and many seafaring references. He also wrote a letter advocating that an account should be written of the Dundee whalers and rebutted a case made in the 'Courier and Advertiser' entitled 'Controlling the weather', in which he drew on his experience of the Arctic.

It is clear that grandpa took a lively interest in matters in which he felt involved, and had no hesitation in writing to MPs or the press, or any person, to express his views on subjects, particularly those relevant to his experiences.

A major interest during grandpa's last years, was the writing and publishing of his memoirs. His first success at writing for publication was in December 1926, when a series of four articles appeared on successive days in the 'Evening Telegraph'. They were entitled 'My 50 Years at Sea, Newport Whaling Captain's Adventures', 'A Man Overboard, Exploits of whaling Days', 'Surprises in Far Off Lands, and Happy Reunions with Exiled Dundonians' and 'My Fame as a Witch-Doctor among Esquimaux'. The first two articles consist mainly of material subsequently printed in Captain James' Memoirs. Material from the fourth article has been incorporated into this text. The articles are impressively presented and lavishly illustrated with pictures of Aurora, eskimos, polar bears, and of Fairweather House in Calcutta. An anecdote from his third article reads as follows:

> "During the years I was calling at ports out east and south, I met an astonishingly large number of Dundee people. They were all very glad to see me and it did me good to see them. On one occasion when landing at a port in the Philippines, I heard a voice saying "You won't get any whales here Captain Fairweather." The voice belonged to an old second engineer of mine when I was on the Aurora. One day I was walking along the jetty at Burnbury, Western Australia and noticed four men splicing a huge hawser, one of them said, "How would this do for a Lowrie Tow, Captain Fairweather?" (A Lowrie Tow is a piece of rope ten feet long given to the men on a sealing steamer to drag the seal skins to the ship), "What do you know about a Lowrie Tow?" I asked. "I was with you on the Active in 1879", he replied. Needless to say it was a happy meeting. These exiled Dundonians were always glad to meet a Dundonian and to hear about the 'city'."[1]

This anecdote must have been omitted from his subsequent work by his editor who was probably an employee of John Leng & Co. Ltd of Dundee with whom correspondence is extant. A letter written by Captain James in

April 1928 would suggest that the full manuscript had been completed in 1926, but only the first four chapters had been published. Nothing further seems to have happened until March 1927 when grandpa received a letter from John Leng agreeing that the stories they had printed could be reprinted in a book (whether privately or for general publication is not clear).[1]

Grandpa was also in correspondence with David Moore Lindsay requesting permission to quote from his book, *A Voyage to the Arctic in the Whaler Aurora*, which was readily granted with warnings about the perfidy of publishers.

In the letter of 4 April 1928 he again approached John Leng after the book was rejected by Messrs Chambers of Edinburgh as being of local interest only. The letter is confusing but the outcome swift. By October 1928 the book had been printed for private circulation, and overlapping with this, five articles, being extracts from the book, were printed in the 'Scots Magazine', the last being in January 1929.

The publication of the articles in the 'Scots Magazine' brought many letters of appreciation and favourable reviews. There was a letter from Dr Rudmose Brown of Sheffield University, who had been a young scientist on the Scotia expedition in 1902 He remembered the *Vortigern* putting into Capetown in 1904 from New York. Grandpa also heard from James Ritchie of the Royal Scottish Museum in Edinburgh, who had reviewed the article in the 'Scottish Naturalist' of August (1928).

There was also a favourable review in 'The Scotsman' of August 30th. This correspondence must have given grandpa much pleasure.[3]

The privately printed book 'With the Scottish Whalers' is however a great rarity, to this day unknown to antiquarian booksellers. Many sections have been printed in this narrative. To me, the work is typical of the man, the fifty-nine pages telling a story by no means chronological but brimming with adventure, humour and humanity. It concluded with six stories written by his son William twenty-four years before. A fitting tribute from a father to his much loved son of whom he was justly proud.

No one knows how many copies of this book were printed. Each branch of the family was presented with one, and ours is charmingly inscribed in his hand:

'To Mrs Stuart Bolton with the Author's Compliments Xmas 1928'.

My birth in 1930 was a belated family event which was followed by a visit to Bonavista. No doubt there were many other family visits during the last three years of his life.

A photograph exists of a well wrapped-up grandpa seated outside Bonavista with grandma serenely beside him. This is my last memory of grandpa.

He died at Bonavista on March the 23rd 1933 aged seventy nine years, and was buried in the family grave at Vicarsford, Forgan with two of his sons, and a memorial to a third.

I conclude with repeating the last paragraph of grandpa's memoirs, describing his return after nearly three years in India:

"It was towards the end of December when we reached the river Elbe, and found it frozen over, which brought some of my Arctic experiences back again to me. We all took very bad with cold after being so long in India. But now that is a thing of the past, and with nothing else to do now but sit in my chair at the fireside and think of the past, forget about the colds and all other past troubles, and, may I whisper, would like to do it all over again."

"In all his fifty-two years of dangerous sea-life,
he lost, with the exception of one man who went
a-missing, neither a single life nor one of his ships."

ENVOI

Grandpa's death left granny then aged eighty one with no immediate family in Scotland. My mother was the only daughter in a position to care for her. Consequently my parents took a large house 'Invermark' in a very pleasant residential area of Halifax. Here the enlarged family could be accommodated in comfort. The household consisted of myself and my parents, granny in her upstairs room, a floating population of boys from Ashville College, and Ethel from time to time until her marriage. A man and wife, Mr & Mrs Rowlands, were engaged to live in. My last recollection of granny was of her eighty third birthday. Rupert Burton (Ethel's husband) was a director of Express Dairies, and provided an enormous cake decorated with blue and white icing. Chunks were handed out to the milkman and other tradesmen.

Granny outlived Grandpa by sixteen months. She died on July 11th 1934, at the age of eighty three and was buried beside Grandpa in the family grave at Vicarsford Cemetery, Forgan.

Erected
by
JAMES FAIRWEATHER
SHIPMASTER
AND HIS WIFE
MARY ANN CRAIK
IN LOVING MEMORY OF THEIR SON
ALEXANDER
WHO DIED AT NEWPORT
2ND AUG 1903   AGED 22 YEARS
ALSO THEIR SON
WILLIAM CRAIK
WHO DIED AT NEWPORT
9TH APRIL 1906   AGED 21 YEARS
ALSO THE ABOVE
JAMES FAIRWEATHER
WHO DIED AT NEWPORT
23RD MARCH 1933 AGED 79 YEARS
AND HIS WIFE
MARY ANN CRAIK
WHO DIED 11TH JULY 1934
AGED 84 YEARS

engraved on one side

ALSO OF JAMES
WHO DIED AT GLASSON DOCK
LANCASTER
11TH OCTOBER 1927
AGED 51 YEARS

Appendix I

1877 The *Victor*, a sealing and whaling voyage

James Fairweather was appointed 1st officer (first mate) of the ship *Victor* on a sealing and whaling voyage in 1877. A fellow crewmember, Hector Adams, subsequently wrote an account of the voyage; this gives us an insight into the working of the ship and its crew, and of the sea conditions and experiences encountered. The following is an abridged transcription of the account as published in the P.S.N.C. Magazine, Sea Breezes.

Whaling Stories

A Sealing Voyage

The ship Victor sailed from Camperdown Dock, Dundee, on 20th February, 1877. The master's name was John Nicoll, the first mate James Fairwhether (sic), second mate Clarke. I am unable to recall all the names, but the spectioneer, who had charge of all fishing guns, lines, harpoons, flenshing and other gear, and was a kind of third mate, was Alex Donaldson. The schieman (or captain of the hold), D. Bruce. There were two engineers, two firemen, boatswain and his mate, carpenter, by name Levey, his mate, and blacksmith, cooper and sailmaker, each having a mate. These mates were picked after sailing. Five line managers, who pulled stroke oar and looked after the boat's gear; four harpooneers - mates and spectioneer were also harpooneers - spectioneer, harpooneer, schieman, are relics of our forerunners, the Dutch. who had 300 sail at the fishing in 1665). Five or six boat steerers - more were picked as required.

A useful man on board.

We had six whale boats in davits and a dinghy across the stern, also two spare boats on skids. The crew numbered about 45, and 15 more were shipped at Lerwick, making a total of 60, which included a doctor and a shipkeeper, the latter being an old veteran, by name Davity Thompson, who in his own way, described himself as being in charge of "Ah thing that everybody else forgot." He was able, on account of his possession of an only mate's ticket, to take any position, as an officer if required, and was a capable man at flenshing or "making off" when necessary. He was popularly known as the "bear slayer" on account of some of his escapades; his name will crop up later. About 15 of the hands were seamen legally, but as there were about 15 or 20 real A.B.'s on board, the rest could be made to pull an oar somehow. The crowd looked strong and healthy, and would make a good show at sea or ashore. Everyone seemed to have a good kit, and in any case could replenish from the ship's slopchest, woollen mitts, scarves, guernseys, caps, etc., which were cheap and plenty of them.

So the sailing of the *Victor* was made lively by the usual parting and by the results of the libations that were offered to the gods of fortune. As I was

17 years of age, and had never seen so many men who so suddenly became of very little use - except as fighting units - I felt a deep feeling of repugnance and dislike at all the shouting and exchange of "pocket pistols." A few were late enough, and so were bundled into a boat as we steamed away, and hauled on board in the river.

Squaring up below.

As I have sailed and steamed over much water since then, and am now 69, my attitude is not now so squeamish about it.   I have, however, on many an occasion seen to it that the half-seas-over bully boys amongst my crews didn't get a whiff of their own Dutch - or Scotch courage after they had once put their foot on board. To continue. I found myself at the wheel, and after we had dropped our pilot off Tay Bar some attempt was made to set the watch, but the decks were now deserted, and the sounds of revelry and fighting that came from the crew's quarters, were not hopeful.

When daylight broke I got very busy, as the crowd below were sleeping off their hilarious "dust up," during which some of the chest lids had been kicked open. Some of my pet property had been badly mauled about; I heartily kicked some of the already bruised and damaged forms, but that didn't bring back the aunt's steak and kidney pie, or the master's plum cake, nor did it restore the contents of the chest to sweet cleanliness.

Neptune was good to us, and the 50 horses, manacled to the ship (under the funnel) kept a-going. The westerly wind freshened, and shortly after daylight some of us were making "square-sail," and trying to get some-thing to eat. Meantime the officers and bo's'un were shaking up the fat-headed ones. I was pleased to find that no one seemed to worry as to how they came by their cuts, general bruises, and corpulent ears, but cherished them as part of a good time, and were already looking forward to having a "hair from the dog" when we arrived at Lerwick.

A month's stores, which consisted of sugar, butter, tea, lime juice, tobacco, dried fruit and coffee, were served out, and all hands (except the cabin aft) had to cook their own breakfast and supper, and supply their own kettles, pans, pannikins. etc.   The cook, and his mate, cooked the dinner and supplied hot water, the coppers being replenished by the boys on watch. We had tinned meat and plum duff twice a week. Suet pudding and salt beef, or salt pork, five days a week and two days rice, or pea soup, and beef, or pork, seals' flippers, white bears' hams, and often salmon, caught in nets made on board, and wild ducks' eggs. The captain at times sent tinned milk, cheese or the tot of rum on Saturdays as a special favour.

The galley range was in the crew's living place, and was kept going all night. The quarters were warm and comfortable. Three men - one in each watch - slept in one bunk, and before retiring. Clothing was rolled carefully, and hung up with a small rope bucket so that if the crew were called to man boats they could take their bundle, get into the boat, and so take turns at dressing while those in the boats rowed away from the ship.

The *Victor* was fitted with a "trunk" at the fore part of the stern post. The propeller was two bladed, and fitted into a frame, or carriage, which could be hoisted up the trunk by a pair of sheer legs, a broken blade could be taken off the boss, and another bolted on. The carriage, or frame, could be then lowered to its working position when it fitted into a socketed flange on the propeller shaft and into a socket on the stern post. The whole was then screwed and wedged down and secured for work. When under sail the two blades were up and down ("feathered"). This arrangement was not repeated in the more modern ships, as they had fixed propellers with three blades, say, in *Arctic* and four blades in *Resolute*. In one case two blades were taken off after the fall fishing, in a West Greenland harbour before leaving the country for the passage home. The *Victor's* people (mate's watch) were able to change propeller blades and be under steam again in 1¾ hours.

This with three watches and three men on one bunk, also two boats' crews and a few to spare in each watch, took a ritual, and carried a lot of secret lobbying and some bargaining with "clothes washing," tobacco and even our possible rum messpots. The main things were to get into a good harpooneer's boat, also to get two bed-mates of cleanly habits, and with good bedding.

But to get back to our arrival in Lerwick. Our men required to complete the crew (all R.N.R.) were alongside, also some cases of slops were bundled on board, and without anchoring, we steamed to sea again. Fort William (about 200 men drilled there each winter) gave us a cheer as the garrison (or crew) stood easy, and then with a stentorian yell continued to "Repel boarders in the starboard bow," etc. So we found ourselves at sea, our bows pointing north, and we bowled away for Jan Mayen, with a whole sail westerly breeze.

Shetland lads satisfactory.

The Shetland hands were sober and clean, well supplied with good clothing, and two of them were harpooneers, and steady old lads they were. They had a ready fund of stories, re warlocks, witches, bogles, etc.

That night I found myself at the wheel, and our captain was stepping it out on the quarter-deck and singing to himself

"Fire up, fire up, fire up, down below,
There's all the bonny lasses waiting for me in Dundee, ye know."

We found that this ditty was a kind of hymn of praise and joy when things were going well. Many a time during the voyage I heard the opposite, viz.

"Erring children, prone to wander,
Lord, I feel it; Lord, I feel it,"

and have speculated on the identity of the erring one and his, or my, chances of proving an alibi.

Anyhow, *"Polaris"* was over our fore-topgallant yard, and our longitude was a little to the westward of Greenwich, so we picked up Northing fast and prepared for the seal fishing. The oil tanks (10 tons each) were full of coal leaving Dundee, and as we proceeded the tanks were emptied and cleaned, the bunkers being kept full. In about seven days from Shetland we made the ice, and after steaming along the loose heaving mush for 24 hours (heading N.E.) we entered the ice, steering to N.N.W., and I had my first experience of ice conditions. The grinding and crashing of large pieces around the bows, the creaking and groaning of the ship as the swell rose and fell, kept me on deck fascinated, until we had worked our way in. We were 10 or 12 miles from the open water before we lost the sea swell.

Off to the Sealing Grounds

We were now equipped with our gear for fishing, Viz., a pick, six inches long on a five-feet shaft, a heavy skinning knife in a large wooden sheath, a rope one inch, ten feet long, called a "lowery tow." which is used to lace up and drag the seal skins to the ship. Booms were hung overside, about two feet. from the ice for the men to jump to the ice or return to ship, etc.

We should now be amongst the seals. which are born on the ice about the middle or beginning of March. These patches of Saddleback seals are the objective of every sealer. Their name comes from a black band that runs from the back of the neck down each side. The young are absolutely white and are known as "whitey coats." The male takes no responsibility whatever in family matters, while the female seems continually consumed about her beautiful white baby. She is apparently never at rest, never mistakes her own when she gets on the ice to suckle it. So, day after day the cubs grow, are taught to take the water, to swim, for themselves. This goes on for five or six weeks from birth. The ships were timed to get on the sealing grounds while the young are still unable to take the water, and many thousands are often killed in a radius of 20 miles. A young seal puts on fat very fast, and ships have lain amongst them and awaited their growth, often weighing the living cubs, to see what improvement has been made. When the young Saddle is a month old he loses his white jacket, and dons a coat of coarse hair, dark grey black spots, and as soon as he takes to the water on his own, instinct guides him and he keeps going north. He attains maturity in his third year; there seems to be no pairing off with the Saddleback seals, but they gather in immense hoards.

The Bladder-nosed Seal as a husband.

The Hood seals of Newfoundland are known as bladder-nosed seals by Scotch sealers. These not only pair, but do not mix with the saddles, and they are so named on account of a large bag of loose skin on the top part of its head. When enraged he can swell this to the size of a football; this is so thick that buck shot, unless at very close range, will not penetrate it. It is thus a protection, and may be used to impress and frighten in private quarrels. The hood or bladder does not appear on the female, and does not adorn the male until his third year, when he seeks a mate. Once paired he regards this a knot tied for life. If bladder-nosed seals are met about the 10th or 20th March, when the young are being born, they will always be in pairs. Kill a female, and the male (if absent) will invariably return to the spot to seek her. If the sealer meets bladder-noses now, he must reckon on the fighting male. The defenceless mother may be killed with a stroke of the pick, but at the first sign of danger, be it man or beast, the male swiftly shuffles across the ice to meet it. He might easily slip into the safety of the water, but prefers to die in defence of his family. The motive in this case is probably not so much affection as his pugnacious nature. The young male will show the same spirit when seven or eight days old, snapping savagely at the club or pick which kills him.

Our captain was now remaining longer in the "crow's nest," and as the ship could not make much headway through the heavy ice the order would be passed along, "Prepare to roll ship." All boats, frappings, and belts would be cast adrift, braces would be slacked, the blacksmith's anvil would be hoisted on the main stay, all hands would be called out, and at the word "Over" from the mate. the crowd would "rush" from one side to the other. After keeping this up for four or five hours we would settle down to "coal shifting" again.

Not a bad day's work.

So for a day or two the ship was butted through the floes, then a couple of boats' crews would be sent ahead of the ship with some of the green hands to get used to ice travelling; if lucky they might fall in with a couple of dozen seals and get "blooded." We picked up 200 pelts here and there, and the skinning and rolling six or eight pelts and lacing them up so that you dragged them with the lay of the hair (each skin projecting half over the other, and then dragging them to the ship, got to be "something like" the thing.

One forenoon all hands were sent out to the N.W., and we walked about two or three miles, in a fall of snow, when we were recalled by the ship's whistle. The propeller had struck a black piece of ice, which had come under the ship, and rising under her counter, had stripped a blade. By the time the people got on board and the roll had been called, the snow was very thick, and with two hands missing and the fresh wind having changed, there was some danger of the ice "opening up," so the dinghy was manned, and the ship kept her whistle going whilst the hands got another blade out of the 'tween decks, and rigged the sheers over the trunk, and in one and a half hours a new blade was fitted, and a cradle or carriage secured. Our two lost men turned up for dinner, and our " quiet" second mate publicly thanked them for their punctuality. The cook pretended that their duff had been whacked out to the living, and so all was well.

The weather cleared 48 hours afterwards, and no seals could be found, although scouts went out for about eighty miles. Bad weather came on, strong gales from westward, which continued for a while. Shortly afterwards a bear was sighted to the eastward. He was approaching the ship with a long lopping gait at almost the speed of an ordinary horse. A few finks of fat, or a piece of shark's liver, which was being rendered down in the stoke hold to be used in lubricating the engines were thrown in the furnaces, to encourage poor bruin. Once he stopped and rose up on his haunches to sniff, then away he came again. A terrible figure, gaunt and starving, that lopeing trot, brought him within 200 feet of the ship, and he arose, erect, on his hind legs, with his great paws extended as if defying the ship, and its puny occupants. He dropped, with a projectile from the mate's "Martini Henry," which went in under his chin and out through his brain.

The old sealers shook their heads as they stripped the pelt off him, and found two pebbles in his stomach. "There's no seals for a hundred miles," said they. His hams were hung on the martingale stay for food, and the skin was salted and packed away.

An unprofitable voyage.

To return to our sealing. Time, April 22nd, 1877. We had drawn the Arctic Ocean through all kinds of ice to lat. 78.40 N., long. 3 E., and south again; it was now evident that we had "drawn it blank," and that our sealing voyage was a failure. Our bag did not exceed 500 seals, three bears and 15 sharks, which were harpooned whilst nibbling the salt junk through a hole in the ice. So the ship was headed south for Dundee, and the refit and store for the whaling to Davis Straits; as we reluctantly came south we sighted Jan Mayan, 40 miles off. The Victor, Jan Mayan, Nova Zembla, Hope, Intrepid and less powerful of the Scotch ships went to this West Ice sealing and it was a few years later given up as not payable. Several vessels from Norway carried on with varying success. In 1909 the Balaena, of Dundee, caught four whales and a few narwhal between 78 min. N., 1 min. W. and 79 min. N., 1 min. E., and lost one whale in dense fog which almost daily hampered the fishing. She sighted several Norwegian sloops out for old seals, narwhal and white whales, walrus, etc.

So we landed the 16 Shetland men at Lerwick, later arrived in Dundee, and very little time was occupied in landing our poor catch. There were people employed in coaling, shipping the whaling gear, storing her with provisions, etc., for every conceivable contingency. Her 200 tons of tank space for oil was supplemented by "shakes" large half-ton casks, collapsed, and hooped to save space which being reassembled and coopered would hold about 70 to 80 tons of oil. Much care was taken to see that all stores were stacked in very stout watertight oak barrels, or casks, and kept handy in case the ship had to be abandoned.

First Whaling Voyage, May 3rd, 1877

We sailed from Camperdown Dock, and as the sealing trip had not been an "El Dorado" - monthly pay, minus a bit of advance and a couple of white stocking-days, which didn't leave much to jubilate about - our farewells were dour as a kirk session. We called at Lerwick to pick up our decent "Shelties" to fill up the crew list, and to replenish the slop chest. The contents of the ordinary ship's slop chest has been held up to contempt, but the Scotch whale fishers — being what they are — knew what was good in sea clothing, and many blessings went up in the Arctic weather for the fleecy gear that protected us.

On arrival at Lerwick we found two other whalers there on our own errand, and by some means some of the men from each vessel got ashore, and after a bit of a mix-up amongst themselves, they then " turned on" to the police. Where the fighting juice came from was at first a mystery, but when the yarns were spun afterwards "an illicit still manufactured the fire-water," and the welcome of the guide and his saga to them and to the old fiddler " Spring thy bow, Joonie; spring thy bow, now, and play up 'Scallaway Lassies,' for here comes them Dundee Scotch lads, what spends der money freely; sit thee doon by the ingle, lad, and tak' thee a tatter and roast it to thysel'."

"Hands to the pumps!"

Anyhow, before finishing up, the gang got into a hat shop, and the special constables and captains escorted them afloat - all hands wearing a varied - assortment of head-gear. The cost of the damage etc. was all slumped together and each ship was debited with one third of it. After sailing, the official log was written up, and a copy nailed up in the half-deck. I found myself, like everyone else, debited with 2/4 as my reward for remaining on board and " missing the fun." After getting away to sea and clearing the land, a strong south-westerly wind with which a high sea sprung up, and the "old man" being in the mind to hang the full courses and main topgallant on to her, made the old ship shake things up a bit. The engines were stopped for economy, and the real " sailors" were busy with preventer stays, also bending a new main topgallant sail, and a jib, to replace the losses. The fore top gallant mast was found to be sprung, and it had to be housed and secured. The yard was sent down, and the watch slithered about in the "wash" and their "Handy Billy" "sweating up" everything under the orders of the leading "afterguards." It was not surprising that the little ship required some pumping after the hard ramming she had endured in the ice on the sealing trip. Anyhow, the mate pointed out that pulling the bell rope on the fly wheel pump was a splendid training for men who were not yet expert at pulling an oar, and so it was ordained that the pumps were manned and relieved by the "bad lads" who got adrift at Lerwick. The sea began to rise from the N.W., and the cross sea filled her decks as she drove into it, and so we all "shook down" to our proper places with two helmsmen and a spare hand "standing by." A good honest summer Atlantic breeze, and the lash of the spray whipping one to healthy action. The "old man," hanging on to the life lines on the weather side of the little quarter deck, quietly watching her ways and lovingly chided her. "Lift to 'em Old Vic.," and sometimes admonished her ladyship with his " Up, my lassie," then as the roaring top of a sea crashed and flew in spray up to the tops, so she lurched to leeward with a quick mad jerk, and pitched on the crest of the wave as it passed under her. A little laugh came out of the night from the figure under the weather topgallant rail, who, like everyone else, had been brought low and lost their legs, " Ye did that fine, ye auld hussy."

Victor Outward Whaling Passage

Our North-Wester blew itself "out" (and so did the next one, and the one that followed it) meantime the stumpy little funnel aft was not "even an ornament," and our canvas, even the " bentic foresail," with its slovenly looking, but handy boom, saved much coal. The deck pump "boxes" clucked, and clinked, merrily, until the old ship's topsides felt the benefit of her immersion, and the planking tightened up. So the pump sucked sooner, and at last was itself an ornament. So the ship was pushed to the north-westward for Cape Farewell. The weather moderated as we approached Greenland, and on inquiring we learned that our "Westing" was helped by the "Polar current" which curves into Davis Straits from Denmark Strait. At last we sighted land, 25 miles off, on our starboard beam. A high rugged coast-line, about one thousand to two thousand feet high, covered by ice and snow. Somewhere about Godhaven. Next day, calm and fog, steaming with sails furled, amongst loose ice. So we continued, and crossed the "Arctic Circle," May 18th, 1877. A few days afterwards there was no night; the sun describing a small circle during the 24 hours and being high in the heavens. After passing many icebergs and much loose ice, we called at Lively Harbour, in Disco Island.

Disco Island.

A Danish trading station on the Greenland side of Davis Straits. The Danes on these settlements were a governor, schoolmaster, cooper, blacksmith, carpenter, their Danish wives and a few of their families. A Danish Government sailing brig used to make one voyage a year, calling along the Greenland coast for oil, furs, ivory, etc. The Scotch whalers were made welcome at these settlements, and the welcoming shout of the Eskimo, "Chimo-Chimo," was proof that for years a good feeling had existed. After permission had been obtained from the Governor, a picked landing party, in charge of an officer, was allowed to "kick up their heels" on a large flat rock. The Eskimo lasses had crude and very strenuous ideas of dancing. The schoolmaster was M.C., and an efficient "Vigilance Committee" of the "rude fathers" of the Innuit Tribe shepherded their fat little "Kudlays" and "Evaloos." We literally dragged them through reels, polkas and any old thing that would fit the occasion. But there was no "sitting-out." We had been allowed ashore to dance, and by the "Great snatch block" there was no time allowed to "rub noses" (the Eskimo equivalent for billing and cooing). So at one a.m. we parted. After thanking the Governor, and after an exchange of threepenny-pieces and sixpences for highly-dyed seal skin, tobacco, fobs, etc., and escorted by the happy-faced little women and their men folk, not forgetting whole troops of dogs, whose barking and howling sent back strange echoes from the hills.

We took to our boats, and back to the ship as she weighed anchor and so proceeded north. Whilst we had been ashore the disgruntled ones had expressed disapproval of the doctor, who had been deputed to "pick" the dance party. The little "medico" demanded a "take back." The hesitation of the "looker-for-trouble" left him on his back " looking" up with unseeing eyes at the doc. standing over him for a few minutes. There were some questions asked aft, and the captain said the men who were especially allowed ashore at Disco, had stayed by the ship at Lerwick, and that was the end of the matter.

It was said that some of the 'ero's of the "hat raid" in Shetland heard the "old man" singing his newest song after sailing from Disco.

> Rob Roryson's bonnet, "lang syne" it was new,
> It's red tooree's awa', and it's gay ribbons, too,
> And its liker a "nose bag" than a bonnet o' blue,
> It sairs for a kale bag and tattee poke, noo;
> And he tried it wi' brose, but it loot out the brew,
> And you've aw heard tell o' Rob Roryson's bonnet,
> You've aw heard tell o' Rob Roryson's bonnet.
> But, it wasna the bonnet, 'twas the head that was in it,
> Made the hale village talk o' Rob Royston's bonnet.

Melville Bay.

We were now steaming along the Greenland coast — about 15 miles off to the northward, and thus avoiding the strong southern drift of the Polar current and its flotsam of large bergs and heavy field ice. To reach Melville Bay and pass through its dangerous area to the expected open water in Smith Sound, and on our fishing grounds, and then follow the ice south, along the western shores of Baffin's Bay and Davis Straits. The Greenland coast was lined by stranded bergs of massive size and fantastic shapes, which our "old hands" recognised as having been there for more than an Arctic whaleman's lifetime. To the writer, young and impressionable, it was a delight to sit forward on the "head" — when not shifting coal or on watch — and forget my losing fights with Jock Mullock, in the blue transparent sea — visible clear down for many fathoms with eider duck, looms and geese, which mesmerised by the rushing, noisy monster which was thrusting aside with its iron-shod forefoot the heavy drifting ice-floes, darting ahead under water, with outspread wings until, becoming tired, they swerve and come up alongside, to dive and swim again and again. Ah! snow-covered blue ice, sunshine all the time, and a sea of sapphire: the teeming bird and animal life of Arctic spring, and health to enjoy it all.

So we passed Upper Navic and zig-zagged to pick up leads of loose ice to work north und keep the coast aboard just able to see the rushing waters in the valleys as the snow and ice melted. So in a few days we see in the clear air a steamer's smoke ahead, and find *Narwhale, Intrepid*, and *Active*, who are stopped by an ice jamb that has piled layer after layer of two-feet cakes of floe, one above the other; they had rammed it for some time and had tried gun-cotton. etc. We are soon busy ramming the neck and "rolling ship," and after a few hours of this, smoke is sighted to the southward, and when the newcomer was seen to be Funnel Amidships, otherwise *Arctic*, our operations were suspended for the assistance of the heavier ship. She had left Dundee some days after us, and was, by some, considered too long for her job, but as she approached one could see that in this ice her power and weight were in her favour. Her usual good fortune she was always a "well fished ship" — helped her, for just as she came up a report was spread from our mast-head that the "pressure" was easing.

An Ice Jamb.

As the *Arctic* approached we backed away and left a clearance for the new arrival to try "his metal" in forcing a passage. So with our "Sunday Ensigns" flying at the peak we awaited the *Arctic*, whose master hailed us, from her nest, and inquired if "there was a wedding." There was a flutter of excitement as she took the neck in her stride, and, with her masts and gear all "a shake" and rattling with the shock, her bow was thrown to starboard with a heavy roll, her head lifted, and bore down on the over-lapped floes, and broke them, and so she screwed, and rolled, her way through into the loose ice of the lead, northward. The other ships followed only after some punching, as the moving floes caused "a nip" that quickly closed the "lead" after *Arctic* had got through. In this connection, an argument on our ship as to the merits and popularity of the various skippers resulted in our "alleged" poet, "The Baazer" having the "last word" by writing on the school slate the following:

Arctic - Your straight, hard punching made our toil a *jest*,
We "cut no ice" - wanting an A.1. "clipper;"
Here's to the *whiskers, brain* and *brawn* that overflows *your*
nest,
Thank Providence who sent a ship, and much the heaviest   skipper.

We gradually fought our way towards, and through, Melville Bay, after being beset at one ice jamb after another, or, we had left some ship beset by heavy ice. The *Active*, being the smallest, and least powerful, was badly used and suffered from the nips, and, on one occasion, was partly covered by the ice driving on and overlapping her. The crew and boats, stores and food, were on the crushing, grinding floes, and the almost capsized ship, whose main hatchway was described as being "diamond shaped," had been "given up"," when the ice ceased "running" and the squeeze died down. After some time she uprighted herself and with some assistance from other vessels was able to (as I heard the story) "prosecute the voyage." Anyhow, there is no "turning back" from Melville Bay. Our little ship *Victor* was no better for the squeezes of "The Bay," but like the rest of the grand old fleet, settled back to her shape with a squeak from her timbers occasionally, as she resumed her normal condition. We had killed four walrus and three bears before sighting McCarey Islands, and our taxidermist (the blacksmith's mate) had caught, and was stuffing, several "snow bunting" to add to his collection of looms and eider ducks. Although we were late in arriving off Carey Islands being the last days of May — permission was given to try and get some eggs, and a boat was sent ashore to do so. Many hundreds must have been brought on board, and stored in a tank in layers of salt. The ducks themselves who sat on the eggs, on the bare rocks, until they were "knocked off" and killed, were brought off by a second boat, and the breasts fried in their own fat were on the menu for three weeks at breakfast, and five or six eggs — a la "panhag" —- for a week or two for tea. Here in lat. 78 deg. N. and long. 73 deg. W., the land and sea "teemed " with life. As the weather became warmer, fog became frequent, and we had, after leaving "Heyes Peninsula," a succession of foggy and overcast days. The ice, however, was loose, and waterlogged, and we proceeded cautiously towards "Devon Land," keeping as good a look out as was possible for whales and drifting bergs. We were now close to the magnetic Pole, and a slight change in our position to the westward produced a large change in the variation (which is nearly 100 degrees), the compass becomes sluggish, and almost useless for making a course in thick weather.

NOTE. — Melville Bay accounted for the loss of 14 whalers in 1819 and for 19 in 1830; of course, these were sailing vessels.

The Whale Boat.

To the modern whale "bomber," with his blubber and whale meat "digesters" and his equipment for "inflating" his easy "quarry," the following details will not appeal, but to those who can appreciate the qualities of head and hand necessary for the hunt of the whale in a 24-ft. boat, they should act as a reminder of the men who did "so much" with "so little." Like the "old has-beens" of "sailor" times, they were proud of doing the lot themselves, and did not ask for handy "little buttons" to "push."

Mainly explanatory, but nevertheless interesting.

The boat is "caulker" built with a bluff, roomy stern to coil the whale-line in (4½ lengths of 90 fathoms say, 400 fathoms of 2½in. hemp requires some space and reduces the boat's freeboard) and a little stiffened forecastle deck is fitted in the bow. The harpoon swivel gun is mounted on a hard wood bollard, slightly on the port bow, on this little deck. A small kid, to hold six fathoms of 2in. manilla, called the "foregoer," projects half over the starboard bow. a 9in. hardwood bollard is fitted between — and just abaft of the gun bollard, and the foregoer kid, or tub. This bollard is used to "wring" the fish, when the harpoon has been fired into it and is "said" to be "fast." The manilla "foregoer" is spliced into the wire shackle of the harpoon, and the end of the 2½ in. hemp (tarred) whale-line is brought from aft, passed above the thwarts, between the crew, on the left of the stroke No. 4 (line manager), right of No. 3, left of No. 2, right of No. 1, and left of harpooner, so that when he stands up to his gun the whale-line will be on his right hand ready (for the use of the bollard), it is spliced to the inner end of the 2in. manilla foregoer with a short splice.

When the gun is fired the "foregoer" follows the harpoon, and if the fish is fastened, the boat-steerer runs out his steering oar, steps off the coiled whale-line (which he has been standing on) into a little foot space in the run of the stern, whips off the canvas cover from the lines, which tows by its lanyard and squats there, only allowing one fake to rise at a time. The crew lay their oars across the boat at the sound of the gun, and lean on them, to keep the line free from jumping when the fish "sounds." The stroke pours water on the line during the rush to avoid the line heating the bollard, and when the fish "easies her sound" the harpooner gets a turn, perhaps two, on the bollard and tries to "wing her." The danger then is that a sudden "sound" will fill the boat from over the bow if too many turns are on the bollard. The longer the fish can be "kept down," the longer she has to stay on top, and gives a second boat an opportunity to get "fast." In shallow water, where the fish cannot "sound" the whale is liable to keep the boats pulling here, and there in attempts to get more harpoons in her, and guessing where she will "come up" next time, for many hours. Ice and bergs are dangerous to boats and hard on whale-lines.

There are five oarsmen, including the harpooner. Everything is done to deaden the noise, and much grease is used at the thole pin to ensure proper feathering of oars. Swabs are laid on bottom boards as a hint that clattering the feet about is not a popular (if noisy) way of warning them. The heavy steering oar is fitted like the rest - with mats and grummits - and with an iron pin on a cross plank, which projects about 18in to port; this gives the boat-steerer power to 'sweep' the boat quickly from his foothold on the canvas cover of the whale-lines.

With her equipment of sail, mast, grapnel, two lances for killing, rocket-gun, hand harpoon, fresh water, whale-line, harpoon gun, bread, canned food and a (so-called) "conjuror" to make tea, etc., and swabs and bailers, she always was to me a wonder, and it was fine to see her in a jump of a sea, "ran up" by her tackle crew, guns, whale-lines, harpoons and gear all in place. The davit tackles hook on to ring bolts in front of the stem, and outside of the stern; there is no rudder or other fitments. Well might the writer's "Sire" an old (84) and experienced whaler, when speaking of the results of a naval polar expedition of that time, remark "They couldn't have done less if they had gone in a whale boat."

The Nest.

Sometimes called "the barrel," is a specially-made elongated "barrel;" it is substantial and securely clamped to the specially-made topgallant mast pole. The hinged bottom rises when the head and shoulders push it up; it is furnished with a flap seat, a wire to the engine-room gong, an iron circular bar to spread a little "dodger." and a signaling disc, like a "frying-pan." Long distance signals to boats are made by the fore-topgallant sail and its clues, also yard, up or down. A substantial wire ladder comes down to the after shroud of the main rigging.

The "North Water."

We were now in comparatively ice-clear water, except for the land ice, which extended in places for many miles from the shore. In some places at the mouth of a stream swollen by the glacier melting in a valley the land could be approached by the ship. So we work our way westward up Lancaster Sound in light winds, and under sail (to husband our fuel), and near the North Devon Land the boats are sent away to a school of White Whales, off an inlet, in a small bay. We "pulled across and across its entrance, making whatever din and noise with mallets, etc., on the boat's bottom boards, that could be made, and after many hours of splashing, rattling of tins and much continuous rowing, we got the school started for the rocky beach at the head of the bay. The idea was to get them in the shallow water at or about high water, where they become stranded, and are killed by lances, as the tide recedes. Many lance shafts were broken by the struggles and "lashing about" of the dying mammals. There were some hundreds in the school, but our bag was about 50. They were 10 to 14 feet long, and the thick coating of blubber had to be stripped off and then towed about three or four miles off to the ship. An arduous and miserable job with all hands, the boats and the beach, a wretched welter of blood and filth. A waterfall, splashing from the high land was although ice cold a godsend. The weather being fairly warm the sea water blood-stained and infested with ground sharks was welcomed as a dipping pool at intervals. The result was about five tons of blubber. A couple of tides afterwards we landed again at the same fiord to try for bears, but had to be content to stick a harpoon into a shark or two, who were busy "cleaning up" the beach; one of those, after being hauled ashore and his tail chopped off, still floundered away, and managed to escape to the water, where his brother scavengers "took him to their bosoms" at once.

"Greenland's Icy Mountains."

The ship is bow "on" to the land floe (ice), off Lancaster Sound, and about 15 miles from the land, which was "low" with mountains in the distance she was moored with an ice anchor on each bow, with a 6in.rope on each, which kept her "stem on." Both sides of the ship were thus, kept clear for boat work. We had been there a couple of days and had all our defects as boatmen proclaimed to " Greenland's icy Mountains" by "long suffering" leather-lunged mates and harpooners. The captain had called on "all his gods" to witness that he had never seen such a gory, blue-speckled lot of crab-catchers. All this, and a few changes and "cut outs," had shaken the crowd down, and now the carpenter is overside on a stage, caulking the topsides. The blacksmith is welding some broken lances. "Sails" is making blubber shoots and pudding bags for the galley, with No. 5 canvas. The bosun has some hands re-mousing the brace-pennant clip-hooks. The writer known as the "Skipper's white-haired laddie" by some of the "hard cases" and whose job on the articles was the high-sounding one of "line-manager," had been made captain's boy by someone, and I was overhauling the seizings on the wood ratlings of the captain's nest ladder, which ran from the main top to the crow's nest at the topgallant masthead. The harpooner in the nest reports "Eskimo sledges coming from the land." Shortly afterwards the captain goes aloft, and I can now see the three teams of sledges and dogs. The crew below hear of "Huskies" (Eskimos) and come up by ones and twos. In a while the dogs can be heard. The captain's glass, however, is not pointing to the land, but is "taking in" the "open sea" right astern, with some ice and bergs drifting south. Suddenly comes the order, "Lower away the watch," and then, "Stop all that row on deck." "Tell the engineer to get up steam." "Chips" tumbles inboard and dumps his gear below. The watch drop everything, and they like the doctor, carpenter and second engineer all jump for the two boats, and away they go towards a little berg, and what looks like a faint little lazy jet of steam in the cold air. Now the Eskimos can be heard exhorting the dogs, "Hush-huck" (to get up) and their welcoming shouts, "Chimo Chimo" is repeated by the women and shrilled by the children. "Philaday — Philaday." The dogs adding their music to the sounds, echoed from the little iceberg in the offing.

There she blows !

The shipkeeper calls the next watch of two boats' crews to "take over" deck duties. The captain, with a disc at the end of a short stick, is signalling the two boats to alter course to starboard, but they have already something else in view. Then the "blast" of a fish can be seen — far to seaward and another; I try to say "There she blows" in an ordinary speaking tone, but it was, somehow, much too loud for the old Peterhead harpooner on the bridge, who growled out "Keep yer breath to cool yer porridge." The order is given from the nest "Call a fall," and someone, anyone, EVERYONE yells down the scuttle, "A fall; a fall." The cook bangs his hand-spike (he keeps it for the purpose) along the decks, and bumps and bawls, "A fall a fall." A stream of men in stocking feet, with their clothing and boots in a "rope bucket," scramble up, and into the four boats, so, amidst the shouts and orders of officers and harpooners, the "chimos" of the arriving Eskimos and the excited "nankooting" (yowling) of their 24 dogs, the boats were "dropped" and the crews "pulled away" in their underclothes to the insistent orders to

"Give way, there," from the harpooners and boat steerers, and "Lay back to it, man," from the nest.

Innuit Eskimo Dogs.

The writer had been, shortly before the "Fall" was called, told to help the steward to hand out some tobacco for Eskimos, four tins milk for the Eskimo women, and a tin of Scotch sweeties for the piccaninnies. Even the dogs were not forgotten, and an ash bucket of very ripe sharks' livers were part of the "job." Interested in this, and excited by the "fish," he just failed to get his place as stroke of the mate's boat. He scurried about," but failed even to get an "oar." Whilst lowering one of the boats, someone in her - a wag it was - yelled an order from the "spectioneer" (third mate) to get a wooden toggle for the "cant" tackle and "grease" it well, ready for when they brought the fish alongside. I could laugh with the rest at the "oily" joke, but inwardly promised to get a "boat" next "fall," if I slept in her for a week to do it. Anyhow; the captain, although much interested in the "fish," took pains to explain to the Eskimos that they were welcome, and spoke to them by name, and in their language said "the ship would return." So I had to dump the oily mess of sharks' livers on the floe for the dogs. The savage, hungry pack evidently looked upon the writer as part of the "feast," and — for a fearful minute or so I felt sure, that like "Daniel in the den of lions whoever said grace after the meal it would not be me. The whips were brought into play by their masters, and with women and children shrieking threats at their animals, they were driven off. As ordered, I unhooked the ice anchors, and shinned up the "head gear" with the loss of a good portion of trouser leg. The last seen of the dogs was three of them jammed in the ash bucket, evidently eating each other, in the attempt to lick it clean, whilst the rest of them tried to haul them out piecemeal.

The Cant Tackle.

The ship backed away from the floe edge, and the boats having got fast to a fish, those of us who remained on board were bustled about by the captain, the shipkeeper, and one of the extra harpooners in rigging the gear to get the blubber on hoard. The most important purchase was the "Cant" tackle. Two enormous wood four-fold blocks had a 5-in. rope rove in them; the upper block was lashed round the foremast head, the lower one was fitted with a double strop and toggle, and was overhauled over the ship's side right down to the whale, which was moored forward by a chain round its tail, and with a couple of grapnels from its lips and "bowsed" tight to abaft the main rigging. The men on the fish, using a sharp spade, cut down through the outer coating of blubber, and its blue covering to the flesh. They lifted up this "flap," which was, say, 3ft. 6in. broad, and cut a hole in it. The lower block strop of the cant was pushed through this hole and the "toggle" put through it. The cant fall, leading from a centre sheave of the upper block, was then led to the windlass and hove on until the upper portion of whale was well out of the water. The whole of this surface blubber having been cut and lifted off by the " after speck" fall and the "fore spec" fall, and were dropped into the between decks to allow the water to get off the blubber and drain away.

The Flenshing.

The top surface having been stripped, the "spade" men cut the "flap" or "strip" of blubber so that, with a good weight being kept on the cant, the strip gradually rolls the carcass round until the top surface can be again cleaned off. So the cant remains on the turning strip until the whole of the round of the fish is cleaned off. At stated positions of the lips, the tongue, the whale bone and fins are removed, and when all is done, the grapnel is unhooked from the lips and the tail is taken on board in sections the chain slips off the stump of the tail and the strip of blubber, which the cant is fast to — sometimes the cant tackle is two blocks (say, 40 feet long) is cut from the flesh, and slowly the carcass sinks. The tail and fins are used as chopping blocks to cut the blubber small at the "making off."

Making off.

The "flenshing" would take about (on the average) eight hours. The work would probably be much interrupted if there were any fish about. The *Camperdown*, at "Ponds Bay," in the previous year killed 16 fish in three days and decided that they had enough. They, however, lost so much time in getting them aboard, on account of bad weather and in "making them off," that the toll taken by sharks and other sea scavengers reduced the blubber so much, and from other reasons, the ship was far from "full" and she never got another chance to get fast that season.

After the blubber has "drained" for 24 to 36 hours it is hoisted on deck and "chopped up," the outer skin and any adhering flesh has to be cleaned off. The whale bone has to be carefully split and cleaned (a tedious and long job); it is put in a cool and dry place. The blubber is put into tanks and requires to be tended as it swells, or lowers, plugs in the top of tank lids, being adjusted to such conditions. A perfect armoury of long cutters, choppers, forks. slicers, spakes, spurs - to stand on the fish with - blubber hooks, can hooks, etc., etc. The work itself takes about nine or ten hours.

The "Fall" may call all hands to the boats more than once or twice in these operations, and probably keep them away for four or six hours without any result.

The Capture.

About the middle of June we had taken three medium-sized whales, some 52 white whales, one male narwhale with eight-feet horn, four female ditto, three or four walrus, three small deer on the high table lands - also we had (after making our own nets) taken at various small streams and Clyde river, many salmon and trout; these were dried in the rigging and, like the venison, were consumed as required. Four bears had been shot on the ice and two on the land. The deer and most of the bears had fallen to our chief mate, Mr. J. Fairweather, a keen gunner and a "merciful" shot.

About this time, and since getting into the "North Water" our sails had again "come into their own," coal was precious. Less ice and more clear water room meant yard trimming, tacking ship, and work to do aloft . . . I admit I always liked a new job, even when it came as an addition to all my other jobs, so when, whilst lacing a paunch mat over the lanyards of the main rigging I was called away, handed a "fowling piece" and hailed by the mate to go with him "after a bear", I just slung his and my own cartridges over my shoulder and "hopped off" after him. A slight mist on the ice made objects loom up a bit, we got away over the bow, the second mate from the nest said (in answer to the mate), "There seems to be three of them," I ventured to ask Mr. F. as we plodded along "What am I to do with a shot gun?' " but got no answer. I tried again with "What's to happen if we meet them?" He gave a grim chuckle and replied, "Ye'r just to round them up to me, till I'll get a mark on them." Something I'd read of being "butchered to make a Roman holiday," but I pushed desperately ahead of him and stopped to look at his face, saw nothing strange there, so plodded on. After walking in a circle for three or more miles to get to leeward of the bears, we saw a boat had left the ship as arranged and it pulled away off and along the floe. So after much sore crouching and scrambling under the lee of the rough overlapping ice to get cover we came to a high hummock. I was told to go round one way and he the mate would go the other. I had not felt much of the thrill of the hunter up to now, and as he turned away I asked savagely if I was to shoot if I met anything, but with some remark about "keeping out of his line of fire," he trudged off. Angry and sore, I blundered ahead, trailing my useless "Duck blinder," and not much caring whether a bear or a dozen came my way. So I ran and stumbled, and when nearly round the hummock I heard a shot, and putting my best foot forward, was glad to see a dead bear, with two well grown cubs snarling and snapping around the mate and their dead dam. The boat's crew arrived and dragged the old bear to the floe edge. The mate and I shepherded and prodded the two needle-clawed cubs towards the water. Soon we got the assistance of the boat's crew, and rounded them up and so, after several "break aways," we got them in the water, secured them with an eye "sling" through the bow and stern ring-bolts of the boat, and with their dead mother towing astern, we went alongside. The cubs were hoisted on deck, and hauled down to a ringbolt in the hatch combings. The old bear was skinned. The cooper and his mate were "turned to" and "made up" two large "shakes" (half-tun casks). The rope sling around the necks of the cubs was passed through the bung-holes in the bottom of these casks, and they were hauled in. The cooper then put hoop iron across the open end, and drove hoops over and "on" to hold these bars in position; the ropes were "let go" and bruin was "at home" with plenty of luscious bear meat to start with; whale, seal or narwhale flesh, and any old scraps to "carry on" with. Occasionally a bucket of pea soup was squirted through the engine-room syringe into the ever-open gullets, and a good wash with the deck hose every morning to keep them white, clean and healthy.

Off "Coutts Inlet," Baffin Land, we had chased a few fish and had lost the run of them in the patches of fog. Three boats were "out," and an occasional whistle fixed their position as about half a mile astern. The ship had been dodging under topsails with a light air of wind. "Forecastle" reported, "ice close to;" topsails were clewed up, and the "floe edge" "brought up" the ship. The ice anchors suspended from the end of bowsprit were dropped by the tripping lines and secured in the ice. While clewing up the topsails, and securing the anchors, a whale "broke water" close alongside, and gave a "full-lunged blast." The surprise and tense excitement of the first 30 or 40 seconds was complete. Then every one rushed to the three boats at the davits one word from the skipper in the nest "silence." This was indeed no time for yelling orders so "Pantomime" and a variegated supply of whispered profanity, plus one's own training, filled up the gap.

The writer had "shinned down" from aloft, and slipping from the fore topmast backstay, scrambled on to the davits and tumbled into the only boat on the port side where the whale had "come up." I found myself in the boat-steerer's place, and although only a "line manager," and I had no right to the "sweep oar," I was intent on hanging on to the job that would put me in the "killing," and hoped to hold it (in the rush) by right of possession.

"This boat," says the second mate in a whisper (and he indicated ours). "Pantomime", from the harpooner, mate and some by myself. A good healthy "blast" from the fish, which was moving ahead right under the boat's keel, "more panto" to "lower the boat," and so she was quietly lowered, with her bow lower than her stern. "Dinna forget yer pin, Sandy," almost whispered the mate. and then a bit louder, "What say year, now," and, as the fish kept on the move and cleared the boat, Sandy Donald, the "man behind our gun," yelled "Let go all," depressed his muzzle, took out his safety pin and as the fish made "a back to" sound, fired into it. The great tail "slashed" out of the water and "lashed up" a few inches clear of the boat's bow, half filling us with water. The falls were "let go" and the movement of the fish's "propeller" (tail) and the manner of her going, washed the boat away off. Then pandemonium broke loose, and " A fall, a fall." I cleared the cover off the lines, cut the after davit fall, which had fouled the lower block, and unhooked the same, dropping it into "Davy Jones' locker," while the whale line was screaming out under the men's crossed oars. Meantime, we had (with mad haste and some foreboding) plied the bailers to get the water out of the boat. Someone on deck was bawling to "pass the end of our whale lines to one of the boats who were coming" (to the sound of our gun) from astern. Sandy growled through his beard, "Pump or sink, this is our fish." Then someone warned us that "there was too much water in the boat," and in a roar that drowned the cautious one's voice, Donald ordered us to " Bail awa', ye deils buckies, yons your fush; hey, a bonny fush."

Just as we had made some impression on the water, "the bonny fush" eased her run, and a half turn on the bollard, (I prefer to think by design) whisked us away from the ship. The speed the fish then "got up" rushed the water aft, and after running out another line to lift the stern up, and avoid shipping water aft, we soon dealt with the water, so the worst of our troubles, viz., the ship, the boats, and the question of handing over the fish (the captive of our harpoon). These were all now behind us, in the fog. There was, of course, some chance of being dragged into collision with "washed" ice, or of losing the ship in the fog.

The harpooner said, "It's no sounding as it ought till, but it's a bonny fush." After an hour of speed with a couple of lines out, the whale circled back "dipping" and rising to blow every few minutes. Some time later we crossed ahead of our boats, one of them had a flying shot at her but did not get her fast. We now made a drogue with the boat's mast, sail, etc., rigged with a "bridle" to try and reduce the speed. It, however, interfered with the sweep of our steer oar and had to be unrigged. About this time her liveliness began to abate, so we were able to "shorten in" and recoil some of our line, and then found ourselves passing near the ship, they sent the dinghy which fired a rocket that glanced off the fish's crown and exploded in the air. Later on another boat got a chance and a second gun harpoon was planted in her, the "shackle" being "butt up."

Eventually the boats gathered around, and as she rolled and lifted her fins the long (two-way cut) lances, were thrust "in" under them again and again on each side; so the lungs and heart being pierced, the breathing organs spouted great clots of blood, which fell covering the sea, boats and men. That was the end; slowly, with great convulsive "sobbings" the immense body turned "belly up," and the harmless mammal one of the "largest of all living creatures" died.

We had been over seven hours "wearing her down" and killing her. It was found that "she" had lately suckled a calf, and had evidently "lost it," which might account for her erratic movements. She was 81ft. 6in. long, and her estimated weight (gross) about 74 tons 18ft. baleen (whalebone). We had now five whales on board.

When the weather cleared up, the *Arctic* was sighted with 10 fish, also *Aurora* and three others. A few days afterwards we got fast to a fish which "sounded," and was supposed to have remained fast in the mud at the bottom in 150 fathoms. After heaving on the whale line and trying all means to get her up it was decided to risk things by steaming around slowly with the line fast on the bow. The line parted and the fish was given up.

A Clean Down.

The summer fishing being finished early in August wherever the Right Whale hid himself during that month, he kept the secret well and so the ships were obliged to work "South," seek harbour in Cumberland Gulf, or according to the state of the season, the Captains compare notes, and prospects, etc., and await developments. (the writer has in mind an occasion when their fiat deprived one of themselves of his command.) The three-cornered scrapers are used to get off some of the blubber grease that with so much risk and anxiety we had put on.

Boats, and all their gear, are hauled up on the sandy beach, canvas and elbow grease being plentiful. All defects are made good and preparation for the fall fishing, with its blizzards and darkness, are made. Meanwhile a boat from each ship keeps a lookout for whales about the harbour heads, an officer on some higher ground being in touch with them.

During this breathing space the ships often shift anchorage (or harbour) under sail. Some good-humored rivalry between our fellows, and the next nearest vessel, *Narwhale* cropped up. Her people (who laughed in derision at our rendering of "Storm Along" while weighing anchor) were promptly challenged by us to "get their anchor," and make sail with a song.

The Bethel.

During the summer, at the floe-edge, the writer had been able, on a couple of Sundays, to slip along to "Service" on board the *Esquimaux*. Captain Charles Yule (who did not fish on Sundays) and his breezy reading of the sermons of Dr. Talmage, the American orator and divine, were in keeping with the captain's strong personality. So, when the ship hoisted the "Bethel" flag here, several boat-loads gathered on her deck. Both her "Medico" and ours were believers in the virtue of our song, so one played the harmonium and the other the violin; thus; we soon all joined in, and our singers (although they failed at praying) enjoyed themselves, and took a bit of stopping. All good things come to an end, and, as we left to rejoin our ships, we lay on our oars while a clear baritone voice from the deck, accompanied by a good violinist, sent us away with an "Aberystwyth" (God be with you till we meet again) that lingered like a blessing.

The Fall Fishing.

With the last day of August the weather has changed; boating is a wet, cold and benumbing job. Gales spring up suddenly, with sleet and snow. High seas are running in the offing. No one seems to take the "fall" fishing seriously. The poor results of the summer season (the *Victor* took only six fish, i.e., 68 tons of oil) warrant us in making an effort and taking some risks to add to our catch. Anyhow, the *Rock Noseing* had towards the end of September yielded the fleet a couple of fish, but neither fell to us.

The young ice had formed on sheltered coast inlets, and on October 3rd a roaring blizzard had raged for a week. While this continued the ships used their engines to ease the cables and "ground tackle" during the hurricane squalls. At last, in a bit of a lull, a few days later (while two boats were still at the "Rock Nebbin") the ship steamed out; boats were hoisted and secured, and under small canvas, with a N.W. gale and heavy snow, which lasted 48 hours, we trundled "out of the country," with two "look-out" men on the fore yard.

Among the Dreaded Icebergs Again.

Six hours later "all hands" were "out" making sail, to clear a big berg which roared with "breakers" under our lee. Its terrible thunderings, as the mass seemed to lurch toward us, and our rolling and tumbling about in the backwash of the awful thing, almost rendered us panic-stricken. Things looked fearsome and black, but the frosted canvas was packed on her by the "crowd" (some of us partly naked), and as the reefed spanker was set, and the sheet of the mainsail hauled aft, the engines began to move; she gave a shuddering roll, luffed to the wind, and rammed her bows into the great breaking sea, filling her decks with water and loose "crash ice."

The bentic foresail was then set, and our fight had begun against the high, topping, breaking seas which curled over us, battering the ship with each lurch towards "The Terror" under our lee. How long might the berg be? Would our canvas, engines and gear hold out?

The bellowing and crashing of our iceberg could plainly be heard above the gale, "well away" on our weather quarter; so we scraped clear, and, reducing our sail, we cautiously "kept away" for home. The old ship was tight as a bottle on the passage, but even if she had soaked it in like a sponge, well . . . we got clear of "Davis Straits;" the forecastle "look-outs" were again kept; the engines put out of commission; and the "watch tackle" came again into its own.

We arrived at Dundee on the 9th of November, 1877, and were paid off with an estimated first pay, and about a week later, when the quantity of oil, bone, etc., had been verified in the "boil-yard," we received a second and last pay.

So we parted with a "noggin," and a song; I, to my old "love," *Fortitude* (a Hartlepool schooner) for the winter.

The writer, and Mr. J. Fairwearter (sic), chief mate of the *Victor*, met at Antwerp in 1893; he was then master of a large steamer, and I was chief officer of the s.s. *Alberta*, a 7,000-ton vessel. I was informed that in consequence of some legal action, as between the managers and shareholders, he had been authorised by the judge to control the necessary expenses for the benefit of the company and all concerned, and to report in regard to the same, to the Admiralty Court; than which (I may say) no greater compliment could be paid to his character and probity as a shipmaster.

During the war he was in command of the Examination Vessel (off the Tay Bar) for Dundee, and barked at the Nation's Gates in good style; my grateful thanks are due to him for what he "unlearnt" me 51 years ago.

CAPTAIN HECTOR ADAMS.

Appendix II

The Shackleton Relief Expedition

Sailing Orders. Lieutenant-Commander J. Fairweather, R.N.R.

M.48425/16.   2nd August, 1916

Sir,
        I am commanded by My Lords Commissioners of
the Admiralty to signify to you their directions, the
S.S. "Discovery" being in all respects ready for sea,
to leave Devonport in tow of the Collier "Polesley"
on such day as that vessel may be ready to proceed
to the Falkland Islands.
        A copy of the orders given to the Master of
the Collier will be sent to you separately.
2.   You are to report your arrival at Port
Stanley, Falkland Islands, to the Admiralty, as well
as your arrival at and departure from any intermediate
port which circumstances may require you to enter,
3.   You are also to report your arrival at Port
 Stanley to the Governor of the Falkland Islands and to
inform him fully of the object of your mission and
the instructions you have received.
4.   Should Sir Ernest Shackleton be at Port
Stanley, you are at once to confer with him as to the
rescue of the members of his expedition left on Elephant
Island. A copy of the Admiralty letter to Sir Ernest
Shackleton is enclosed for your information, from which
you will see that the "Discovery", under your command,
is placed at his disposal, and that, subject to the
safety and welfare of the Officers and men committed
to your charge and to the risk to the ship inseparable
from such service, you are to take him on board and
carry out his wishes as far as possible in regard to
all measures he may advise, to effect the rescue of
the party.
5.   You are guided by his advice as to the
treatment of the rescued persons who may be helpless
or disabled. If any of the party have died and been
buried since their landing on the Island, you are to
make suitable arrangements to mark their graves, but
their bodies are not to be embarked.
6.   Should it be found that the party has left
Elephant Island, the time during which the search is
to be continued and the distance to which it is to extend
is left to your discretion, provided that the "Discovery"

is back at Port Stanley by the 1st December, 1916.

7.   A full record of the first landing party, the
time of your visit and the names of those rescued and
brought away,packed in a watertight cylinder, is to be
placed in a Cairn built on some conspicuous point of the
island.

8.   On your return to Port Stanley, the rescued men
are to be landed and transferred to the charge of Sir
Ernest Shackleton, but if you are ordered home you are
authorised to give a passage in the ship to any of those
who are willing to accept the accommodation which is available
and who are certified by the Medical Officer
of the ship to be fit to undergo the voyage home.

9.   In the event of Sir Ernest Shackleton's not
being at Port Stanley on your arrival from England, or,
in the event of his not being able to accompany you, you
are to proceed, with as little delay as possible, to
carry out the rescue to the best of your ability, and,
in accordance with the preceding instructions.

10   It is their Lordships intention that you
should return to Plymouth as soon as you have completed
the work of rescue, but definite orders will be sent to
you after the receipt of your report of the result of
your expedition, which you are to telegraph to the
Admiralty immediately on your arrival.

            I am, Sir,

            Your obedient Servant,

        (Signed). W.GRAHAM GREENE.

C O P Y   O F   T E L E G R A M.
FROM   ADMIRALTY.
TO   COMMANDER—IN—CHIEF, DEVONPORT.
DATE   6th August 1916.   No.956.

Following for Lieutenant—Commander Fairweather, R.N.R.,

            H.M.S. "DISCOVERY".

        A copy of your sailing orders, Admiralty Letter
M.48425 of 2nd August, with letter to Shackleton, and
conditions of publication, should be made and given to
Governor, Falklands, on arrival, as it is doubtful
whether the copies which have been posted from Colonial
Office will arrive before you.

Admiralty
Sir Ernest Shackleton, G.V.O.   2nd August 1916
Sir,
I am commanded by My Lords Commissioners of the
Admiralty to acquaint you that consequent on the failure
to obtain a suitable vessel in any of the South American
Ports, H.M. Government has directed that a vessel should
be sent out from England to rescue the members of your
Expedition from Elephant Island.
2.   The Antarctic Ship "Discovery" has accordingly
been manned and fitted out with all dispatch and has
been put under the command of Lieutenant- Commander
James Fairweather, R.N.R., an Ice Master and seaman of
proved experience and ability.
3.   The "Discovery" will leave Plymouth on the 5th
August, and, owing to the urgency of the case, the
Lords Commissioners of the Admiralty have decided that
she is to be towed to the Falkland Islands.
4.   On her arrival at Port Stanley, Lieutenant Commander
Fairweather will at once confer with you as to the steps
to be taken to effect the rescue of the party on
Elephant Island. He has been directed to take you on
board and to carry out your wishes as far as possible in
regard to all measures you may advise to effect the
rescue of your men, but the command of the ship, and all
who may be on board as well as the responsibility
for the action he takes, must be in his hands.
5.   A copy of the orders given to him is enclosed
for your information, from which you will see that,
in the event of your not being at Port Stanley, or
not being able to accompany him in the ship, he is
to carry out the rescue of the party to the best of
his ability.
6.   A copy is also enclosed of a condition, under
which all the Officers and Crew of the "Discovery"
have been engaged, respecting the publication of
matter relating to this Expedition, which My Lords
must ask you to consider as binding on yourself.
7.   On the return of the "Discovery" at Port Stanley,
the rescued men will be landed and transferred to
your charge, except that passage home in the "Discovery"
will be given to such as are willing and fit to undergo
the long voyage in her.
          I am, Sir.
          Your obedient Servant,
             (Signed)
             W. Graham Greene.

Appendix III

Obituary of Captain Alexander Fairweather.

'Dundee Advertiser', 23rd July, 1896.

DEATH OF DUNDEE WHALING CAPTAIN

A feeling of sadness prevailed in shipping circles in Dundee yesterday when it became known that Captain Alexander Fairweather, master of the Dundee whaler Balaena died on 31st May. This feeling was accentuated by the absence of details regarding the unexpected event, the only information obtainable being from the hastily written letter received from Captain Davidson, on the Polar Star, now prospecting the Greenland fishing. Few persons could at first bring themselves to believe that the hale and hearty skipper who sailed from the city on the 4th April last, looking forward to a successful cruise, was no more. To the shipping community he had been long and intimately known, and his personal worth and amiable qualities had secured him a large circle of friends. With Dundee and its shipping Captain Fairweather had been connected for 40 years. A native of the city, he had followed the sea as a profession since boyhood. His first voyage was in a small coasting vessel when he was only 10 years of age. He subsequently became bound apprentice, and completed his term when 16. A spirit of adventure and the desire to see as many parts of the world as possible, led him to join the whaler Tay in the spring of 1863, and it was on board that vessel that he received the first of the training which was to prove so valuable in after years. Although this voyage in the Tay was successful enough, he did not return to the Arctic seas the following year, and he accordingly shipped on a cruise to China and the Indies. For three years he sailed to various parts of the world, but finding himself once more in Dundee he joined the whaler Camperdown as harpooner, and again visited the frozen North. This was in 1866. Curiously enough he had not yet become enamoured of the whaling industry, and a further period of four years passed ere he again sailed to the North. In the meantime, however, he had pushed himself forward in his profession, and had obtained his certificate as first mate.

In 1870 the Camperdown was without a chief officer, and Mr Fairweather was asked to take this second command on the voyage upon which she was just setting out. As chief mate of the Camperdown, and also of the Victor which he joined the following year he added to his experience of Arctic navigation; and when Mr Leigh Smith, the well-known explorer, fitted out an expedition for the relief of Baron Nordenskjold Captain Fairweather was asked to take command. For a young sailor of six and twenty the position was an important one; but the manner in which Captain Fairweather handled the Diana, the steam yacht conveying the expedition, and also the sagacity and resource he displayed in relieving the Norwegian party, more than justified the confidence reposed in him. During the time the Diana was in Spitzbergen - fully three years - Captain Fairweather assisted in taking many observations of much scientific value, and here it may be stated that on many subsequent voyages he made careful studies of the currents, the fauna, and the flora of the Arctic regions, and from the Meteorological and other Scientific Societies he again and again received flattering acknowledgments of his valuable services. On returning to Dundee in 1874, he was appointed to the command of the whaler Active.   Under Captain Fairweather the Active made five voyages to the ice, and every autumn the vessel came home full. Subsequently the captain was transferred to the whaler Our Queen, but in this command he was unfortunate. With the produce of 16 large whales on board and the season well advanced, the ship was badly crushed and went to the bottom. The crew were brought home by the other ships in the fleet. Captain Fairweather's next command was the Aurora, which at that time was looked upon as the finest whaler afloat.   He made several most successful voyages in that craft, as also in the Thetis and Terra Nova, both of which vessels, under his able management, brought home lucrative cargoes.

Towards the close of the 80's Captain Fairweather had serious thoughts of retiring from the sea altogether.   His friends were also of opinion that he should rest from his labours and take up life ashore. This he decided to do, and for one year the fleet sailed for the North without him. When at home however he felt, as the saying goes "Like a fish out of water," and the ensuing year saw him once more in harness. This time his interest was more than that of a master, for along with friends he had invested part of his savings in the purchase of a smart little steamer the Balaena, which was fitted out for the fishing enterprise. Although the venture proved a success the profits were not so large as in former years, and the idea was mooted that the scene of whaling operations might be changed with good results to all concerned. According to the reports of Antarctic explorers the black or bone-yielding whale was to be met with in large numbers in the frozen waters south of the Falkland Islands, and it occurred to the owners of the Balaena and other Dundee whalers that it might be as well to fit out an expedition to hunt the cetacean in these southern latitudes. Captain Fairweather took a most active part in the enterprise, and sailed in the Balaena to the Antarctic in company with three other Dundee vessels. The expedition excited much interest all over the kingdom, and the movements of the little fleet were watched very keenly on both sides of the Atlantic. Promoted and arranged on purely commercial lines, the expedition also partook of a scientific character. Two well-known scientists accompanied the ships, and the observations made by these gentlemen proved of the utmost importance. But the main object of the enterprise was unsuccessful. No black whales were sighted during the entire voyage, and several of the captains expressed doubts as to the existence of the bone-yielding cetacean in these waters. Seals, however, were met with in great abundance, and the ships filled up with these and returned home. The voyage to the Antarctic was not, however, without its interesting side, but it was found that the risk, danger, and expense of sending steamers so far south were so great that the promoters would not be justified in continuing the venture.

In 1894 and last year Captain Fairweather took the Balaena to Davis Strait, and on both voyages he met with a fair return; and this year, as stated, he was looking forward to a good season's fishing at Greenland, the whaling grounds of which he had not visited for several years. He intended this to be his last voyage before settling down at home. Captain Fairweather was a fine type of the British seaman. Short, stout, vigorous, and active, he had a suggestion of the salt water in all his movements. He had the knack of drawing round him large circles of friends, and when he was in port there was probably no more pleasant place in which to spend a profitable hour than the cabin of the Balaena, where the genial captain was generally to be found recounting his adventures and experiences to his landsmen friends. By his death there is removed another of those skilful and intrepid Arctic navigators who in great measure built up the whaling industry, and if that industry is now becoming less remunerative, the circumstances may be attributable to the havoc that was wrought by Captain Fairweather, and men like him, when whales were far more numerous than at the present day. Captain Fairweather who was 52 years of age, leaves a widow and family, for whom the deepest sympathy is felt. To him the public of Dundee are indebted for many important contributions to the Museum. His gifts took the form of interesting curios from the Arctic regions, and two years ago he brought home a few relics of an unfortunate Esquimaux party which perished in Prince Regent's Inlet. These also find a resting-place in the Museum.

In the city, at the shore, in Newport, and wherever the daring whale hunter was known, the news of the death of Captain Fairweather of the Balaena called forth sorrow and sympathy.

A strong, hardy sailor, the very type of man to stand the strain of severe weather in the frozen North, Captain Fairweather looked fit for many a whale hunt.

Shortly after his return from his season's voyage he spoke to me as if he was tired of the work, and felt inclined to take a spell of rest. But I suppose, as time for starting drew near, he became restless, and could not make up his mind to remain at home while the ships were off again on the quest which he had followed so long and so venturously.

Like Captain Adams, Captain Fairweather was a daring hunter and explorer, and like the famous of the Arctic, Captain Fairweather for long was remarkably fortunate.

The genial, kind-hearted sailor has gone to his rest amidst the icy waters which he sailed so long. He will be sorely missed by those who loved him, and for the widow and family sympathy will be genuine and general.

THE BURDEN OF THE BALAENA

Yesterday the steam whaler Balaena arrived at Dundee from the
Greenland fishing.
The steamer had on board the body of Captain Alexander
Fairweather,
who died on May 31st after an illness of six days.

Home is the sailor, home from the sea. *R. L. Stevenson*

Flag at half-mast!
So sailors tell the story
Of grief and pain.
And by the coast, all in the sunset glory.
The old ship steers again;
But not with ensign flying overhead,
As when she bore out free.
To-night her gallant mariner lies dead
The sailor is home from the sea!

Across the bar!
And past the lighthouse shining,
By sandy shore,
And where the old familiar river, twining,
Leads homeward as of yore.
But not again for him the well-known lights,
The welcome at the quay.
Past all the anxious days, the stormy nights
The sailor is home from the sea!

No more, no more!
The wave-washed deck at morning,
The white caps racing by.
No more at stormy night the danger scorning,
The gale, the starless sky.
No more for him the icebound wastes around,
The bergs, the pathless snow;
He comes to rest upon familiar ground,
Where daisies grow.[1]   N. S.

[1]Undated cutting in Captain James' Scrapbook

Appendix IV

Obituary Notice of Captain James Fairweather

The 'Courier', Dundee   FRIDAY, MARCH 24, 1933

LINK WITH DUNDEE WHALING DAYS

DEATH OF VETERAN SHIPMASTER

Captain James Fairweather's
Adventurous Career in Arctic

One of the few remaining links with the old Dundee whaling days was snapped by the death of Captain James Fairweather yesterday at his residence, Bona Vista, Norwood, East Newport, in his 80th year.

Captain Fairweather spent an adventurous career in the Arctic. He made a name for himself as one of the most courageous and skilful navigators and shipmasters in the whaling industry.

Born in Dundee, Captain Fairweather joined the Dundee Barque Stork in 1867 as ship's boy. In 1871 he joined the whaler Tay, and subsequently became mate of the Victor.

His first command came in 1878, when he was appointed to the then well known whaler Active. Later he commanded the Thetis and the Aurora.

He had many exciting adventures, but in all his 52 years of sea life he never lost a ship, and with the exception of one man who went amissing he never lost a single life under his command.

BACK FROM RETIREMENT

Captain Fairweather retired in 1913 but came back from his retirement in the spring of the following year, at the request of the owners, to make a final voyage to the Arctic in the Morning. The purpose of the voyage was to investigate the possibilities of new fishing grounds.

Captain Fairweather's seafaring experiences were not confined to the Arctic. He sailed the seven seas, but particularly was familiar with the East.

On the decline of the whaling industry he turned his attention to other parts, and commanded various steamships, including the Dundee-owned vessel Drumgeith. He made many trips to Calcutta, and with that great port his name is inseparably associated.

Fairweather House stands in Calcutta as a monument to his memory. He collected funds to equip the building as a social club for marine officers and engineers, and it was named after its founder. Thousands of seafaring men have sheltered under its friendly roof.

When war broke out Captain Fairweather was given a commission as Lieut.-Commander in the Royal Navy.

His work was mainly in the North Sea, looking for enemy submarines and sweeping for mines.*

Captain Fairweather was a man of genial personality and had a great fund of Scottish humour.

He could talk interestingly on his adventures at sea, and he had the knack of being able to write about them as well. He wrote a series of articles for the "Scots Magazine" in 1928-29, which dealt not only with whaling but also with his experiences in various parts of the world.

Captain Fairweather is survived by his widow, two sons, and three daughters.

Three sons predeceased him. One of them was Captain James Fairweather, who served for many years with the Booth Line.

* Inaccurate information, see chapter on War Service.

Appendix V

A Drama of the Sea

The Fate of the *Active* and of the *Morning*

By Bobbie Jamieson

DURING the First and Second World Wars the Admiralty commissioned every vessel that could be used in any way for war work. Several more put to jobs they were entirely unsuitable for resulting in the loss of many lives.

I suppose some of the men who were responsible for sending unsuitable ships to sea in winter were men who were only accustomed to office work and had not had any sea experience.

One ship in particular I want to tell you about was one of the old Dundee whalers, named the "Active" which had been laid up in port many years waiting to be scrapped.

The whalers were propelled by a combination of sails and a small steam engine, which could only drive them about 4 or 5 knots an hour.

It was Christmas week in 1915 when the Active left Dundee for, of all places, the White Sea. If you look at a map of Europe, you will see the distance she was chartered to go with a cargo of war material. She would have had to go around the North Cape of Norway. then on to the White Sea in the north of Russia.

I'm not sure how many of a crew she had. The skipper was Willie Leask. I Think he came from Sandsound and was married to a Janet Manson from Bigton. The one I know best about was the mate. He was Jamie Scott Jamieson (no relation of mine) from Longhill. Bigton.

They had not been long out of Dundee when a gale suddenly sprang up from the southeast which soon strengthened to hurricane force, accompanied with blinding snow.

The old ship soon found the mountainous seas and the gale were too much for her old timbers and she sprung a leak.

The crew battled to keep her afloat by pumping all they could but it was of little avail and they eventually saw she was foundering and would soon be under the waves.

The mate, Jamie Scott, 36 years, already mentioned, saw all hope was gone of any of the crew surviving much longer in such conditions. He got a sheet of paper and a pen and wrote a letter to his father and mother and brother and sisters and also made his Will to them.

He was a real Christian of outstanding Christian qualities who had committed his life to God. It was only a man with such Christian courage and facing such a tragic death in a few hours, or perhaps only a few more minutes, who could have put pen to paper under such trying conditions.

I have a copy of the letter he wrote and put in a bottle and threw into the raging sea as the ship sank under them. You will notice a few bits are missing. No wonder!

"Finder please post Andrew Jamieson, Longhill, Bigton.

Dear family, this will be my last letter to you. We are sinking to the North Fast of Lerwick. God bless you all as he has given me strength to die. My soul is resting on the finished work of Jesus. A Navy boat passed us and we told him we were sinking. I have been under the boat all night trying to get water out . . . filled . . . again. The water is at my knees on the cabin floor. Don't mourn for me, meet me in heaven, Mother, father, Agnes, Andrew, Ann, Margaret, Coventry. Again God bless you all. I leave everything among you. ta ta. James S. Jamieson."

You will notice he said in the letter he had been all night under the boat trying to get water out. I think this must have meant that he had been there all night working a hand-operated bilge pump that was fixed under the boat on the main deck.

Instead of being, as they thought, NE of Lerwick, they must have foundered very close on the east side of Orkney as the bottle message and two bodies were washed ashore there soon afterwards. One of them was that of Jamie Scott and he was buried in Orkney. A wallet containing £10 or £12, his watch, and a letter his sister Agnes had written to him, were found in his pocket. The money was in good condition so it was clear it had not been long in the water. If I remember right, I think the letter was dropped in the sea on a Friday and it arrived at his home the following Friday.

I wish to convey my thanks to a niece of his, Mrs Margaret Laurenson who lives at Navy Lane, Lerwick. She very kindly wrote me a copy of her uncle's letter and posted it on to me.

Margaret also lost her husband in World War Two through the sinking of his ship by enemy action and she was left with three small children, the youngest only six months old. Captain Laurenson was mate in a tanker that was lost in the Atlantic.

At the time, a story was told that the first crew who signed on to sail in the "Active", refused to go to sea in her. When they saw her condition, they decided that she was not fit to be put on such a trip in the middle of North Sea winter.

For refusing to sail in her, they were sent to jail for 90 days. Apparently the crew that was lost with the ship was the second crew.

There were two sister ships sent on the same voyage - the other was called the "Morning". She was lost near the Faroe islands with the loss of all her crew, except the mate and one seaman.

It appears that some oil tanks that were used for storing whale oil when the ships were engaged in whaling, had been removed to make room for cargo. It was thought that this had weakened the structure of the vessels.

The *"Active"* was lost on Christmas Eve 1915. I remember the south-east gale and accompanying snow storm quite well, as I was almost 17 years old at the time.

Acknowledgements

I would like to record my thanks to my cousin Jim Fairweather for permission to use Grandfather's journal and other papers. Jim also provided many photographs, including the reproduction of his fine painting of *Aurora*.

I am most grateful to many people in Dundee, in particular David Henderson, who taught me about whales and seals, and gave me consistent kindly support; and Norman Watson for proof reading the manuscript, and giving helpful advice and assistance. Both David and Norman gave permission to quote from their writings, for which I thank them. William Owen tracked down the Fairweather homes in Newport, and identified my mother's birthplace. The Tay Valley Family History Society and their researcher Mrs Helen Beat have been on hand with help and instant information. I thank Nigel Gatherer for his good wishes and permission to quote the ballad 'The Old Polina' from his book 'Songs and Ballads of Dundee'. I am grateful to Ann Savours who has consistently helped me over the years, for permission to quote from her book 'The Voyages of the Discovery.' Dr. Gillies Ross of Canada some years ago used his expertise to identify the location of photographs taken during the 1914 *Morning* expedition, for which I am most grateful.

We have received much assistance and information from our friends in Calcutta, and I would like to thank Mr Manik Jain for information about Fairweather House, and also the present officials of Fairweather House, the President of the Fairweather Institute, Mr A. Bhaskarachar; the Honorary General Secretary Mr S,K, Dey, and their colleagues.

Members of my family have given valuable information which has been incorporated into the text, in particular my late cousin Ethel Burton. The younger generation of cousins have helped in various ways; in alphabetical order: Christopher Burton, Rosemary Head, Janet Hobbs, Diana Kelly, and Ruth Todd. Pam Radford recalled memories of her late husband Duncan Corr. Pam Lazenby undertook useful family history research in Australia. I am grateful to them all. I thank the Bolton Family for the use of Captain James' papers relating to the Shackleton Expedition, and for the photographs taken on the 1914 *Morning* voyage. I thank Mr Roland Huntford for allowing me to quote from his book 'Shackleton'.

I also thank The Royal Scottish Geographical Society for permission to publish their portrait of Captain Alexander Fairweather; the National Maritime Museum for permission to reproduce two photographs; the Abertay Historical Society, for permission to quote from their publication 'Dundee and its Textile Industry 1850-1914'.

Finally, a special thank you to Mary Roby and Judith Crampton for checking the text.

Notes and References

Introduction

1   Norman Watson, *The Dundee Whalers*, Tuckwell Press 2003. p. 166
2   Captain James Fairweather, *With the Scottish Whalers*,
    printed for private circulation, October 1928.
3   *The Scots Magazine*, 5 monthly articles September 1928 – January 1929.
4   David Moore Lindsay, *A Voyage to the Arctic in the Whaler Aurora*, Boston,
    Dana Estes & Company, Publishers, 1911.

Family Background

1   Letter in the possession of the Mackay family.
2   Material drawn from: *Dundee and its Textile Industry 1850 – 1914*,
    Bruce Lenman, Charlotte Lythe, Enid Gauldie, Dundee Abertay
    Historical Society Publication no. 14 1969, Chapter V,
    and David S. Henderson, *Fishing for the Whale*, a Dundee Museum
    and Art Gallery Publication Catalogue no. 2 1972.
3   Letters in the possession of Jim Fairweather.
4   Captain James Fairweather, op. cit.
5   Information from Keith Mackay.
6   The 'Dundee Advertiser', 23 July 1896.

The Career of Captain James Fairweather.

1   Census return 1861
2   Captain James op. cit., p. 3
3   "   "   op. cit., p. 42.

Whaling and Sealing, a short history.

1   David S Henderson, op. cit., p. 7.
2   Captain Hector Adams, *Whaling Stories, Sea Breezes,*
    The Pacific Steam Navigation Company (P.S.N.C.)
    Magazine, no. 111 Vol. XII, February to August 1929.
3   David S Henderson, op. cit., pp. 8, 10, 11, 14, 15, 23.
4   Captain James op. cit., p.43.
5   Information about Whales from *Marine Mammals of the World*,
    Jefferson, Leatherwood and Webber U.N.E.P. Rome 1993.
6   Norman Watson, op. cit. p2
7   Lenman, Lythe & Gauldie, op. cit., p. 39.
8   D.S.H., op.cit., p. 24,
9   ibid. p. 25.
10 Captain James Fairweather, op. cit., pp. 6, 7.
11 ibid., p.10.
12 *Chafes Sealing Book*, 3rd edition, St John's, Newfoundland,
    Trade Printers & Publishers Ltd. 1924, Scotch Records p. 13.
13 Basil Lubbock, *The Arctic Whalers*, Brown, Son & Ferguson

Nautical Publishers, 52-58 Darnley Street, Glasgow, 1937,
p. 461.

14   Captain James Fairweather, op. cit., p. 11.
15   447, 903 from Captain James, op. cit., p.10.
      139,885 from D.S.H, op. cit., p. 17.
16   Information on seals from *Mammals in the Sea*,
      F.A.O. Fisheries Series, no. 5 Vol. 11.
      United Nations, Rome, 1979.
17   *Chafes Sealing Book*, op. cit., Species of Seals
      hunted in the North Atlantic, p. 4.
18   Information from D.S. Henderson.
19   David Moore Lindsay, op. cit.
20   Lenman Lythe & Gauldie, op. cit., p. 39.
21   B. Lubbock, op. cit., pp. 40-42

1872 to 1881   The *Victor* and the *Active*.

 1   Newspaper articles, Dundee Central Library, Wellgate.
 2   The 'Dundee Year Book' ibid.
 3   Tay Whale Fishing Company records.
      Archive Records Management and Museum Services,
      University of Dundee.
 4   No trace has been found of this publication.
 5   Letter to the author dated 22 January, 1988.
 6   Information provided by David Henderson.
 7   Captain James, op. cit., p. 18.
 8   "   "   " "   pp. 18-20.
 9   *Sea Breezes*, the magazine of the Pacific Steam Navigation Company
      (P.S.N.C.)
10   Captain James op. cit., p. 16.
11   "   "   " "   p. 6.
12   "   "   " "   pp. 40-42.
13   "   "   " "   p.18.
14   Letter in the possession of Jim Fairweather of Australia.
15   *Sea Breezes*, p. 8. For further accounts of the
      loss of the *Victor*, see the 'Dundee Advertiser',
      of August 31, and of September 10, 1881, p. 5.
16   Basil Lubbock, op. cit., p. 451.
17   Letter in the possession of Jim Fairweather.
18   ibid.
19   *The People's Journal*, a former Dundee weekly
      newspaper and The 'Dundee Year Book' 1881.
20   Captain James op. cit., p.24.
21   Letter in the possession of Jim Fairweather.
22   Captain James op. cit., p. 6.
23   Captain James op. cit., pp. 8 & 9.

Aurora

1   Captain James' scrapbook.
2   Comment by Jim Fairweather.
3   D. M. L., op. cit., p. 17.
4   ibid., p. 119.
5   ibid., p. 23.
6   B. Lubbock, op., cit., p. 413
7   D. M. L., op. cit., p. 154.
8   Captain James, op. cit., pp. 42 - 44.
9   B. Lubbock, op. cit., pp. 414 - 417.
10   D. M. L., op. cit., p. 34.
11   ibid., pp. 35, 36.
12   Captain James, op. cit., p. 13.
13   D. M. L. op. cit., p. 81, 82.
14   Captain James op. cit., p. 9.
15   ibid., p.37 – 40.
16   D. M. L. op. cit., p. 210.
17   Norman Watson, op. cit., p. 112.
18   Captain James, op. cit., p. 22, 23.
19   B. Lubbock, op. cit., pp. 418, 419.
20   Letter to the author from William Owen, 13 December 1994.
21   Captain James, op. cit., p. 24 – 26.
22   D. M. L., op. cit., p. 196.
23   'Dundee Evening Telegraph', 15 December 1926.
24   'Dundee Advertiser', 9 April, 1888.
25   Captain James, op. cit., p. 29 – 33.
26   Testimonials dated 26 & 28 November 1898, in the possession of J. Fairweather.
27   Roland Huntford, *Shackleton*, Hodder & Stoughton Ltd, 1985, p. 339.
28   ibid., p. 370.
29   ibid., p. 638.
30   ibid., p. 642.
31   *Sea Breezes*, op. cit., p. 9.
32   Captain James's scrapbook.

The State of Alabama

1   Reference dated 28 November, 1898 in the possession of J. F.
22   Captain James, op. cit., p. 49.
3   'Dundee Evening Telegraph', 13 December 1926.
4   Captain James, op. cit., pp. 45 – 47.

The Kentigern

1   Correspondence with E.P. Babtie, manager of Arch'd McMillan & Sons Ltd., in the possession of J.F.

2   The compensation paid for the detention of a ship
during loading or unloading beyond the scheduled time
of departure.

3   Captain James, op. cit., p. 49 – 53.

4   Letter of 9 December, 1896 in the possession of J.F.

5   ibid.

6   Information from J.F.

Captain Alexander Fairweather

1   Article in the *Pall Mall Budget* of 20 June, 1893 entitled
The Dundee Antarctic Expedition.

2   W. G. Burn-Murdoch, *From Edinburgh to the Antarctic,*
Longmans, Green & Co London, 1894.

3   The *Pall Mall Budget,* op. cit.

4   Undated cutting in Captain James' scrapbook.

5   Letter in the possession of the Mackay family.

The Vortigern

1   Captain James, op. cit., p.54.

2   *About Fairweathers & Craiks* by Ethel Burton, August 1988.
Typescript copy in the possession of the author.

3   Press cutting from Captain James' scrapbook in the
possession of J.F.

4   Captain James, op. cit., p. 54 – 59.

5   M.H.Beattie, *On the Hooghly*, the reminiscences of a
River Hooghly Pilot, published by Philip Allan,
69 Great Russell Street, London 1935.

6   op. cit., p. 208.

7   Letters from M.H. Beatie to Kathleen Duncan,
8 March & 23 April, 1938.

8   Captain James, op. cit., p.58.

9   Article in the 'Dundee Evening Telegraph', 15 December,1926.

10   Press cuttings from Captain James' scrapbook..

11   H.C. De Mierre, *Clipper Ships to Ocean Greyhounds*, p. 163, publisher
Harold Starke Ltd, circa 1911.

12   Captain James' scrapbook, undated cutting, J.F.

13   Captain James, op. cit., p.59.

14   Captain James' scrapbook, undated, J.F.

15   ibid.

16   Letters in possession of J.F.

17   Captain James' scrapbook, undated, J.F.

18   Letters from E.B. Babtie, 26 January, 1903,
12 &14 October, 1904, J.F.

19   Captain James, op. cit., pp. 48,49.

20   *People's Friend*, a Dundee weekly magazine, still extant.

21   Letters in the possession of J.F.

The Morning

1   Photographs , the property of A.S.G. Bolton.

2   Letter from Dr W. Gillies Ross to the author, 1 July, 1993.

3   Lloyds obituary of Captain James, 25 March, 1933.

4   Basil Lubbock, op. cit., p. 451.

War Service

1   Documents, in the possession of J.F.

2   *Sea Breezes*, op. cit., undated p. 267.

3   Ann Savours, *The Voyages of The Discovery*, p. 150, Virgin Books 1992.

4   J.F., correspondence with the author.

5   Documents in the possession of J.F.

Shackleton Relief Expedition

1   The 'Evening Telegraph', December, 16, 1926.

2   Ann Savours, op. cit., p. 149.

3   Unattributed press cutting in the Bolton *Discovery* file.

4   Letter from Kathleen Duncan to Keith Mackay, 5 July,1981.

5   Roland Huntford, op. cit., pp. 615,616.

6   Documents in the possession of the Bolton Family.

7   ibid.

8   Ann Savours, op. cit., pp. 151, 152.

9   Document in the possession of the Bolton family.

10   Ann Savours, op. cit., p. 152.

11   Hector Adams, op. cit., p. 269.

Retirement

Family information from Ethel Burton, Jim Fairweather,
Rosemary Head, Janet Hobbs, Diana Kelly, Pam Radford
Nancy Rycroft and Ruth Todd.

1   'Dundee Evening Telegraph', 15 December, 1926.

2   Correspondence in the possession of J.F.

3   ibid.

List of Illustrations

Maps
The Polar Regions
>   Basil Lubbock, *Arctic Whalers*

Track of the Whalers at Davis Straits
>   The 'Dundee Year Book', 1881

Family Trees
Fairweather

Fleeming and Duncan

Illustrations
The *Aurora* nipped in the Ice off Cape York, Melville Bay
>   D.M. Lindsay

Captain James Fairweather, as a young man
>   Jim Fairweather

The *Arctic*, with boats fast to a 'Fish'
>   A Whaling Cruise to Baffin's Bay, Albert Hastings Markham 1875

The *Active* berthing in the Dundee Docks
>   Basil Lubbock

The *Aurora* at sea
>   Jim Fairweather

St. John's Harbour in Spring
>   D.M. Lindsay

The *Aurora* in St. John's Harbour
>   D.M. Lindsay

The *Thetis* and the *Bear*
>   D.M. Lindsay

The Fairweather Family, circa 1895
>   Jim Fairweather

Captain Alexander Fairweather
>   Royal Scottish Geographical Society

The *Vortigern*
>   Jim Fairweather

Fairweather House
>   'Evening Telegraph', 15 December,1926

Fairweather House (2)
>   Keith Mackay

Memorial Stone at Vicarsford Cemetery, Forgan
>   N. Rycroft

Mary Ann Craik
>   Fairweather Family

Elizabeth (Lizzie)
>   Fairweather Family

Mary Ann (Tan)
    Fairweather Family
Helen (Ella)
    Fairweather Family
The Morning
    Bolton Family
Eskimos, on Baffin Island
    Bolton Family
Captain James Fairweather,1916
    © National Maritime Museum
Captain James Fairweather, in command of *Discovery*
    © National Maritime Museum
To the Rescue of the Explorers, 1916
    'Daily Mirror', 9, August, 1916
Captain James in later life
    Fairweather Family

Bibliography

Adams, Captain Hector, *"Whaling Stories", Sea Breezes,*
  The Pacific Steam Navigation Company (P.S.N.C.) Magazine.

Beattie M.H., *On The Hooghly*, the Reminiscences of a River Hooghly
  Pilot, published by Philip Allan, 69 Great Russell Street, London, 1935.

Burn-Murdoch, W. G., *From Edinburgh to the Antarctic,*
  Longmans, Green & Co, London 1894.

Burton, Ethel, *About Fairweathers & Craiks* 1988, (Typescript).

Chafe's Sealing Book, 3rd Edition, St John's, Newfoundland.
  Trade Printers & Publishers Ltd, 1924.

De Mierre H.C., *Clipper Ships to Ocean Greyhounds,*
  publisher Harold Starke Ltd, circa 1911.

Fairweather, Captain James, *With the Scottish Whalers,*
  printed for private circulation, 1926.

Gatherer, Nigel, *Songs and Ballads of Dundee,*
  John Donald 1986.

Henderson, David S., *Fishing for the Whale*, a Dundee Museum
  and Art Gallery Publication, Catalogue no.2, 1972.

Huntford, Roland, *Shackleton*, Hodder & Stoughton Ltd, 1985.

Lenman, Bruce; Lythe, Charlotte and Gauldie, Enid;
  Dundee and its Textile Industry 1850 – 1914,
  Abertay Historical Society, publication no.14, 1969.

Lindsay, David Moore, *A Voyage to the Arctic in the Whaler Aurora,*
  Boston, Dana Estes & Company, publishers 1911.

Lubbock, Basil, *The Arctic Whalers*, Brown, Son & Ferguson,
  Nautical Publishers, 52 – 58 Darnley Street, Glasgow, 1937.

Savours, Ann, *The Voyages of the Discovery*, Virgin Books, 1992.

Watson, Norman, *The Dundee Whalers*, Tuckwell Press, 2003.

Additional sources

Census Returns for Dundee 1841,1851,1861.

The 'Courier', D.C.Thomson & Co Ltd., Dundee.

The 'Dundee Advertiser', John Leng & Co., Dundee.

The Dundee Street Directory, 1850.

The 'Dundee Year Book', John Leng & Co., Dundee.

The 'Evening Telegraph', DC Thompson & Co Ltd, Dundee.

Mammals in the Sea, F.A.O. Fisheries Series no.5 vol. 11.
    United Nations, Rome, 1979.

Marine Mammals of the World, Jefferson, Leatherwood & Webber.
    U.N.E.P., Rome 1993. F.A.O. species identification guide.

Old Parish Records, (O.P.R.).

The Pall Mall Budget, 20 June 1893.

The People's Friend, John Leng & Co, Dundee,
    now D.C.Thompson & Co Ltd, a still extant weekly magazine.

The People's Journal, John Leng & Co, Dundee,
    a weekly newspaper.

The Scots Magazine, D.C. Thompson & Co. Ltd., Dundee.

The Tay Whale Fishing Company records,
    Archive Records, Management and Museum Services,
    University of Dundee.

Records and correspondence held by the Bolton, Burton,
Fairweather, Mackay and Rycroft families.

Nancy & Christopher Rycroft with their family
and Keith MacKay on board *'Discovery'*.
Discovery Point, Dundee, July 2002